THOSE OF US WHO MUST DIE

EXECUTION, EXILE AND REVIVAL AFTER THE EASTER RISING

DEREK MOLYNEUX & DARREN KELLY

The Collins Press

FIRST PUBLISHED IN 2017 BY
The Collins Press
West Link Park
Doughcloyne
Wilton
Cork
T12 N5EF
Ireland

A CIP record for this book is available from the British Library.

Paperback ISBN: 978-1-84889-325-2

Typesetting by Carrigboy Typesetting Services
Typeset in Garamond Premier Pro
Printed in Poland by Drukarnia Skleniarz

THOSE OF US
WHO MUST DIE

EXECUTION, EXILE AND REVIVAL
AFTER THE EASTER RISING

DEREK MOLYNEUX and **DARREN KELLY** are close friends with a passionate interest in Irish and military history. They administer the popular Facebook page 'Dublin 1916–1923 Then & Now' and are authors of *When the Clock Struck in 1916* (2015). Derek has an intimate knowledge of Dublin's streets, based on many years as a motorcycle courier, and understands how the same streets have preserved so much history. He now works in the Department of Foreign Affairs. Darren, who has been interested in Irish revolutionary history since the age of ten, is a technician in the music industry.

Follow the auth‚ 923 Then & Now

To our wives and children for your continuing patience,
love and inspiration

Contents

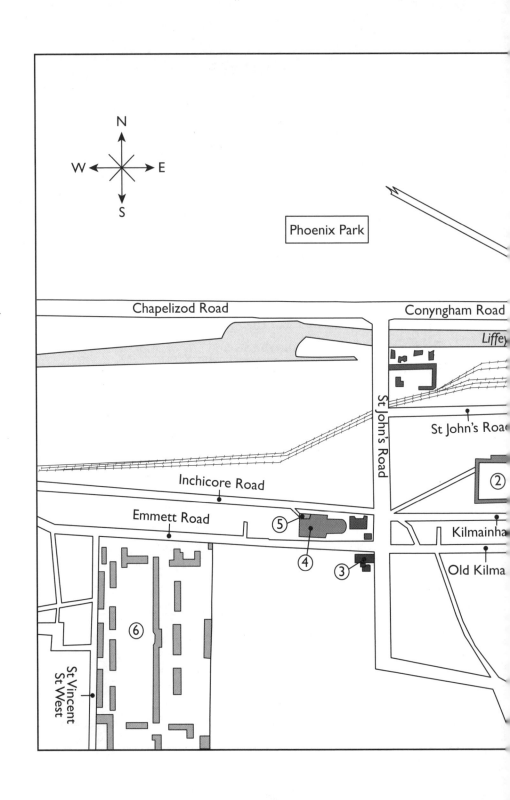

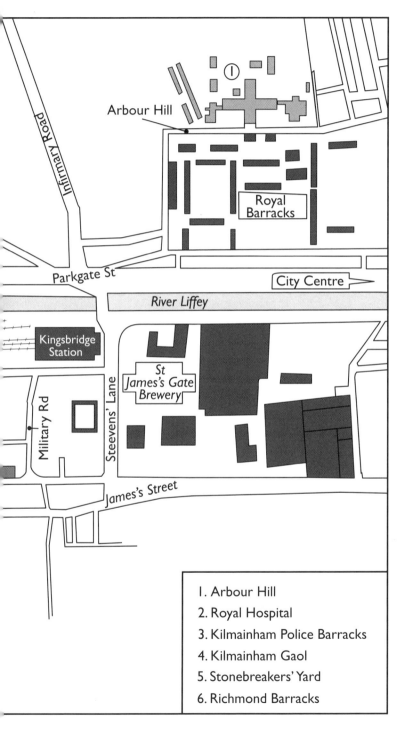

Map of west Dublin in 1916 showing the positions of Richmond Barracks, Kilmainham Gaol, The Royal Hospital Kilmainham and Arbour Hill.

Arbour Hill

Royal Barracks

Parkgate St

City Centre

River Liffey

Kingsbridge Station

St James's Gate Brewery

Steevens' Lane

Military Rd

James's Street

1. Arbour Hill
2. Royal Hospital
3. Kilmainham Police Barracks
4. Kilmainham Gaol
5. Stonebreakers' Yard
6. Richmond Barracks

Kilmainham Gaol,

7.5.'16.

My dear Annie and Lily,

I am giving this to Mrs. Murphy for you; she'll not
mind to hear of what is happening, and she'll get you
all to pray for those of us who must die. Indeed you
girls give us courage, and may God grant you Freedom
soon in the fullest sense. You wont see me again,
and I felt it better not to have you see me, as you'd
only be lonely, but now my soul is gone and pray God
it will be pardoned all its crimes. Tell Christy and
all what happened and ask them to pray for me.

Goodbye, dear friends and remember me in your prayers.

Your fond friend

C. O Colbáird

The letter of 27-year-old Captain Con Colbert to Annie and Lily Cooney written the day before his execution. ANNIE O'BRIEN WS 805

Introduction

The 1916 Rising is one of the most written-about episodes in Ireland's turbulent history. Less well documented, however, is what happened in its immediate aftermath. Many publications cover the courts martial, deportations and executions as a footnote to a wider subject matter, or take a biographical viewpoint of the leaders, either collectively or individually. A small number of books deal exclusively with the courts martial. We felt, however, that the overall narrative of Ireland's revolutionary period was missing a hugely important and no less fascinating focus: the in-depth story of the post-Rising events in Dublin, as well as what followed, from the perspective of those on both sides who were actually there.

For a great many of the participants, what happened in the days, weeks and months after the Rising was probably worse than the fighting itself. In some ways, the combat seen in Dublin and elsewhere during Easter Week was, for those who took part, as exhilarating as it was traumatic. The same could not be said of what came in its wake. Some expressed the wish that they had not survived the insurrection when they found themselves incarcerated in conditions that drove them to the brink of insanity – and, on more than one occasion, beyond.

Yet the period between May 1916 and the autumn of 1917 saw the rebirth of the Irish Volunteer movement. Shattered as it was following its military defeat, and reeling from the executions of its leaders, by late 1917 it was beginning, against all odds, to reshape itself into a formidable force which now had a considerable strategic advantage compared with the rebel units who had turned out on Easter Monday 1916. The Volunteers now had widespread public support, shown by the jubilant welcome they received from thousands of civilians when they returned from imprisonment and internment.

Following the final Republican surrenders in Dublin and elsewhere after Easter Week, the men and women of the Irish Volunteers and Irish Citizen Army were staring into the dark abyss of defeat. Many were unable to comprehend why they had capitulated. They felt a sense of desolation at the shattering of the dream for which they had trained so long and fought so tenaciously. The angry reaction of a huge section of Dublin's civilians towards them came as a great shock that added immeasurably to their anguish. Dublin had divided loyalties at the time of the Rising. Despite significant support for the revolutionary cause from many quarters, thousands of Dublin's civilians took the opposite view. Many who had relations serving in the British Army saw the insurgents as traitors; others were happy to be part of the British Empire; another significant cohort were content with the promise of Home Rule at a later date, however hollow that promise had proved to be. The Volunteers knew this, and had accordingly expected some backlash, but nothing approaching the levels of venom spat at them, to the point where, more than once, enemy soldiers had to intervene to protect them.

The rebel prisoners who were initially detained in Richmond Barracks in Inchicore faced horrendous conditions. They were kept in overcrowded cells with inadequate ventilation, very little water and abysmal hygiene. Fighting men and women who had not eaten, drunk or slept in days had to face the backlash from cruel and hostile enemy soldiers. They then witnessed the pitiless selection of their more prominent figures by detectives for the military courts. The deportations that followed were both terrifying and stomach-churning. Loaded onto stinking cattle boats, many of them expected to be sunk in the Irish Sea by an enemy determined to take revenge. Some were so dejected at this point that such a fate would have been considered a blessing. Then the authorities exacerbated the trauma of defeat with the executions of the rebellion's leaders and more prominent participants.

The courts martial that preceded the executions were swiftly convened, and carried out with equal haste. Despite official records being incomplete, our extensive research has enabled us to gain a reasonably comprehensive picture of the more prominent trials, as well as a picture of what the British officers overseeing them thought of their adversaries. Much of it is surprising. The reactions of the Volunteers to the trials varied. Some wanted nothing to do with them and effectively refused to acknowledge their authority. Others were aghast at the apparent disregard for due process afforded them, a sentiment shared by their most prominent prosecutor, Lieutenant William Wylie.

The executions that took place following the courts martial have been well documented in terms of their victims' personalities, their histories, and their positions in the revolutionary movement. Their chronology is generally well known. However, we felt that there was still a dearth of literature about what happened when the actual executions took place. This is something we have endeavoured to put to rights in this book. Seven of the 14 men shot in Kilmainham Gaol were, after all, in effect the founding fathers of the Irish Republic, having signed the proclamation that underpinned it. Much has been spoken and written of their and the other condemned men's lives, and indeed of their poignant final hours, but comparatively little has been written of what actually took place in the Stonebreakers' Yard when they were put to death. There are, of course, numerous detailed written accounts recorded by the monks who ministered to the condemned men as their final hour approached, but from the perspective of those who had the unpalatable task of carrying out the executions there are comparatively few details.

The principal reason for the lack of official written records from the British side is that anonymity was afforded to both the officers and enlisted soldiers who oversaw the executions. At an administrative level, meticulous records were kept on the condemned men, but the opposite is the case when it comes to those whose boots were on the ground, who carried out the sentences. To remedy this, we have painstakingly trawled through the available accounts from those who were there. Significant detail was passed on by word of mouth, often years later, as well as being recorded in diaries or memoirs. Such sources have yielded knowledge of how these momentous, historic events unfolded. Additionally, while there was no clear-cut manual on firing squads in the British Army at the time, there was a protocol that could be adapted to any given situation, whether on the Western Front or in Dublin. By comparing shootings on the Western Front with those in Kilmainham we could see that, with some exceptions, the same basic protocol was followed. Unfortunately, some officers in charge of firing squads in Dublin were pitifully lacking in any instruction on the protocol, as were their men. This would have horrific consequences. Having approached our research in this way we feel that we have managed to convey to the reader not only how mechanically gruesome the execution procedure itself was, but also how disturbing it was for many of the infantrymen who formed the firing parties, and their officers. In this regard, we hope to have rectified a historic disservice to the men who faced the firing squads, as well those who reluctantly formed them.

The accounts of the executed men are compelling. The stoicism they displayed was admired by many of the soldiers who faced them from the butt end of a rifle, as well as their officers, who at least respected the integrity of their cause and their courage in pursuing it. The following quote, recorded in 1920 by the regiment that provided the firing squads, attests to this.

> 'That is why every Sinn Feiner who was condemned to death stood in the courtyard at Kilmainham before the firing squad, drawn from a sister Battalion to our own, steadily, like men, without flinching, and without support. All faced the rifles not as craven rebels, but like men dying for a great idea. Soldiers who were present, ever susceptible to courage whenever they find it, acknowledge this.'[1]

Inevitably, the trauma that befell the rebellion's participants – on both sides – brought forth the human face of war. In numerous cases during its aftermath, unexpected acts of kindness were shown to the surrendered insurgents by their British Army captors, some of whom came from the very units that had suffered the worst at their hands during the fighting. It was not only the rebellion's leaders who showed astonishing fortitude. The spirit and sheer tenacity displayed by both the officers and rank and file of the Volunteers greatly impressed many of their captors.

Another striking characteristic that was evident in the ranks of the Irish Volunteers, the Irish Citizen Army, the Fianna, and Cumann na mBan was camaraderie.[2] It was needed. These people had trained and fought hard together, knowing that going up against the might of the British military could prove fatal to them, and catastrophic for their families. Nevertheless, a significant number, living as they did in a city with the worst slums in Europe, and the highest rate of infant mortality, felt they had little to lose from a system that offered scant opportunity for the ordinary man and woman. Many of their countrymen who fought in Dublin and elsewhere felt the same. Those Volunteers of better financial and social standing – of whom there were many – felt that recent developments, such as the flagrant disregard of legally constituted

Home Rule, in favour of the Unionists who sought to usurp it, with arms if necessary, shone a light on where they really stood. Few of them hated the British – far from it – but equally, they would die before bowing down to its empire, which they saw as the root cause of so many of their country's woes.

Not all of those who had fought against the British Army during Easter Week 1916 were killed or captured. There were breathtaking escapes under fire; some evaded imprisonment by both pluck and luck; others simply melted away. But over three thousand prisoners, including innocent civilians, were rounded up and processed by the detectives of Dublin's G-Division. Their enthusiasm for their work was not forgotten during the War of Independence that began three years after the Rising, and in which several of them were gunned down by assassination squads.

Our story begins with the Republican surrenders at the end of Easter Week itself, and the immediate aftermath. We then deal with the rounding up and processing of prisoners, the courts martial that followed, and the leaders' executions. We do our best to transport the reader back to the city as it must have looked, sounded and even smelled. We wanted to convey the events in as visceral a manner as possible, as we did in this book's predecessor – *When The Clock Struck in 1916: Close-Quarter Combat in the Easter Rising* (The Collins Press, 2015). Our unflinching accounts are at times not pretty, but we have no wish to sanitise history. We assume the reader will have some degree of prior knowledge of the background to the insurrection itself and its fundamental reasons.

After looking at the incarcerations, courts martial and executions, we touch on the surviving insurgents' fascinating journeys into exile in England and Wales, where they were imprisoned or interned in various camps and prisons, testing their physical and psychological resilience to breaking point. Many of their captors were similarly tested when confronted with their determined and wily Irish adversaries.

Finally, we provide a brief window on their return to Dublin – to a completely different political landscape – where the Volunteers immediately took up the baton under new leadership, only to suffer another devastating loss when Thomas Ashe died on hunger strike in September 1917. His funeral became the rallying cry that saw Volunteers once again assemble in uniform on the streets of Ireland's capital.

We have followed the same thread of characters as those featured in *When The Clock Struck in 1916*, as well as adding some new ones. Ordinary men and women from all walks of life – the 'butchers, bakers and candlestick makers' – took on the biggest empire the world had ever known, an empire on which 'the sun never set'. Their extraordinary stories are gripping. What they experienced in Richmond Barracks, Kilmainham Gaol and in England was just as important in a historical context as the events they lived through during the Rising itself, and in the years that followed.

The area of west Dublin where Richmond Barracks and Kilmainham Gaol are situated still echoes today with the history that haunts the former barracks' open acres and rustic structures, as much as it does the cold, bleak Stonebreakers' Yard in Kilmainham Gaol. It was here where the shape of Ireland was changed irrevocably and for ever. It was, fundamentally, the secretive and legally suspect nature of the courts martial, and the executions, that eventually turned the tide of public opinion in Ireland in favour of the Republican and nationalist causes, and drove a great many whose prior allegiances were either ambiguous, or directed in varying degrees towards the Crown, into the arms of those who sought to subvert the same Crown's authority in Ireland. Indeed, it is often argued that General Maxwell – the man the Crown placed in charge following the insurrection to suppress the cause of the nationalist enemy – ended up doing a great deal more to advance it.

What followed the Easter Rising would lead three years later to the bitterly contested War of Independence. The anguish of the Rising's defeat and the desperate uncertainty as to the future of the nationalist and Republican movement was gradually overcome by the rejigging of the Irish Volunteers under the very noses of the authorities. Frongoch internment camp in north Wales became known as the 'Republican University', the Irish Volunteers' equivalent of Sandhurst Military Academy, which has trained British Army officers for over two centuries. Prisons such as Lewes, Dartmoor, Maidstone, Broadmoor and Portland ended up serving a similar purpose. From these bleak places emerged new leaders, such as Thomas Ashe, Éamon de Valera, Harry Boland, Liam Tobin, Michael Collins and Richard Mulcahy, ready and eager to fill the void left by the orators and visionaries who had been executed the previous year, and who were equally willing to lay down their lives if necessary. Following their deportations and imprisonments the

Volunteers and Citizen Army returned, hailed as heroes, to a different Ireland. The same men and women then set about seizing the initiative handed to them by the actions of the military under General Maxwell, who, like his Prime Minister, Herbert Asquith, had completely misjudged Irish sentiment in May 1916. The propaganda victory Asquith and Maxwell handed to the Republicans was not wasted. The nationalist skill in public relations was then employed with similar, if not greater, effect in September 1917, when the Volunteers, the majority of whom had by then returned to Ireland, paraded once again in public for Thomas Ashe's funeral. Commandant Ashe's death was the result of no less brutal treatment by the authorities than the executions in Kilmainham the previous year.

Many of the same rank-and-file members of the Volunteers, Cumann na mBan and Citizen Army endured not only the Rising and its aftermath but also the continuing struggle for Irish independence in the years beyond. Their stories are tremendously important both to Ireland and to Britain. One of our principal sources, the Bureau of Military History in Cathal Brugha Barracks, offers an unequalled wealth of human history in revolution. The bureau holds thousands of first-hand accounts of the suffering endured when ordinary people set out to change history. They are laced with intensity, tragedy and, often, hilarity. It has been a privilege to present these unforgettable stories and, once again, we hope we have done them justice.

Derek Molyneux & Darren Kelly

Prologue

'Sure we have had a fine fight'

At 2 a.m. on Friday 28 April 1916, a Royal Navy destroyer crept slowly up the estuary of Dublin's River Liffey. British Army General Sir John Grenfell Maxwell stood on its wooden deck along with his retinue. The 56-year-old general had been charged by his political and military masters in London with stemming the Easter Rising in Ireland, now entering its fifth day. His mandate was to crush enemy resistance in both the capital and the country, and to see that those responsible were punished. He was then to ensure that order was restored to Ireland as quickly as possible. This was particularly urgent given the pressure that Britain and its empire were under as the Great War escalated.

Each man who stood with the general on the ship's deck was transfixed by the spectacle of the burning city ahead of him. Central Dublin was an inferno, having been under British artillery fire for two days. The destroyer's sleek form cut through the narrowing river as it entered the city. The figure of Commerce at the top of the Palladian dome of Dublin's Custom House was outlined clearly by the flames consuming all in their path in Sackville Street a half mile to the north-west. At North Wall Quay the ship drew alongside a smaller vessel with a gun mounted on its bow. When it was tied up, gangplanks were thrown across to the other vessel, and from there to the dock. Then a British Army staff officer came aboard the destroyer. As he approached the general and his entourage, they noticed the Military Cross ribbon on his chest – this was a man to be reckoned with. The officer saluted the general, and told him in a pronounced Irish accent that his cars would arrive shortly. Some of the officials accompanying the general enquired, in equally distinctive English public school accents, about the fighting in Dublin. The officer replied, 'Sure we have had a fine fight.'[1]

Soon afterwards, two motor cars pulled up at the dock. The general and his attendants disembarked and made their way to the cars, whose engines were ticking over quietly, their passenger doors held open by saluting drivers. Their destination was the Royal Hospital in Kilmainham, the British Army headquarters in Ireland, situated two miles to the west of the burning city centre. Their route, however, would be an indirect one – along the North Circular Road – because the rebels continued to occupy the General Post Office (GPO) and the Four Courts, both of which stood in their path. The drivers picked up speed passing the bombed-out shell of Liberty Hall. Lieutenant Alfred Brucknill – an Admiralty barrister, who sat next to the general – looked on as Maxwell re-read his orders, and he glimpsed the words: 'To take all such measures as may be necessary for the prompt suppression of the rebellion in Ireland'.[2] He also noticed the instruction that civilians could be tried by courts martial under the Defence of the Realm Act (DORA). As Maxwell's legal adviser, Brucknill knew that, despite his orders, the general had limited powers – the Act did not provide in any way for the event of armed insurrection. It appeared to him, therefore, that once they had overwhelmed the insurgents, they would need to find a means of charging them with 'aiding the enemy' – the Germans and the Central European powers – in order to permit the imposition of maximum sentences, i.e. executions.

They reached the Royal Hospital at 3 a.m., having had only one hair-raising incident en route when the lead car had not slowed down quickly enough at one of the numerous British Army checkpoints that had sprung up all over the city since the British military had established its stranglehold. The alarming sight of over a dozen raised rifles alerted the driver just in time for him to bring the car screeching to a halt and avoid a hail of bullets. British infantry throughout Dublin were in a high state of alert and would open fire at the merest hint of the enemy.

Several hours later, having rested and now enjoying a splendid breakfast, Maxwell was brought fresh news from England: the British cabinet in Westminster had declared that the entire island of Ireland was now under martial law. His own powers had now increased; in effect he was master of his own small kingdom. Stepping away from the table for a moment, he peered out of a huge window towards the South Dublin Union, the clear morning sky revealing an enemy flag hanging from one of its vantage points. The Union was just one of half a dozen Republican garrison areas in Dublin city that were still holding out. Maxwell declared loudly: 'Two guineas to the man who brings that flag in!' The green Republican symbol would, however, remain securely fastened in place at the Union until the following Sunday, and the general failed ultimately to get his hands on it.

1

The First Prisoners – Richmond Barracks and Kilmainham Gaol

'Anyone want to see the animals?'

On the night of Saturday 29 April 1916, Dublin's Easter Rising was all but over. As darkness fell on the smouldering city centre, roughly four hundred dishevelled, exhausted rebel prisoners were herded into the enclosed Rotunda Hospital grounds in Rutland Square, to the north of Sackville Street (now O'Connell Street). They were made up of the Irish Volunteer headquarters (HQ) garrison who had surrendered to the British in Moore Street earlier in the day, as well as most of the men from the Volunteers' 1st Battalion, who had also surrendered that evening at the Four Courts. Fifty-eight other men from the 1st Battalion were still holding out in the North Brunswick Street area to their west, while in other city areas the remaining Volunteer Dublin Brigade battalions were also holding fast. Nevertheless, it was now only a matter of time before they too capitulated. The chilly night air was thick with smoke and dust from the once-picturesque boulevard of Sackville Street, now a post-battlefield ruin of smashed concrete, metal and broken glass.

Edward (Ned) Daly, the 25-year-old Commandant of the 1st Volunteer Battalion, moved among his comrades, ensuring that discipline was still sound, until he was pulled out from among them and thrown to the ground by his captors. He collected himself and glanced around. He now sat among the staff officers of the Irish Volunteers and their aides-de-camp. The men were penned in like sheep and surrounded by a cordon of men with bayonets. Behind the men pointing their 17-inch-long blades were formidable railings and walls, beyond which were additional platoons of enemy soldiers who, following a week of intense street fighting, felt little sympathy for their prisoners. Daly took a few moments to take in the unexpected turn of events. He could not understand why he and his men had been ordered by their commander-in-chief Pádraig Pearse to lay down their arms. His own battalion had been so well fortified in the Four Courts and North King Street areas that the British had found it impossible to dislodge them.

Daly was the youngest of the Irish Volunteers to hold the rank of battalion commandant. Raised in Limerick, he had joined the Irish Volunteers at its inception in November 1913 – ironically, in the same complex that now confined him and his comrades. He had quickly risen through the Volunteer ranks, displaying a military aptitude that, when tested in combat, had frustrated the enemy to such a degree that they had vented their fury on civilians, massacring many non-combatants. The 58 men from Daly's battalion who were still holding out were now under the command of 19-year-old Patrick Holohan. A ceasefire was, however, in place.

Daly's eyes fell on the youthful but weary face of 20-year-old Dubliner Seán McLoughlin. The last time they had met, McLoughlin, from nearby North King Street, had been acting as a runner between the Mendicity Institute, an outpost on Usher's Island, a mile or so to their west, and Volunteer HQ in the GPO. Now the young man was among the rebellion's subdued-looking leaders, having, unbeknownst to Daly, been promoted to the rank of commandant general the previous night. Daly asked McLoughlin what had happened and why they had surrendered.[1] McLoughlin told Daly that he should ask Seán MacDermott – one of the rebellion's chief architects – who was sitting nearby. Just then, a British officer noticed Daly and McLoughlin speaking and became angry. He shouted that if either of them uttered another word it would be his last.

Watching from not far away was 25-year-old Captain Michael Collins, aide-de-camp to another of the Volunteer leaders – 28-year-old Commandant Joseph Plunkett, the Volunteers' Director of Military Operations – who lay next to him. Plunkett was dying of tuberculosis, and after a week of frenetic intensity and combat was now in a pitiful physical state. Two Cumann na mBan members, Winifred Carney and

Julia Grenan, wrapped Plunkett in two overcoats, one of which belonged to Commandant James Connolly – the man in overall charge of the Volunteers' Dublin Brigade – who had earlier been taken to Dublin Castle on a stretcher. Carney had been Connolly's secretary. One of the overcoats was laid out on the ground beneath Plunkett, the other placed over him as a blanket.

As the long cold night dragged into the early hours of Sunday morning, the air was filled with groans, coughs and splutters from the prisoners huddled together and surrounded by the horseshoe-shaped hospital buildings. Sleep, a fitful luxury enjoyed only by those who could simply no longer remain awake, was frequently disturbed by loudly barked reminders that the men were surrounded by guards and that any escape attempts would be met with a speedy and lethal response from the machine gunners and riflemen positioned on the nearby rooftops. The ring of steel remained solid all through the night. Gunshots cracked in the distance. The Volunteers were packed in so tightly in places that men had to lie on top of one another. They were not permitted to stand up to relieve themselves. One particularly vicious British officer – 29-year-old Captain Percival Lea Wilson – darted from place to place among the Volunteers, striking matches in their faces and shouting at his men, 'Anyone want to see the animals?'[2] Lea Wilson had only recently left a nearby public house, which had reopened immediately after the fighting had finished to meet the demands of thirsty soldiers. He was quite drunk. He was wearing a smoking hat with a tassel attached, and looked somewhat ridiculous. When Volunteer Frank Henderson rose to his knees to urinate, Lea Wilson struck him on the back of the head with the butt of a rifle he had grabbed from an infantryman.

At one point, Commandant Daly asked a passing British non-commissioned officer (NCO) for permission to reach across several feet to where his personal belongings lay on the ground. The NCO obliged by picking up the items himself and handing them to Daly. Enraged by this simple act of kindness towards the enemy, Lea Wilson ran at the soldier, berating him and calling him 'a bloody servant to the rebels.'[3] He then approached Daly himself and dragged him to his feet. As soon as the battle-weary commandant was standing, Lea Wilson ripped the epaulettes from the shoulders of his tunic, before ordering a nearby soldier to perform another search on him, which resulted in Daly being stripped half naked.

The unhinged Lea Wilson then turned his attention to Daly's brother-in-law, Tom Clarke, the 58-year-old rebel leader, raised in County Tyrone, who had been the first to put his name to the Proclamation of the Irish Republic, which had been read aloud outside the GPO the previous Monday. That seemed a different world now. Clarke, worn out and frail, and nursing a gunshot wound that pre-dated the insurrection, was pulled out from those surrounding him and dragged to the steps of the hospital's main entrance. There, the captain had him stripped naked. Noticing several horrified nurses looking on at the humiliating spectacle from the upstairs windows, he roared up at them, 'Nice general for your fucking army!' Then, turning back to Clarke, he berated him again. Clarke may have appeared physically frail, but during his life his mental constitution had already withstood sustained and unimaginable assaults. His body was weak, but psychologically he had, by now, been tempered to the point of near impenetrability. He leaned in and whispered something to the captain that further enraged him and resulted in Clarke getting a slap from one of the officer's gloves across his gaunt, wrinkled face. An angry cry came from among the surrounding Volunteers. Some began to get up, their eyes fixed squarely on the demented enemy officer. They then heard several unmistakable metallic clicks. The soldiers were preparing to fire. Commandant Daly quickly brought his men under control, fearing that any fracas would result in a massacre.

Captain Lea Wilson then ran towards a section of his soldiers, shouting wildly at them: 'Whom do you consider the worst, the Boches or the Sinn Féiners?'[4] The soldiers replied with varying degrees of enthusiasm that the 'Sinn Féiners' were the worst. Lea Wilson played to the gallery, asking what they should do with them. 'Shoot 'em, stick a bayonet in 'em,'[5] was the reply from one man. Some of the infantrymen watched in disgust. Others looked uncomfortably at one another, wondering if the officer had gone mad. When Lea Wilson turned his attention to Commandant Plunkett, Michael Collins, in desperate frustration, said, 'This is a very sick man – will you leave him alone?' Collins also made sure to take in as much information as he could about the enemy officer.

On the same Sunday morning, two miles west of the Rotunda, the far more salubrious setting of the Royal Hospital in Kilmainham was a hive of activity. On the top floor, British riflemen and Lewis gunners had concealed themselves behind the twenty or so windows that opened

The Royal Hospital Kilmainham, British Army headquarters in Ireland. NATIONAL LIBRARY
OF IRELAND

from the huge roof facing the still embattled South Dublin Union – one
of the four Republican garrison areas still holding out south of the River
Liffey. Any visible enemy movement within the Union would draw
immediate fire from here. On the ground floor below this lethal cordon
General Maxwell and his staff stood around a large table on which lay
several unrolled maps. Adjutants interjected periodically with updated
estimates of enemy numbers, while fingers hovered and pointed at
various map positions. The officers were trying to figure out where to
concentrate, and subsequently deal with, the anticipated huge hauls of
Volunteer and Citizen Army prisoners from the city. More prisoners
were also expected to be taken throughout the entire country and
marshalled in the capital once it was properly secured.

Richmond Barracks, the biggest barracks in Dublin and less than a
mile to the south-west of the Royal Hospital Kilmainham in Inchicore,

was soon chosen for its sheer size. Its hundred-year-old barracks square, normally the scene of square-bashing by the boots of the Royal Irish Regiment, measured over a dozen acres and its enclosing walls stood 30 foot high in places. This, together with its numerous buildings and outbuildings, made it ideal for containing a large number of prisoners. Its proximity to Kilmainham's Royal Hospital and – equally important – Kilmainham Gaol, presented additional advantages, as did its closeness to Kingsbridge (Heuston) railway station. Dispatches were now sent out to the barracks' officers and men telling them to prepare for what was to come.

A significant problem facing the British command was how to distinguish the enemy ringleaders from their rank and file. In one sense their task so far had been made easier: many of the leaders had identified themselves and led their men and women to the surrender points in Sackville Street the previous evening. The downside, however, was that the British officers and soldiers would be unable to pick out any of the main players in the Volunteer movement other than those who presented themselves voluntarily. Maxwell decided that the best course of action would be to use the Dublin Metropolitan Police (DMP), particularly G-Division, to help identify the ringleaders. G-Division was a detective unit based in Great Brunswick Street (Pearse Street). It had had been keeping tabs on the movements of the Volunteers and Citizen Army since their inception three years earlier. The unit, which had been on standby, was quickly summoned. It was then decided that once the insurrection's ringleaders and instigators had been identified and separated, the remainder would be deported to prisons and camps on the other side of the Irish Sea. The requisite transport could be commandeered and the authorities in England would be notified. Round-ups would follow to capture those who had either escaped or had not risen with their comrades the previous week. In this way, the British hoped to destroy once and for all an enemy they considered a many-headed snake.

At 8 a.m., back in the Rotunda grounds, the British NCOs ordered the bone-weary, half-starved men of the GPO and Four Courts garrisons to form into ranks four deep. They were then marched out of the gates facing Cavendish Row, where they found two long lines of enemy soldiers, on either side of the road, awaiting them with bayonets fixed. Three regiments were represented: the Royal Irish Rifles, the Royal Irish

General Sir John Grenfell Maxwell, at the centre of picture, accompanied by his retinue in Dublin. Lieutenant Brucknill is third from left. COURTESY OF KILMAINHAM GAOL ARCHIVES

Regiment and the Staffordshire Regiment. They numbered almost two men to each prisoner.[6] The rebels and their leaders marched between the enemy infantrymen until they reached the head of the two lines. As soon as the Rotunda was empty the soldiers turned to face forwards. The officer overseeing all of this had received a dispatch ordering him to march the prisoners to Richmond Barracks. Sitting astride a fine bay horse, he rode arrogantly up and down the line of assembled men before finally issuing the order to move out. The British sergeants then bellowed the command to their troops – 'Forward march!' The Volunteers kept in step. The sound of hundreds of marching men soon echoed around the surrounding area and was met with silent stares from scores of gathered civilians. A low melodic hum began to be heard among the ranks of Volunteers – the tune 'God Save Ireland'. It was quickly taken up by more of them as they raised their heads. Soon, the entire column were singing the old rebel song. Some held back tears; others looked defiant, bolstered by the growing melody accompanying the tramp of their feet. As the head of the column reached Lower Sackville Street the eyes of soldier and Volunteer were stung by smoke from the fires in gutted buildings. Commandants Daly and McLoughlin congratulated their men at maintaining such fine order, and issued repeated commands to the men to keep their heads high and their spirits up. Volunteer Maurice Fitzsimons of the 1st Battalion was marching next to his comrade Éamon Dore, a medical student from Limerick. He turned to him, asking if he was feeling downhearted. Dore replied to his fully uniformed friend that he was not – he was proud. Fitzsimons then cried out to the rest of the surrounding men: 'Are we downhearted?'[7] Moggy Murtagh, marching in front of him, answered at the top of his voice, 'No!' A prod from a British NCO's bayonet, however, warned Murtagh to keep his mouth shut. Fitzsimons was stabbed in the behind by a more forceful lunge of the same razor-sharp blade.

Joseph Plunkett had somehow found the strength to keep up with the marching column. He was helped on his way by Michael Collins. Seán MacDermott, on the other hand, following close behind the tail end of the column, which was still on Upper Sackville Street, found it impossible to keep up. He had earlier been relieved of a walking cane he had used since contracting polio in 1912. Captain Lea Wilson had taken it in a final act of cruelty. He explained why he was limping to a Lieutenant Ruxton of the Royal Irish Regiment. Ruxton was intrigued by the sight of this crippled and kindly faced man dressed in civilian clothes. He asked him: 'How did you get into this affair?' He was unaware of MacDermott's position as a principal agitator of the rebellion. MacDermott, from Kiltyclogher in County Leitrim, was the secretary of the Irish Republican Brotherhood's (IRB's) Supreme Council.[8] For many years he had been the Volunteer movement's best-known personality, and he had been a military member of the movement, albeit without an officer's rank, since its foundation. He replied: 'We all have our place in the organisation.' The British officer appeared sympathetic, and detailed a corporal and a section of men to guard MacDermott. He was then permitted to walk at his own pace. Winifred Carney and Julia Grenan were allowed to remain at his side.[9] They marched off slowly, taking turns supporting him, surrounded by soldiers.

The surrendered GPO and Four Courts garrisons crossed the River Liffey at O'Connell Bridge, overlooked by the huge statue of another Irishman who had striven to free his people, albeit in a less violent fashion, during the earlier part of the previous century – Daniel O'Connell. The 'Liberator', as he was known, was today riddled with bullet holes and surrounded by devastation. The group then passed

Winifred Carney, James Connolly's 26-year-old secretary, who helped tend to the desperately ill Joseph Plunkett in the Rotunda grounds during the night of 29–30 April. The following day she assisted Seán MacDermott after his walking cane was taken from him by Captain Lea Wilson. COURTESY OF KILMAINHAM GAOL ARCHIVES

along Westmoreland Street, between Trinity College to their left and the old parliament building to their right, before marching into Dame Street, where clusters of civilians lined the route, some staring silently, others shouting words of support. Many more hurled abuse. Curiously, standing among them were men in civilian clothes with white and blue striped armlets, and carrying batons. Charles Saurin, of the 2nd Volunteer Battalion detachment that had fought in the Sackville Street area, guessed that they were Special Constables, or plainclothes policemen, back on the streets after having been withdrawn for their own protection the previous week.

As the sun began to bathe the city, some of those on the march began to collapse from exhaustion and hunger. Their comrades picked them up and supported them. Michael Collins took turns with several other men to support Joseph Plunkett. Some of the soldiers flanking them took pity and offered them their water canteens, only to be scolded by their own comrades, who looked with contempt upon such acts of empathy towards a hated enemy.

The torment intensified when they reached Francis Street's junction with Thomas Street, just to the west of Christchurch, where larger crowds had gathered on both sides of the road, forming a hate-filled gauntlet. Screams and shouts that the rebels were 'murderers and starvers of the people'[10] were hurled at them. Soldiers had to hold the mob back at bayonet point as they pressed forward, launching missiles and spitting. The Volunteers were perplexed. These were the very people they had tried to set free. Many of the residents of the Francis Street area were vexed that these men had taken up arms against the army in which many of their husbands, sons and fathers served – simply, in many cases, to put food on their families' tables. The officer in charge rode up and down their ranks on his horse, amused at the local people's attitude to the prisoners. At James's Street they were ordered to turn right to avoid the South Dublin Union – still in rebel hands – which was roughly five hundred yards to their front and left. Soon they were descending between the huge flanking walls of Steevens' Lane towards Kingsbridge Station, where they turned left onto St John's Road. The eight-foot granite walls of the Royal Hospital Kilmainham were now on their left. Behind the walls, on the raised grass banks, stood dozens of British soldiers shouting insults at them – one proclaiming loudly to Volunteer Captain Frank Henderson that their 'friends' – the Germans – had just been badly mauled by the British Army. Many of the British soldiers, not to mention the Irish civilians, had suspected the Germans of having masterminded and financed much of the Rising.

The Volunteers eventually reached Kilmainham crossroads, where they turned right onto Emmet Road. Within minutes, at approximately 10 a.m., they were marching through the entrance gates of Richmond Barracks. Volunteer Lieutenant Oscar Traynor, the 30-year-old from the 2nd Battalion detachment that had fought in both the Fairview and Sackville Street areas, noticed a Capuchin monk in his sombre-looking cassock standing outside the gates, crying and saying over and over the word '*Misneach*'.[11] The British soldiers looked at him with curious frowns, little realising that the word was Irish for 'courage'. He was trying to give the men heart for what they were about to face. They would need it.

The barracks square of Richmond Barracks – home to the Royal Irish Regiment, where rebel prisoners were processed and their leaders selected for court martial. It was a scene where both cruelty and kindness was shown to prisoners by their captors. NATIONAL LIBRARY OF IRELAND

Minutes later, the head of the column reached the centre of the barracks square. The officer in charge dismounted from his bay horse and went to hand over command of the prisoners to Lieutenant-Colonel Fraser. Fraser was Provost Marshal,[12] and was in charge of prisoners at Richmond Barracks. A large crowd of off-duty soldiers and what appeared to be their wives, some of whom were carrying babies and children in their arms, gathered to examine the ranks of rebels. Abuse quickly followed. One group of soldiers launched an attack with their fists and feet, but were eventually pushed back by the guards.

As the Volunteers stood in lines, one of them, Arthur Shields, pulled a cigarette from his pack. As he went to light it, a British corporal roared, 'Stop that! Do you know where you are?' A sergeant appeared and laughingly boasted to the corporal, loud enough for most of the Volunteers to hear, that he had been digging graves since early morning. The sergeant then approached Shields, eyeing him with a look of contempt, and said, 'I hope I'll be on the firing party to-morrow'.[13] Shields, despite his sudden trepidation at the sergeant's menacing comment, denied him the satisfaction of a reaction. The two NCOs then moved away.

Meanwhile, two miles to the east, in Ship Street Barracks, situated at the rear of Dublin Castle, three Volunteer captains – Liam Tannam, Michael Staines and Diarmuid Lynch – were lined up in its yard with several other prisoners who had just been ordered out of their cells. Among the others were four Volunteers who had helped to carry the badly wounded Commandant Connolly by stretcher to Dublin Castle the previous day, before being detained themselves in the castle. The three officers and the four other men had since shared a cell with several Citizen Army men who had been captured alongside Dr Kathleen Lynn while fighting in the adjacent City Hall. Lynn and the others had themselves been taken prisoner after the ferocious battle there on Easter Monday. Dr Lynn had assumed command of the City Hall garrison after two of its officers were killed by enemy fire. She was now being held with some other Citizen Army women in a stinking, lice-ridden cell beneath Dublin Castle's cobblestones. The Citizen Army men now stood close to Captains Tannam, Staines and Lynch.

Soon after they had assembled in the yard, the gathered men were looked over by DMP detectives and intelligence officers. The policemen took great satisfaction in breaking the news to them that the rebel HQ had officially surrendered.

Liam Tannam, 21 years old and from Wilton Place in Dublin, had joined the Volunteers in 1914 and the IRB in 1915. He had been introduced to the former, and sworn into the latter, by Éamonn Ceannt, the commandant of the Volunteers 4th Battalion. Tannam himself served as commander of E Company, 3rd Battalion. He had been at the forefront of the recent fighting on Sackville Street and Moore Street.

Tannam and his two fellow officers cursed quietly. They had protested vigorously at their detention in the castle the previous day, insisting that they had come there under an escort during a ceasefire to transport a wounded officer – Commandant Connolly – into enemy custody, and that, as per the rules of war, they should then have been released to their

KILMAINHAM JAIL. DUBLIN .3118 W L

The forbidding walls of Kilmainham Gaol, built in 1796. NATIONAL LIBRARY OF IRELAND

units. Their protests had fallen on deaf ears. The surrender now boasted of by the officers and detectives came as no great surprise, especially considering the ruins they had left behind and the subsequent sight of massed enemy troops, not to mention their artillery. However, they strongly felt that they should have been permitted to return to the men under their command, whose fate – whatever it might be – they would be content to share. Shortly after the detectives had finished gloating, soldiers ordered the assembled men to march out.

The haggard-looking group eventually reached the forbidding stone walls of Kilmainham Gaol. Kilmainham had ceased operating as a prison in 1910, but since the outbreak of the Great War it had been used as a military detention centre. The prisoners were taken inside the gaol before being split up and shoved into cells, three men to each. The cells' whitewashed walls were smeared with blood,[14] suggesting that brutal treatment was being meted out. The prisoners soon discovered that the prison warder on duty that day had little affection for the recent arrivals. He taunted them continuously. Lynch, 38 years old, took offence at this and insisted they be treated as prisoners of war. The warder's response was a vicious blow to Lynch's jaw with his baton.

Captain Staines was thrown into a cell already occupied by two looters, who were sitting on the only bed. Staines, the son of a Royal Irish Constabulary (RIC) officer from County Mayo, quickly collected himself and glared at them. He had no love for looters, having seen at first hand how they had pillaged Sackville Street on Easter Monday. He had served as the GPO garrison's quartermaster, and was also an IRB member. When he and his fellow officers had witnessed the looting carried out by hordes of Dublin's desperately poor slum-dwellers, they had felt disgusted, considering the looters to have thus brought their rebellion, and the tricolour flag he had raised on the GPO's roof, into disrepute. Both looters stood up straightaway and offered the battle-hardened rebel officer the bed.

Back in the Sackville Street area, at approximately 11.00 a.m. the 2/6th Sherwood Forester Infantry Battalion, which had been engaged in the recent heavy fighting in the area, received fresh orders following the earlier departure of the Republican prisoners from the Rotunda. A small detachment was sent to the eastern side of Sackville Street to the nearby Summerhill area with orders to reopen Kennedy's bakery and distribute bread. This was urgent – the population was beginning to starve. The remainder of the battalion would search houses and buildings for hidden or wounded rebels, or their arms, and remove the many dead.

The men of the 2/6th moved nervously forward from their barricades in the Moore Street/Capel Street/Great Britain Street (Parnell Street) area. Despite the previous day's surrender the dry cracks of rifle shots and the sharp staccato of machine-gun fire could still be heard from across the city. D Company moved out from Great Britain Street, filtering into the lanes and alleyways around Moore Street. One detachment from A Company moved into Cole's Lane and Denmark Street. Every house and building had to be searched from top to bottom. B Company concentrated on Capel Street, while C Company made their way into Upper Abbey Street.

A lieutenant named Brace, and a 12-man section from D Company, found themselves in Sackville Lane at the northern end of Moore Street. Amid the detritus of battle scattered all along the narrow lane they saw

COURT-HOUSE & JAIL.KILMAINHAM.5518.W.L.

Kilmainham Gaol, seen from the front with the courthouse to the left of picture.
NATIONAL LIBRARY OF IRELAND

three dead bodies. A sergeant stopped, knelt, and searched each body in turn while the remainder of the section moved on, scanning every nook and cranny for danger. On one of the bodies the sergeant found a bloodied letter which began 'Written after I was shot,' and ended 'Goodbye darling.' There was also a communiqué from Commandant-General James Connolly. Then, as the sergeant looked up at the wall above the body, he frowned – the word 'O'Rahilly' appeared to have been written on the wall in blood. This was the Volunteer captain who had led a charge into enemy fire on Moore Street the previous Friday. Reading the letter again, the sergeant saw that it included a delivery address. He handed it to Lieutenant Brace. One of the sergeant's section members then called out in alarm when he noticed a rifle poking out from the roof of a nearby public house. The troops rushed at the building, forcing the door, then made for the roof, calling on the enemy rifleman they assumed was there to surrender. There was no reply. Carefully moving onto the roof with weapons at the ready, the infantrymen found to their relief that the position was unmanned. Ominously, however, they discovered that the recently departed sniper had enough food to keep him going for several days, a daunting prospect considering the number of buildings yet to be cleared, any of which could conceal a well-supplied sniper.

Captain Edmunds, in charge of the infantry detachment from A Company, was disgusted by the squalor he found while searching some of the houses on Denmark Street, which sat between Henry Street and Great Britain Street. The captain was seeing at first hand the festering tenement conditions in which almost thirty thousand people were forced to exist, and which, for a great many of those who had killed and maimed his comrades, was their justification for taking up arms – they were seen as the enforcers of the system that kept them in abject poverty. The dispositions of the people living in these crowded tenements varied. In one room, Edmunds and his men were greeted by screeching and hysterical women and children. In the next, the occupants just stared, in a daze, as his men searched around them. When they came across a former sniper's nest in one particular building they were both disturbed and impressed by what they found. Bricks from an outer wall at the back of a fireplace had been removed, along with the fireplace itself, and sandbags put in their place in such a way that the sniper within the room could remain concealed behind the sandbags while he had a clear view of the street below through the aperture created by the missing bricks. The soldiers were tremendously relieved that the fighting in this area was over.

2

The Prisoner Selections Begin in Richmond Barracks

'England's difficulty ...'

In Richmond Barracks, as the Sherwood Foresters were beginning to comb Dublin's slums, the men of the GPO and Four Courts garrisons awaited their fate in the barracks square. They were stupefied with exhaustion. Many struggled to remain upright. Some were becoming delirious from lack of sleep.

An army lieutenant named Jackson appeared from a nearby building.[1] He ordered a section of the 3rd Royal Irish Regiment to move in and search the Volunteers for any hidden weapons the earlier searches at the Rotunda might have missed. This opportunity was not wasted on some of the infantrymen carrying out the searches. They stole any valuables the rebels had. When Volunteer Séamus Kavanagh was searched, the soldier suggested that he may as well hand over everything, adding that since he was going to be shot he would have no further need of his belongings. Seán Kennedy watched in disgust, when his turn came, as an NCO took his money, counted it and pocketed it, saying, 'You won't want that.'[2] Then, perhaps stricken by remorse, he returned a couple of shillings before moving on to the next man.

Shortly before noon, Seán MacDermott, Winifred Carney and Julia Grenan slowly entered the barracks square, still surrounded by British soldiers. Charles Saurin looked on from a distance as MacDermott was stopped and separated from the two women, who were taken off the square and into a guarded room. They were told that they would not be alone for long. MacDermott limped over to his comrades. He still appeared to be in good spirits, despite everything. This was more than could be said of many Volunteers. Some had collapsed from dehydration and weariness, others from the unbearable pain of not having being allowed to perform their bodily functions for nearly 24 hours. One of the first to fall was Commandant Joseph Plunkett. Desperately weak, he could simply take no more. He was dragged by the shoulders out of the line to a nearby footpath and given water. He soon revived. Volunteer Thomas Dowling, who had also fainted, was put beside Plunkett. When he came round he saw a young British soldier trying to pull a ring from Plunkett's finger. Plunkett refused to give it up, summoning what little strength he had to wrest the soldier's hand from his own. The soldier eventually gave up.

As the minutes turned to hours the unseasonal heat of the early afternoon sun led to more groans and thuds as men collapsed onto the stone surface of the barracks square, relieving themselves in the process. Those still standing grappled with the overpowering desire to let go. Men's heads rolled on their shoulders; knees and limbs swayed and shook in protest. An old NCO from the Royal Irish Regiment looked on as the torture continued. Soon he had had enough. He grabbed a bucket and mug, filled the bucket with water, pushed his way through the cordon of soldiers and began passing the water to the Volunteers. He did this several times – backwards and forwards he went with his bucket. The Volunteers thanked him fervently each time he returned. Some began pressing their last possessions on him by way of thanks, assuming they would soon no longer have use for them. They expected to be shot, and the soldiers' taunts and jibes did little to assuage their fears. Another soldier quickly spotted an opportunity and copied the NCO. His was not a mission of charity, however: he would only give water to those who could pay. If the offering was not enough, there would be no water. But luckily for the Volunteers the old NCO kept up his rounds. Eventually, everyone was given a drink.

Suddenly, whistles and commands echoed around the enclosing walls as the Volunteers were divided into groups. This was followed by a shout from an officer: 'You four – move!' as he pointed at an archway underneath a clock tower to the east of the square. Four Volunteers ran

The gymnasium of Richmond Barracks with its distinctive roof cupola to the centre of picture. It was here that the rebels were singled out by the detectives of Dublin's G-Division. NATIONAL LIBRARY OF IRELAND

under the archway, helped along by boorish assurances from surrounding soldiers that if they hesitated they would be shot on the spot. As soon as they were out of sight, however, a burst of machine-gun fire sounded from beyond the archway. Another four were ordered to run through. They waited, terrified. Nearby troops presented their rifles, shouts and orders were hurled and almost involuntarily the second group of four began their ragged dash through the archway. Soon afterwards there was another burst of fire. A sense of dread descended on the surrendered men. Were they all going to be shot out of hand?[3]

Charles Saurin and Arthur Shields stuck close together. They were next. Following a shout of 'At the double!' they set off with another two men, their stomachs churning with fear as they ran under the arch. To their surprise, waiting for them beyond the arch were two burly NCOs, who searched them and then escorted them to a smaller building opposite, where they were met by Lieutenant Jackson, now seated at a desk. Behind the lieutenant stood a plainclothes detective from G-Division. The four disoriented rebels were summoned to the desk. Saurin noticed a small pile of documents and papers on the ground held down with a paperweight, and watched as his Irish Volunteers membership card was flung on top of it. The officer demanded his name and address while the next man was searched. All the while the G-man eyed him suspiciously. Saurin looked at his comrades. They were filthy, bearded and bedraggled following a week of fighting. He would have been surprised if the detective recognised any of them. His own fear had abated – he was simply too worn out to care any more. Then, with a flick of dismissal from Lieutenant Jackson's hand, he was passed through another cordon of soldiers and shoved into the barrack's gymnasium to his left. Once inside, he saw that no firing squad awaited. The machine-gun fire, it appeared, had come from further into the city.

The GPO and Four Courts garrisons now followed Saurin and Shields, one by one, into the gymnasium, a large rectangular room. Each man who went in passed a wooden and glass partition to his left, unaware that he was being scrutinised by G-men from the other side of the partition. Other detectives in the spacious room stood, for their own protection, next to soldiers with fixed bayonets. More soldiers surveyed the gymnasium from a gallery above the entrance, beneath which was a latrine. When Seán MacDermott was searched on his way in, the NCO searching him found a mobilisation order signed by MacDermott himself with his Irish surname – MacDiarmada – and dated 23 April. This was passed to Colonel Fraser, who positioned just inside the entrance. Then, when Lieutenant Jackson asked MacDermott his name, he replied 'John MacDermott', which Jackson wrote down. MacDermott then limped past the desk, followed by Seán McLoughlin. When McLoughlin entered, he came face to face with a G-man who was notorious among the Volunteers: Detective Sergeant Johnny Barton. Barton smiled mockingly at McLoughlin, saying sarcastically in his Kerry accent, 'Here's one of the gallant scouts!'[4] Barton's cohorts looked on and laughed. McLoughlin had been a Fianna officer, had joined the Volunteers in 1913, and was a member of the IRB. He assumed from Barton's remarks that the policeman already knew all this. McLoughlin sensed he could be in serious trouble, however, if Barton discovered his current position – commandant general in the Volunteers – which was far more significant than that of a Fianna scout. When he had been commissioned with his new rank in Moore Street during the fighting, he had been presented with a yellow ribbon to tie around his upper arm as a means of identifying his rank in the absence of more formal insignia. The ribbon had since been removed by a British officer. Whether or not that had been done deliberately, it had saved him, at least for now, from what was to come. The act would more than likely save his life.

Soon the gymnasium was full. The Volunteers were ordered to sit on the right-hand side of the room when they entered. The warm air stank of soiled and unwashed garments and equally grimy bodies. Most of the Volunteers had been wearing the same clothes for a week – a week in which their physical and mental endurance had been tested beyond anything they could have imagined. They had had little or no sleep and few opportunities to wash as the fighting escalated to all-out war during the latter part of the Rising. Latrine runs were then organised in the gymnasium.

After things had settled down the detectives appeared en masse, swooping on the unsuspecting Volunteers like birds of prey. Those chosen for further scrutiny were singled out with the sharp instruction, 'You – you – over that side!', accompanied by a forceful jab to the shoulder with a walking stick or umbrella. Those chosen were then made to stand while G-men eyed them up maliciously, their breath brushing against their faces. Then they were commanded, 'Over the other side' or 'Sit back down.' It went on and on. Patrick Rankin, 27 years old, from Newry in County Down, who had cycled the 70 miles from his home town to fight at the GPO, noticed that each of the detectives had a large flower in the buttonhole of his coat. He could not help but think that the flowers, accompanied by the beaming smiles on their faces, made them look as if they were all going to a wedding, concluding to himself that this was what it felt like to them – a joyous occasion.

Slowly but surely, those the authorities really wanted were picked out: Tom Clarke, Joseph Plunkett, Leo Henderson, Seán McGarry and Seán MacDermott, among others. They took their places on the left of the room. More prisoners began to filter in, but the G-men quickly took advantage of the spaces left by those they had singled out, moving among the Volunteers for a closer look, and selecting more: Joseph Plunkett's brothers, Jack and George; Joseph Gleeson of the Kimmage garrison, who had lived in and trained at Plunkett's home, Larkfield House in Kimmage. As the selections went on, two policemen stood for a moment in front of Patrick Rankin. Listening in on their conversation, Rankin overheard one of them ask the other, 'Is that Daly?'[5] while pointing at the drooping-eyed, moustachioed commandant who sat among a cluster of his comrades. The other replied that he was not sure. The one who had posed the question walked over to the man. 'Are you Ned Daly?' Commandant Daly stood up dead straight and confirmed that he was. He was ordered to take his place among the selected.

Pádraig Pearse's younger brother, 34-year-old Willie, was sitting beside 26-year-old Volunteer Seán MacEntee when a red-faced, rather stout detective stooped above the pair, having noticed a yellow tab on Pearse's uniform. Pearse held the rank of captain in the Volunteers. The detective asked him his name. The reply made him immensely proud of his find. Wide-eyed and beaming from ear to ear, he ordered Pearse to the other side of the room. This would, within three days, cost Pearse his life. Moving on, the same detective spotted Arthur Shields, and demanded his name and place of work. Shields identified himself and, rather apprehensively, gave the Abbey Theatre as his employer, fearing a backlash should the detective be aware of the theatre's status as a hotbed of nationalism, but the policeman moved on to seek another victim.

Three miles to the east of Richmond Barracks during the same early afternoon, the 58 Volunteers of the 1st Battalion, led by Patrick Holohan, stood assembled in rows in the upper yard of Dublin Castle. They had been led by Holohan, who was from Summerhill in Dublin, after their captain, Nicholas Laffan, had been shot in the head the previous day in North Brunswick Street. On Sunday morning they had surrendered separately from the rest of Commandant Daly's battalion. Standing now beneath the castle's 60-foot-high clock tower, they were harried and roughly searched for over an hour. Patrick's brother, 21-year-old Garry, was among them. Both brothers were seasoned Fianna members who, under the command of Lieutenant Paddy Daly, had helped plan and execute a daring raid on the Magazine Fort in the Phoenix Park at the outset of the Rising.

In front of them were several broken windows, which looked distinctly out of place in the ornate surroundings of the nerve centre of British rule in Ireland. There had been no time to repair the damage caused during the previous Monday's Citizen Army assault on City Hall, the whitewashed walls of which bore the scorch marks of exploded hand grenades. Gunfire had been exchanged throughout the upper yard for over 24 hours during a particularly ferocious clash as the battle there had drawn to a close on Tuesday. Holohan's men had spent the previous few days in another area of the city, 500 yards to the north of the Four Courts, engaged in their own desperate battle. They had kept an 800-strong battalion of South Staffordshire infantry at bay during 30 hours of unrelentingly vicious street fighting. The South Staffordshires had then rampaged through the area's houses, massacring civilians.

When a dispatch arrived at the castle confirming that Colonel Fraser in Richmond Barracks was ready to receive the small detachment, the order to move out was given. The men were led between the castle's enclosing walls towards its Ship Street entrance, where they marched through a cordon of enemy soldiers. As soon as they had halted on the cobblestones in Ship Street, several dozen infantrymen alighted from the barracks and began taunting them. One of them was so abusive that Volunteer Patrick Kelly was sure that if he had his way he would have shot them all on the spot.[6] Eventually, to Holohan's relief, the officer in charge of the prisoners shouted the order 'Quick march!' and they began their march to Richmond Barracks.

An hour later, at roughly 1.30 p.m., the same 58 men found themselves halted in the centre of the recently emptied barracks square, where they were searched once again. This time, however, those doing the searching were the same soldiers who had earlier stolen from the men's Volunteer comrades. Relishing the prospect of additional bounty, they were much more enthusiastic than the guards in Dublin Castle. Bayonets were shoved into the sweating faces of men who were at the point of collapse. The soldiers demanded that rings and watches be handed over. When Patrick Kelly refused to hand over his watch, a soldier presented the business end of a rifle barrel. Kelly did not react kindly to the gesture. Luckily, a passing British officer noticed the developing altercation and intervened. Kelly asked him sarcastically if it was obligatory to hand over such personal items as watches. The officer reprimanded the soldiers and ordered them to return anything they had taken. He then ordered most of them to join the other sections of troops darting about under the raucous shouts of NCOs. A small number of guards remained.

Any relief that Holohan's Volunteers had felt was short-lived, however. They were now ordered to remain standing where they were in the bright sunshine for what seemed like hours. Thirst began to torture them. When they were eventually approached by a soldier bearing the insignia of the Royal Irish Fusiliers, who looked very drunk, they feared another tirade, or worse. The soldier stopped, half-frowning, almost as if he did not know what to make of these peculiar-looking combatants. He stepped sideways to their front, passing Holohan, a smile appearing on his face. He then announced that he was an Irishman and proud of it, and he admired the way they had fought.[7] Then he asked if there was anything he could do for them. The answer was grateful and immediate – water. The soldier gathered himself and rushed away, returning soon after with two buckets of water and some tin cups. Patrick Holohan and his comrades gratefully gulped the water, quenching their thirst, before offering the soldier some money for his kindness. The fusilier refused at first, but then changed his mind. After collecting a small fortune in coins, he sped off. He soon returned with armfuls of packs of cigarettes and biscuits, which he began to distribute among the Volunteers.

As Holohan and his men ate the biscuits, Seán O'Duffy noticed a policeman he knew – Detective Joseph Cavanagh – watching the group from close to the clock tower. The detective walked towards them. O'Duffy quietly warned his comrades. Cavanagh stopped in front of him. 'Hello, Mr Duffy. How are you?'[8] O'Duffy smiled and replied in the colloquialism of the time, 'Oh, I am game ball.'[9] Cavanagh then asked O'Duffy if he would like him to deliver a message to his father. O'Duffy, suspicious of an ulterior motive, replied that he did not. When Cavanagh insisted, however, O'Duffy relented and wrote a short note to his father telling him he was okay. Detective Cavanagh then asked if anyone else was from the 'Barn' area, meaning Dolphin's Barn, a suburb to the city's south-west. O'Duffy, still suspicious, assured him that there was nobody else.

A short time later, a lieutenant named O'Brien, a subaltern stationed in the barracks, gave the order to move towards the gymnasium. At its entrance, Garry Holohan stepped forward and gave his name at the desk. He then looked on as another officer erroneously wrote the name Nolan on the list. It was a mistake that would save Holohan from a court martial – and perhaps his life. Holohan, a Fianna member for six years and an IRB member for the previous four, was considered a priority target for capture since he had shot an unarmed civil servant who had attempted to alert the authorities outside Phoenix Park on Easter Monday.

The Volunteers were then ordered inside. When they entered the gymnasium, they were sent to the right. Garry Holohan sat down and looked over to the opposite side. His eyes fell upon Tom Clarke and Seán MacDermott. His smile was warmly reciprocated by the pair, as though they were trying to reassure him. Holohan did not know it, but this would be the last time he set eyes on either of them. Patrick Kelly sat down close to Holohan, having calmed down since his confrontation with the soldier in the yard. Kelly smiled across the hall and raised his hand to acknowledge Ned Daly. Daly's kind smile in response belied his ruthlessly astute mind. Daly's men had tremendous respect for his leadership abilities, proven to them beyond doubt in a cauldron of close-quarter combat surrounding the Four Courts. On this day, however, it looked to Kelly the saddest smile he had ever seen.

Then the G-men swooped again. This was to be a busy day for them. More Volunteers were sent across the room: Maurice Collins, Jack Shouldice, Piaras Béaslaí. Anyone the detectives did not like the look of or who did not answer their questions satisfactorily was sent over. Harry Boland, who had fought in Sackville Street, was sent across; Liam Tobin, from the Four Courts garrison, followed. Any protests that they were innocent, having simply obeyed orders, counted for nothing. Detective Smyth simply replied, 'What do you think you have been doing for the last week?' The selected group continued to swell.

Shortly afterwards, 21-year-old Tobin – a hardware apprentice in civilian life – recognised a British Army major who had just entered the gymnasium. Tobin had taken the same officer prisoner, along with the soldier and writer Lord Dunsany, on Easter Monday close to the Four Courts. Now the major passed along the line of rebel prisoners until he drew level with Tobin. Tobin said hello, and the major immediately recognised him and smiled. Shortly afterwards, the major was asked if he recognised any of the prisoners. He answered 'No'. Following this episode, more former prisoners of the Republicans were brought in to identify the surrendered men. Twenty-three DMP constables arrived, having themselves been held captive in the Bridewell Barracks behind the Four Courts until the previous day. Not a single man among them identified a prisoner. Others, however, were not as forgiving. Private James Murray, from the Royal Irish Regiment, who had been held captive in the GPO, identified his former captors as soon as he saw them, as did a lieutenant named King. King had been captured on the previous

Tuesday, before being released with the rest of the prisoners from the GPO on Friday evening, when several among them had subsequently been machine-gunned by their own side. He was especially eager to pick out anyone he had seen in a position of command. Other former captive soldiers and policemen were brought in to see if they could pick out more men. Some took great satisfaction as they did, savouring the fact that the boot was now firmly on the other foot. Others were sickened by the apparent circus and, like the major and the Bridewell policemen, deliberately overlooked men they clearly recognised.

Michael Collins and Joe Good, a 21-year old electrician and Irish Volunteer from London, were huddled together on Collins's overcoat to protect them from the cold floor, when a British NCO who knew Collins approached them. 'What has you here, Collins?' he asked. Collins had a notoriously short temper, which had not been improved by recent events. His rasping reply was, 'England's difficulty ...',[10] alluding to the well-known nationalist maxim that England's difficulty was Ireland's opportunity. The sergeant walked away.

A short time later, a British officer entered the gymnasium and, looking around, shouted to the G-men to hurry up; he needed the space for another batch of prisoners, and they had already had more than enough time for their task. He then ordered some soldiers to set up a table and chairs near to the exit door at the right-hand side of the far end of the building. He told Detectives Barton and Hoey to sit at the table while he himself prepared to clear the room. Another two detectives joined them and were soon taking fingerprints from prisoners who were hurried to the table before being taken to the exit. Names, addresses and occupations were demanded. More men were singled out. Those who avoided the selections were now escorted past the desk and into rooms in a cluster of two-storey barrack buildings beyond the gymnasium. Séamus Kavanagh was called to the desk and his fingerprints taken. He gave his name but refused to answer anything further. His interrogator angrily ordered him to the selected lines, but moments later turned his head away. When another policeman pointed to him to pass beyond into the barracks, Kavanagh seized the opportunity. He had escaped selection.

Once each barrack room was full of prisoners, hard biscuits and buckets filled with tea were brought in. This was the first food many of the rebels had seen in almost 48 hours; for some it had been even longer.

In the room containing Frank Henderson, a soldier bringing tea and biscuits declared that he was from County Clare. He then asked if there was anything he could do to help. One Volunteer asked him what would happen to them. He said he did not know, but guessed that they might be sent to France to dig trenches.

The barrack room doors were locked and guarded, but intermittently would be opened to admit the despised G-men. Each time they looked from man to man as they exclaimed, 'You – you – you – out!' The selection seemed never-ending.

3

Round-ups, More Selections and Civilian Backlash

'Shoot the Sinn Féin Bastards'

The Easter Rising had spawned combat between the Republicans and the Crown forces outside Dublin as well as within the capital itself. In County Galway, the Volunteer brigade under Liam Mellows had at times controlled hundreds of square miles of countryside to the east and south of Galway city. There had been exchanges of gunfire in Enniscorthy in County Wexford as the Volunteers attacked the town's RIC barracks before taking over most of the town. There had also been fighting outside Tyrrellspass in County Westmeath, as well as actions in Counties Louth and Laois. It was the Volunteers' 5th Battalion under 31-year-old Commandant Thomas Ashe, however, that had enjoyed the most success outside the capital in terms of enemy casualties. They had fought in Swords, Garristown and Donabate, as well as elsewhere in north County Dublin, but their most stunning victory was when they engaged a large RIC force just outside Ashbourne in County Meath on Friday 28 April. It was the only occasion during the Rising when the Irish Volunteers had comprehensively defeated the enemy during a strategically significant engagement. Vice-Commandant Richard Mulcahy, aged 29, had risen to prominence during this particularly brutal battle. His ability to co-ordinate men under fire was displayed at a critical moment when all seemed lost. Mulcahy had opted to attack rather than retreat, and ultimately swung the battle in the Volunteers' favour. They had inflicted over 25 casualties, at least eight fatal, on the enemy. They then took over sixty policemen prisoner, later releasing them in the name of the Irish Republic, on the assurance that they would not take up arms again on behalf of the English king against their fellow countrymen. But now, on Sunday 30 April, the tables had turned.

Shortly after 2.30 p.m. on Sunday, Mulcahy – a post office engineer by profession, a Volunteer since 1913, and an IRB member since 1908 – climbed into the back seat of a motor car driven by an RIC officer. Mulcahy and his new battalion were positioned a dozen or so miles to the north of Dublin city centre. He had actually been a lieutenant of C Company, 3rd Battalion, but he had sought out the 5th Battalion when he became cut off from the city while on operational duty on its north side on Easter Monday. Now, he sat silently in the car as the men of his new unit watched the car drive away from the picturesque area of New Barn, Kilsallaghan, on the Dublin/Meath border, where its men had mustered following their recent action at Ashbourne.

After a 45-minute drive the car pulled up outside Irish Command HQ in Parkgate Street, next to the Phoenix Park, leaving its engine running. Mulcahy remained silent. A British officer came out of the building and climbed into the car, ordering the driver to drive on. Within minutes the car had pulled up once again, this time less than half a mile away, in the forecourt of Arbour Hill detention barracks, situated just to the rear of the Royal Barracks, a mile to the west of the city centre. Mulcahy entered the prison and was escorted down a corridor to a row of cells. Ahead of him he heard the creak and clatter of an iron-reinforced cell door being pulled open, followed by a sharply barked order to the prisoner inside: 'Get up!'

Mulcahy stepped inside the cell and immediately stood to attention. Commandant Pádraig Pearse, the cell's 36-year-old occupant, told him to stand at ease before warmly shaking his hand. Pearse had been brought here the previous day after officially signing the general surrender order during a meeting with General Maxwell in the building that Mulcahy had just left. Pearse, recently declared the Irish Republic's president, was a qualified barrister, but had followed a teaching career. He owned and ran St Enda's school in Rathfarnam in Dublin. The building was also his family home. Pearse's nationalistic passion and impressive oratorical skills had ultimately led him to his position as the Republic's president.

He was a founding member of the Irish Volunteers, as well as a member of the IRB's Supreme Council.

Pearse, usually so meticulously groomed, looked drawn and dishevelled. Mulcahy unfolded and handed his commander-in-chief a piece of paper that had been presented to Commandant Ashe earlier that morning in Kilsallaghan – the order of general surrender. He asked Pearse if this was indeed his order. Pearse replied that it was. Mulcahy asked if the order applied to Dublin or to the whole country. Pearse's subdued reply was that it referred to the whole of Ireland. Mulcahy continued, alluding to the 5th Battalion, which was still in the field, 'Would it be any use if a small band of men who had given a good account of themselves during the week were to hold out any longer?'[1] Pearse's answer was 'No'. Mulcahy saluted his commander and whispered, 'God's Blessing on you.'[2]

Mulcahy was then taken to see General Lovick Friend back at army HQ. There, the 60-year-old general, assuming from Mulcahy's recent prison visit that he was an important man, asked him to use his influence to stop the bloodshed.[3] He said that with the insurrection all but over in Dublin, British soldiers would be freed up to move against the Volunteer positions in the surrounding counties and further afield. Mulcahy kept his cards close to his chest at first, but eventually conceded that his commanding officer's orders would be obeyed. If those orders included surrender, so be it. Seizing the opportunity to move things along, another staff officer instructed Mulcahy to turn himself and his men in to RIC District Inspector Smyth at Ashbourne. Friend interjected: 'Unfortunately the District Inspector has been killed and the County Inspector is severely wounded.'[4] The officer bit his lip. It was eventually agreed that they would surrender to a squadron of the 5th Lancers, who were deployed close to Kilsallaghan. Mulcahy was then taken away in the vehicle waiting outside. Arriving back at New Barn at roughly 5 p.m., he informed the 5th Fingal Volunteer Battalion: 'It is all up, boys.'[5]

A mile to the east of Arbour Hill, meanwhile, the ranks of the Royal College of Surgeons/St Stephen's Green Irish Citizen Army garrison, under the command of 42-year-old Commandant Michael Mallin, having surrendered some time earlier in the day, had by now been marched into the narrow, enclosed avenue at the rear of Dublin Castle's lower yard. Most of its members had not eaten properly in days. They were ordered to halt opposite the normally picturesque castle gardens.

Two large pits had been dug in the lawns. Many of the rebels expected to be shot and buried in the pits. The men of the Royal Dublin Fusiliers who had come from Ship Street Barracks did nothing to allay their fears. One sneering private approached 21-year-old Sergeant Frank Robbins, pointing at the two large pits, laughing as he said, 'In an hour's time some of yiz will be in it!', much to the amusement of his comrades. Captain Richard McCormack, standing close by, shouted back defiantly: 'If I'm for one of them, I'll call for three cheers for the Irish Republic as they are about to shoot me!'[6]

The Fusiliers then turned their attentions to the enigmatic Countess Markievicz, the labour and feminist activist who had turned her back on her aristocratic roots and wealth to align herself with the socialist goals of the Citizen Army and its leader, James Connolly. The soldiers began mocking the plumage adorning her hat. She ignored them. Eventually, following another dispatch confirming that Richmond Barracks was ready for its latest prisoner contingent, the order to march was given by the officer in charge – Lieutenant Orelim – and the captive garrison was led westwards to the barracks.

Garry Holohan was standing in a cramped barrack room in Richmond Barracks when, roughly 45 minutes after the Citizen Army had set off from Dublin Castle, he heard the tramp of their feet as they entered the barracks square. Looking carefully out of the window while trying to remain concealed from the sentries just outside, he could just make them out as they came to a halt. Lieutenant Orelim then handed them over to the custody of Lieutenant O'Brien. Countess Markievicz, who had earlier declined an offer of transport to the barracks, had maintained her position at the head of the ranks next to Commandant Mallin. Now she and the other women of the garrison were segregated from their male comrades and taken away. Garry Holohan, still looking on discreetly, could not help but admire her as she was marched away in her full uniform with a glare of defiance on her face. Then, as she was led into in the same barrack room as Julia Grenan and Winifred Carney, a British officer called out: 'Remove that woman!'[7] The 48-year-old countess was taken away and placed in a heavily guarded room on her own.

Out on the square, when the official searches for ammunition and intelligence, and the more lucrative unofficial searches for personal belongings and valuables, were completed, the Citizen Army men moved towards the gymnasium. On the way in they saw Lieutenant

Jackson berating several of his men while pointing to a pile of items – rosary beads, watches, and other pilfered personal belongings – lying on the floor nearby. He reiterated sharply that the soldiers were only to confiscate documents and loose ammunition.

Commandant Mallin's men turned left and filtered inside. It was now their turn to face the wall of G-men, among whom stood Inspector Love, and Detectives Bruton, Halley and Smyth. However, due to his increasingly heavy workload, the patience of the British officer in charge of the room was wearing thin, and it was decided to perform the selection at the entrance door. Commandant Mallin was the first man selected.

Mallin was known to the detectives. He had himself served in the British Army, and had been posted to India. He was a silk-weaver by trade and his trade union activities had led him to the ranks of the Citizen Army following the notorious Dublin Lockout of 1913. His previous military experience led to him being put in charge of the army's training, and he was eventually appointed as its chief of staff. He had since overseen the Citizen Army's defence of the Royal College of Surgeons following its redeployment under heavy fire from St Stephen's Green.

Soon, others followed Mallin into the gymnasium, both to the left and the right. Another Volunteer, by the name of Séamus Kavanagh, in this case from D Company, 2nd Battalion, had fought with the Citizen Army during the previous week. When he was selected and told to go to the left-hand side, his friend, 41-year-old Joseph McGuinness, called out to him. McGuinness had been in action at the Four Courts but had since been misinformed that Kavanagh had been shot. He was greatly relieved to see that he had not. The men began conversing until a soldier separated the two, ordering McGuinness to the left and Kavanagh to the right. Kavanagh protested that it should have been the other way round, but to no avail. The mistake was to have huge ramifications for McGuinness. Thomas O'Donoghue, of the Citizen Army, then entered the gym. Detective Sergeant Bruton, who seemed to be enjoying his work immensely, pinched his arm and began interrogating him, increasing the pressure of his pinch with each question. O'Donoghue was eventually sent to the right. When all of Mallin's garrison were inside, the G-men moved among them. Detective Barton had stepped up from his desk to join them, eager to ensure that no one was overlooked.

Stopping in front of Captain Joseph Connolly, Barton asked him his name. He already knew the answer. Joseph was the brother of Captain Seán Connolly, who had led Easter Monday's assault on City Hall. Barton took great satisfaction in telling him that his brother was dead. Connolly looked at him with contempt, saying, 'He died for his country.'[8] Barton replied dismissively that the dead man was nothing but a disgrace to his country. Connolly's angry reaction to this earned him a place among the selected ranks. Barton seemed delighted with this result, and now moved on to Michael Donnelly, pointing at him and stating: 'I know you.' Donnelly replied: 'So well you might.' Barton studied him momentarily before explaining that Donnelly had laughed at him when their paths crossed recently. Donnelly replied: 'Hasn't the cat leave to laugh at the king?'[9] Barton said, 'I suppose so' before returning to his desk, unaware that Seán McLoughlin, who had still not been identified as holding a senior rank, was watching his every move.

At roughly the same time, during the early evening on Sunday, Volunteers Vinny Byrne and James Carbury stood between the hallway and kitchen of a stranger's house near St Stephen's Green, while the woman who lived there vigorously brushed the flour that had become caked into their overcoats during the week. They had only recently taken flight from Jacob's biscuit factory following its garrison's surrender. The woman had dragged the two anxious Volunteers into her house to escape from an angry mob that had gathered in the area. She feared that 15-year-old Byrne and his 2nd Battalion comrade would be torn limb from limb if the mob got hold of them, and knew that the flour would identify them as rebels from the factory.

When the mob moved on, the woman checked that the coast was clear before allowing the grateful pair to continue their escape. They made for Grafton Street, soon reaching the junction with South Anne Street, which was to their right. Byrne felt a great sense of relief. He was now within yards of his home in nearby Anne's Lane. He offered Carbury the option of hiding out there with him for a few days. Carbury declined and set off, telling Byrne that he would try to make his own way home but would return if his route was barred. Byrne wished him good luck.

Byrne quickened his pace as he entered South Anne Street. Suddenly, he realised that a patrolling British infantryman was standing in the street. The soldier turned towards him, raised his rifle and pointed it at him. Byrne froze. Then a shot rang out, echoing around the walls of the street's three- and four-storey town houses and shops. The soldier collapsed. The shot had been fired by a sniper. Byrne, unable to believe his luck, edged forward, looking cautiously for movement from his stricken enemy, but there was none. A pool of blood formed on the cobblestones beneath the fallen soldier as a few of his comrades appeared from Duke Lane just behind him, but, fearing another shot from the same sniper, they remained in cover. The young Volunteer's way was once again clear. Within moments Byrne was banging on his own front door. When his mother opened it she broke down crying, telling him she had thought he was dead.

Half a mile away, Vinny Byrne's comrades in the surrendered 2nd Battalion from Jacob's, under Commandant Thomas MacDonagh, were mustered on the enclosed 150-yard stretch of Bride Road, close to Christchurch. They were now joined by the 4th Battalion under Commandant Ceannt. The 4th Battalion had surrendered sometime earlier in the South Dublin Union. Both battalions were now to be marched to Richmond Barracks. The small roadway was flanked on one side by the red-brick five-storey Iveagh Trust buildings. This huge complex was home to workers from the nearby Guinness brewery, which was not known for its love of revolutionary nationalism. Civilians crowded into the windows, some staring silently, absorbing the spectacle, others calling out streams of insults to the surrendered men and women in the street beneath them. The Volunteers remained silent, listening to the taunts, whistles and curses echoing in the street.

A British sergeant towards the front of the column took a pistol from Major John MacBride. Major MacBride, a Boer War veteran, had taken the position of second-in-command of the Jacob's garrison. He now stood next to Commandant MacDonagh. MacDonagh's brother John stood on his other side.

After momentarily examining the name engraved on MacBride's pistol, the British sergeant went to his commanding officer, who was standing nearby, awaiting orders to move out with the prisoners. Handing the officer the pistol, he pointed at MacBride and said, 'Major MacBride, Sir – he fought in the Boer war.'[10] The officer looked over the NCO's shoulder at the imposing 47-year-old prisoner. 'With us or against us?' The sergeant replied, 'Against us'. MacBride had led the Irish Transvaal Brigade in South Africa against the British, achieving several victories and leading his men with the same élan that had made him a legend among the Irish Volunteers. The British officer then marched over to MacBride and questioned him about his recent activities. MacBride's responded with silence. The officer then stepped away and returned MacBride's pistol to the sergeant. Close by was a British Army major named Armstrong. Armstrong was intrigued by the commanding demeanour of MacBride, who was dressed in a roughed-up blue suit. He turned to Lieutenant William Wylie, and asked if MacBride was on the list of unarmed detainees – those who had surrendered without weapons. This list had recently been compiled by Lieutenant Wylie himself – being fewer in number, the unarmed prisoners from both battalions were easier to track than those carrying arms. The logic was simple – if a prisoner was not on the unarmed list he must have been armed. Wylie, a barrister by profession, confirmed that MacBride had been armed.

At 6 p.m., when all the prisoners had been searched and the men had their names taken, and the appropriate orders had arrived, the surrendered men and women were ordered to march. This was followed by a final fusillade of mocking cheers and a deluge of missiles from the scores of civilians in the Iveagh Trust buildings. When the volume of projectiles increased the soldiers guarding the prisoners were ordered to turn their rifles towards the windows. The sharp commands of several NCOs to load and aim put a stop to the abuse.

Roughly 20 minutes later, as they marched towards Mount Brown, the column drew level with the South Dublin Union, its forbidding walls to their left. They continued down the hill towards Old Kilmainham, where a single Volunteer began to sing hoarsely, 'God Save Ireland'. The tune was quickly taken up by several hundred comrades.

The marchers' morale lifted as the singing swelled, filling them with a sense of fortitude they would soon need. A huge angry crowd had filled the streets of Kilmainham ahead of them. Then the onslaught began. Insults were hurled; there were shouts of 'Shoot the Sinn Féin bastards!' A volley of missiles followed. Almost everyone from F Company, 4th Battalion, whose members had been recruited from the surrounding area, had their names called out individually by the mob. Nineteen-year-old Robert Holland, a sharpshooter and Fianna member since its inception in 1909, and an IRB member, feared more for his life than he had during all the fighting of the previous week when he heard someone cry out:

'There is Robert Holland and Peadar Doyle – shoot the bastards!' As the mob worked itself into a frenzy of hatred, a dozen or so lunged at the column. This escalated quickly into a full-scale assault before the British soldiers guarding the march intervened, their officers hoping to prevent a riot. A great sense of relief came over the surrendered ranks when, at 6.45 p.m., they approached the gates of Richmond Barracks and were told to wait outside. Their reprieve, however, would be short-lived.

That evening, outside the city at Kilsallaghan, the forty or so Volunteers of Thomas Ashe's 5th Battalion sat along the hedgerows as a mounted squadron of 200 troopers from the 5th Lancers approached – as pre-arranged by General Friend and Vice-Commandant Mulcahy earlier in Parkgate Street. Lieutenant Joseph Lawless looked on as the troopers trotted towards them, concluding to himself that the Rising was over for sure.

After Commandant Ashe, a school headmaster by profession, had ordered them to lay down their arms, the Volunteers formed into two columns facing east along the Ashbourne–Swords road. The lancers then divided into three troops. After they had secured the surrendered weapons, two troops took up positions on the Volunteers' left and right flanks, the third taking up the rear. They then moved east towards Swords. One Volunteer looked up at the lancer next to him, saying: 'Pity you delayed so long in getting here.'[11] The lancer appeared intrigued by the remark but did not reply. The hooves of his mount clattered on the road in almost perfect time with the other horses while he kept his eyes to his front. Those marching alongside, however, knew precisely what their Volunteer comrade had meant – they had been waiting in ambush for this unit the previous night. The overall demeanour of the lancer troop was belligerent, but some were surprisingly jovial. Lieutenant Lawless, however, cursed his luck at having to listen to the constant complaints of the horseman next to him, who protested that he had spent two years in the trenches without getting a bullet, only to take his leave in Dublin and very nearly get shot. Then, as the column made its way through an area known as Killosory, the same lancer looked at 21-year-old Lawless as if he had gone mad: Lawless, an engineering apprentice with a strong interest in Irish history and folklore, who had been a Volunteer from the beginning, was saluting towards a nearby graveyard. He was paying his respects to his grandfather and grandmother, who were buried there. Lawless wondered if his dead forebears could see them from beyond the grave; if they could, he thought, they would be proud of their grandson and their two sons – Frank and Jim Lawless – who were also in the ranks of Volunteers. His musings were cut short by the lancer's ranting. The march continued.

Inside Richmond Barracks, as Sunday evening moved into night, two British officers had been tasked with entering each individual detention room containing the prisoners who had already passed through the gymnasium – once again to separate the Volunteers. Patrick Kelly looked on as his comrade George Butler and several others were picked. After a time, Kelly concluded that they were segregating the younger from the older captives. The grime and dirt caked into the faces of many, however, made it difficult for the officers to determine their ages. Sixteen-year-old William Oman of the Citizen Army was called out, as was another Fianna youngster, who needed to be led out because he was nearly blind. Astonishingly, the same half-blind youth had been allowed to shoot a Lee-Enfield rifle at the enemy during the fighting in St Stephen's Green. Eventually all those under the age of 18 were placed in a separate barrack room.

In another room, meanwhile, Éamon Dore and the dozens of others locked in with him had been relieving themselves into several slop-buckets that had been left there earlier. The buckets had been quickly filled, a fact that was promptly brought to a guard's attention. The buckets were then passed out while the Volunteers pleaded for water. Soon afterwards some water buckets were passed in. Dore, however, was certain that they were the same slop-buckets that had simply been emptied and refilled with water. Many were so desperately thirsty that they drank from the buckets. Dore, however, chose to endure his thirst.

Back at the gymnasium's exit door, Detective Barton rose from his desk and spoke briefly to Inspector Love. Love then summoned the other G-men in the room and explained to them that he wanted to post a detective at each of the barrack rooms beyond.

Soon afterwards, a British subaltern entered the gymnasium and spoke to the officer at the entrance desk. The subaltern shouted to the sentries, 'There's far too many people in the place, some will have to go!',[12] and pointed back towards the barracks square. It appeared that the barrack rooms were at risk of becoming swamped with prisoners and it now made more sense to bypass them with the current batch. At this point the barracks commanders had received word that a steamship –

the TSS (Twin-Screw Steamer) *Slieve Bloom* – was waiting in Dublin's docks to transport several hundred prisoners. They felt it more expedient to send those currently in the gymnasium straight back out to the square and to follow with the men in the barrack rooms, rather than overfill the already crowded barrack rooms before sending them all out from there and risking a breakdown in order, as well as a loss of precious time.

The soldiers ordered the prisoners on the right-hand side of the gymnasium to their feet and towards the exit desk. Seán McLoughlin seized his chance to evade Detective Barton's attentions and positioned himself at the head of the line. He passed through and eventually made it back to the barracks square. Ranks were quickly formed. Moments later, Inspector Love and Detective Barton returned to the gymnasium, and Barton went back to the exit desk. McLoughlin, at least for now, had evaded the detective's grasp.

Back inside, Patrick Rankin joined the shuffling line of prisoners behind James Ryan, one of the medical men of the GPO garrison. As Ryan approached Barton and had his fingerprints taken, he was asked his name, address and occupation. He was about to pass through when Barton piped up: 'I have a charge against Ryan,' addressing the subaltern, who gave him an impatient look. Barton was too busy conferring with a colleague as to what charge they could bring against Ryan to notice. This held up the rest of the line, at which the young officer lost his patience, bellowing at Barton: 'I am in charge here!'[13] Then, turning to Ryan, in a calmer tone he instructed him to proceed outside and into the square. Rankin followed behind, as did the others from the right-hand side of the gymnasium.

Back at a barrack room window, meanwhile, Charles Saurin watched a large number of soldiers fall in outside with full equipment. They were then inspected by an officer. The door of Saurin's room was thrown open. An NCO and a detective stood in the doorway and shouted: 'Up on your feet!' Similar commands could be heard all along the corridor as other doors were flung open. The NCO in Saurin's doorway began calling out names. Then, as Saurin's fellow inmates filed past the NCO, the G-man next to him gave each man one last look, picking out a man here and there to remain. Seán O'Duffy was called out of another room, and as he passed Detective Cavanagh in the corridor, he asked him where they were going. Cavanagh replied: 'You will be all right – you are off to England,' adding, with a look of foreboding, 'But I pity those who are being kept back.'[14] Cavanagh shook O'Duffy's hand and moved on, but he was unsettled at what the detective had said.

Volunteer Harry Nichols, who had fought in St Stephen's Green, passed out from another room into the square, where he saw a friend of his in a British officer's uniform. He then asked his officer friend if he knew where they were being sent. The officer replied: 'Across the water,' and they parted company.

When there were sufficient numbers of prisoners on the square, NCOs moved among them distributing tins of bully beef and dog biscuits. Each tin was to be shared between two men and there were four biscuits per man. They were told to conserve them; there would be no more food for a considerable time. This was no lie – the infantrymen themselves were now on the same meagre and unpalatable rations as their prisoners due to the disruption in the food supply caused by the recent fighting.

Within minutes of their assembly, an officer ordered soldiers of the Staffordshire Regiment to move in on either side of the gathered men. Another order – 'Royal Irish to the rear!' – was called out and a strong rearguard was put in place. The officer then addressed the Volunteers in a surprisingly cordial fashion, 'Now, I am sure all you men know the drill.'[15] He then called them to attention, at which roughly two hundred pairs of rebel boots clattered in almost perfect time with their British counterparts. Seemingly impressed by this, he called, 'Close up and turn left – two deep!' The officer then went up and down the lines of his own soldiers telling each man which prisoner he would be responsible for.

The order to march was then given, and at 8 p.m. on Sunday evening, the first batch of Republican prisoners marched out of Richmond Barracks. More were being assembled on the square behind them. On their way out they saw a large group of prisoners from the recently arrived 2nd and 4th Battalions sitting and lying on the grass that bordered the barracks, awaiting their turn to go in, and wondering where their comrades were being marched off to. They stood up. Waves and salutes were exchanged. Seán McLoughlin breathed a sigh of relief as he passed out of the barracks. He had escaped the G-men. He wondered what was next.

As the second group formed up on the barracks square the same rations were distributed to the men, with the instruction not to eat them yet as they were going on a long journey.[16] It now began to dawn on some of those assembled that none of their leaders was present. Word had also spread of what Detective Cavanagh had said to Seán O'Duffy about pitying those being kept back, which increased their concerns for the men who had been selected. Many feared the worst – in 14 cases these fears would prove justified. Then the order was given from a different officer, who was on horseback: 'Attention and form up!' Once this was done, and each soldier had been given his man to mark, another order was shouted, this one directed solely at the soldiers: 'Load rifles!' There was a soft metallic double rattle[17] as scores of rifle bolts were pulled back, allowing the breech of each rifle to be filled with a cartridge. Then: 'Left turn – march!' The officer rode up and down the ranks, impressing upon his men that they should not waste time on any prisoner who stumbled or fell.[18] The Volunteers fully understood his meaning: anyone who fell out of line was to be shot on the spot.

After the first prisoners had left Richmond Barracks, Major Collis at the RIC barracks in Swords – he was in command of a squadron of lancers now taking up most of the length of Swords Main Street – received a phone call telling him that as soon as the Volunteers under Commandant Ashe had arrived they were to be sent to Richmond Barracks. A small fleet of flat-bed trucks stood close by the barracks. The barracks itself still bore the scars of the attack launched by Commandant Ashe's battalion the previous Wednesday, during which they had captured the building. When the prisoner column and its escorting lancer troop eventually reached Swords village at roughly 8.30 p.m., the Volunteers were loaded onto the trucks. Soldiers with fixed bayonets leaned up against the backs of the drivers' cabs, guarding the prisoners as they sat on the floor facing rearwards. Each man sat between the legs of the man behind, so that the last man had to use his hands to prop himself up. The trucks then lumbered off to Richmond Barracks, 15 miles away.

In Kilmainham Gaol, meanwhile, Liam Tannam and the other prisoners who had been locked in the bloodstained cells earlier in the day were taken out of the cells and ushered into the gaol's main concourse. They were lined up and greeted by three corporals who appeared to be greatly relishing their moment of power over the enemy. One of them looked enviously at Diarmuid Lynch's pigskin gaiters.

Captain Lynch, 38 years old, an agricultural wholesaler in civilian life, originally from Cork, had spent years in London and New York promoting the Irish cause. He was a member of the IRB's Supreme Council. Very highly regarded in the Republican movement, he counted Tom Clarke among his good friends. Lynch had been pivotal in organising the rebellion. Pádraig Pearse had given him the responsibility of selecting a landing zone for a large consignment of arms that had been shipped by Imperial Germany to support the Rising.[19] He had chosen Fenit Harbour in Kerry. During the fighting itself, Lynch had served as Commandant Connolly's aide-de-camp. This had placed him front and centre of the tumultuous week. His face and uniform, covered with soot and grime, betrayed his recent tribulations. Now he glared balefully as an enemy corporal untied his gaiters, taking them as spoils of war. The corporal's mocking laughter resounded around the concourse as he added insults to his act of theft. Then an officer called the first prisoner in line into a nearby room. Lynch quickly gathered himself, straining to hear the interrogation he assumed was now taking place in the room. On his instruction, word was passed down the line of prisoners that they were not to answer any questions when their own turn came.

Tony Makapaltis, a Finnish sailor, had, somewhat astonishingly, convinced Captain Tannam to let him join the GPO garrison on Easter Monday. His unorthodox intention had been to fight against the occupier of his own country – Russia – by proxy against its ally, Great Britain. Tannam, aware that they needed all the help they could get on the day, had admitted him to the GPO. Now the Finn was in Kilmainham Gaol. Makapaltis had a poor command of English, and when his turn came to be summoned to the room, he had a hard time understanding his interrogator's questions. Consequently, he did not answer any of them, much to the officer's frustration. Eventually, when he finally realised he was getting nowhere with Makapaltis, not to mention the rest of the prisoners, he had them removed to a disused room in the old prison infirmary. Their cells would soon be used for a contingent of female prisoners due to be transferred from Richmond Barracks the following day. With no female warders to look after the women, it was considered best to lock them in the cells when they arrived. The looters, meanwhile, were all crammed into a single cell.

Back in Richmond Barracks, the 2nd and 4th Battalions were ordered into the barracks square, where Lieutenant O'Brien waited to receive them. The women were separated from the men and led to the first floor of the barracks' married quarters by an NCO and a guard, and placed in a large room. Then the NCO made an unusual request. He asked them to give them their word of honour not to try to escape or to break any glass.[20]

When they gave their word, he asked if they had any guns on them, adding that they were likely to be searched later. Rose MacNamara, aged 30, assured him that they did not. The women were then separated into two different rooms. The NCO brought a bucket of hot tea and some dog biscuits into each room, apologising for the poor food. He then locked the women in for the night.

After a time, the women began to discuss what to do with a number of handguns they were concealing. Many of the male prisoners had earlier given the women their pistols to hide, thinking that they would be released more or less immediately. Release now, however, seemed unlikely. One Cumann na mBan member pointed to a fireplace, which, after some probing, was found to have recesses in its chimney. All their guns were eventually hidden there. The same scenario was repeated in the other room, before both groups of women settled down for the long evening and cold night.

Back out on the square, Lieutenant Jackson, having by now dispatched the male 2nd and 4th Battalion prisoners to the barracks, sent in search parties drawn from the Royal Irish Regiment. There were to be no further selections that night. Instead, following the searches, the prisoners were housed in barrack rooms until the morning. Roughly fifty men were crowded into each room. There was no space to lie down. Exhausted men sat back to back, supporting each other, while others stood to allow their comrades to sit in shifts. More buckets were brought in to act as latrines. Tea and dog biscuits were then brought in in separate buckets.

Inside the gymnasium, the work of the G-men was done for the day. The rebellion's leaders, and those selected for further scrutiny, were ordered to their feet before being taken into different rooms, some of which already contained the younger Volunteer members who had been segregated earlier. There they waited.

4

The Deportations Begin

'If they let you live six months ...'

As the ranks of dishevelled prisoners who had been marched out of Richmond Barracks for deportation on Sunday evening approached Dublin's city centre, the darkening streets were completely deserted. A deathly silence[1] was punctuated only by the tramp of shoes and boots on the cobblestones and the occasional distant bark of a machine gun. The men were utterly worn out. Michael O'Reilly, who had been stationed at the GPO and subsequently in Moore Street, thought as he looked up that even the seagulls flying overhead or perching on lamp posts held their tongues in shocked silence. As they approached O'Connell Bridge on Westmoreland Street, Frank Robbins, a dockworker by trade, began humming a Volunteer marching tune. Several dozen men took up the song until a British NCO ran up and down their ranks ordering them to stop. Lieutenant Robert de Coeur, of the Citizen Army, then broke the silence with his own whistled version of the tune, only to elicit a similar response.

The column was halted at the southern end of O'Connell Bridge. It seemed that their captors were offering them one last look at the devastation wrought on the smoking city. To their front and right, the entire length of Eden Quay was a bombed-out ruin. Fires still blazed. Behind the O'Connell monument, Sackville Street was filled with the detritus of war: collapsed shells of buildings, wrecked barricades, broken and smashed vehicles and the decomposing bodies of horses. Joe

Good stood among the Volunteer officers. The previous Monday, at the Rising's outset, he had taken up a position at the opposite end of the same bridge. The devastating effects on manpower of Eoin MacNeill's countermand order[2] had seen Good left single-handed to man the bridge, more than fifty yards wide, armed only with a shotgun and an axe, but ready nonetheless to fight the empire. Looking around, having for now lost that fight, he could not help but admire his officers as they stood defiant and proud in their dusty, soiled uniforms. To him they looked as dignified as any of the British officers in the escort. Turning to Éamon Morkan – Battalion Quarter Master (BQM) for the 1st Battalion – he suggested the reason for the unexpected halt was so that the enemy could provoke a reaction from them. Morkan replied: 'If they let you live six months you will see the reaction.'[3] Then came the order to move on. The column turned right onto Burgh Quay, where the pavements were covered with broken glass and small lumps of brick and concrete gouged from buildings during the recent rifle battles. Further along, they crossed over Butt Bridge. The ruins of Liberty Hall confronted them as they then turned right onto Custom House Quay to find it thronged with troops. Some were colonial troops from New Zealand, identifiable by their slouch hats and broad accents. The Volunteers were surprised when the New Zealanders cheered them on and wished them good luck. Unbeknownst to those marching, these soldiers had been guarding a contingent of their comrades in the Custom House since the previous Friday. Their charges included captains Frank Thornton, Séamus Daly and William Brennan-Whitmore. The New Zealanders had initially been misinformed that the prisoners under their watchful eyes were mere arsonists, not revolutionaries, and had set the city on fire because of an industrial dispute; and when they discovered the truth they showed considerable enthusiasm for the bravado of the Volunteers, feeding them with the best rations available and suggesting boisterously that they themselves should organise something similar in New Zealand.

No such cheer awaited the marching column of prisoners, however. They continued for a half mile or so along North Wall Quay. The River Liffey, to their right, was calm as the sky darkened. They eventually arrived at the red-brick London North-Western Railway building. Here they were moved to a subway filled with waiting soldiers. A loud command of 'Halt!' brought them to a stop. While they waited here for further instructions Seán McLoughlin turned to the soldier nearest him

Eden Quay in ruins following the Rising. Many of the Volunteers were awestruck by the damage caused to the city centre when they saw it for the first time on their way to deportation. COURTESY OF KILMAINHAM GAOL ARCHIVES

and asked if he could provide a drink of water for the wounded man beside him. The soldier pulled out his canteen and handed it to the wounded Volunteer. When the same soldier was scolded by a comrade for doing this he colourfully told the man to mind his own business. Then came the order to move on.

Minutes later, the front ranks of the four hundred or so Volunteers took what many of them thought would be their final steps on Irish soil as they mounted the wooden gangway of a 300-foot steamship. Once on board they were herded below decks through open hatches into a huge stinking cattle hold. The smell was overpowering. Their captors packed them in as tightly as possible but also made sure to account for ballast – so men were crammed in on either side. Patrick Kelly tripped over another prisoner as he descended a ramp into the odious cesspit. He raised himself up to find his hands and his garments covered in rancid slime. A nearby Volunteer added to his misery by cursing at him: 'Look where you're going!' Kelly turned towards his comrade, intending to give as good as he got, only to find it was Tom Rath – his civilian work colleague at the Grand Canal Goods Company for the previous two years. Astonishingly, neither had known the other was a Volunteer. More prisoners were then crammed in. When the pens were filled, the ship's cargo hold was used. This was luxurious by comparison. Charles Saurin and Arthur Shields were lucky enough to find themselves placed there, where they found some life jackets. Some of their comrades put these on; others used them as makeshift mattresses or pillows. They were cramped but comfortable, which was more than could be said for their comrades in the cattle hold, who cursed profusely at the conditions.

The talk among the unfortunate men struggling to stay on their feet in the cattle hold eventually turned to their future – or whether they had a future. Garry Holohan believed they were going to be press-ganged into the Royal Navy. One Volunteer's less optimistic question, however, articulated what most of the men feared: 'Are they going to sink us in the Irish Sea?'[4] Another man suggested that if the British did sink them, they could easily blame it on a German submarine. No more rebels – no more problem. Sean Prendergast of the 1st Battalion added: 'Wish they would, couldn't be much worse than this.'[5] The comment was met with wry smiles until another man suggested that getting torpedoed was a realistic prospect. The smiles disappeared for a moment. Then someone said: 'Well, then the Tommies would be in the same boat as us.' His pun was well received. Another wondered aloud: 'In that event, would they try and save us?' Several fatalistic sighs summed up the negative consensus on that question. Fergus de Búrca, of the GPO garrison, meanwhile, gave in to the filth beneath his feet. No longer able to stand from exhaustion, and racked with sickness due to the stench, he sat down on the fetid floor. The man behind did the same until the two men's backs supported each other. De Búrca began to doze, thinking that he no longer cared what happened. Buckets of water were then given to the men in the cargo holds, most of the contents being spilled as they were passed down. This luxury was denied to those in the cattle hold. They would have to drink from dirty troughs. Then, at 10 p.m., with a sudden shudder, the steamer's twin engines started, and the TSS *Slieve Bloom*[6] moved away from the dockside. Charles Saurin recognised a Volunteer officer he had last seen accompanying the HQ staff during the fighting on Moore Street. The officer looked up through the open hatch and shouted in Irish: 'Goodbye, Ireland.'[7]

Volunteer Michael Flanagan and several other comrades found themselves on board a different ship; a British War Department sloop.[8]

Luckily for them, they were allowed to remain on deck surrounded by an army guard. Soon, it too pulled out from the dock to follow the *Slieve Bloom*. Flanagan had been at the forefront of some of the previous week's most vicious fighting in North King Street, where his brother had fallen to an enemy machine gunner. He felt no love for the enemy, and his unpleasant experiences since the fighting had ended suggested that this sentiment was likely to remain. To his surprise, however, British sailors brought out chunks of bread with cups of coffee and cocoa, which were passed around the prisoners. Those who had already fallen asleep were woken for the unexpected feast. Then, to Flanagan's astonishment, the sailors apologised for not having enough mugs to go around, suggesting they took turns. Flanagan ate and drank his quota before drifting off to sleep as he thought about his fallen brother.

Meanwhile, on the south-eastern side of Dublin city, the men of the Irish Volunteers 3rd Battalion, under Commandant Éamon de Valera, were making the most of their captivity in the Royal Dublin Showgrounds, having been marched under guard through its Anglesea Road entrance several hours earlier. The 3rd Volunteer Battalion had been the last to capitulate in Dublin. On their journey from their surrender point in Grattan Street they had been flanked by several hundred civilians, who looked on more silently than those in Kilmainham and Francis Street had earlier in the day. They appeared content to observe quietly the men who had wrought carnage on the British soldiers sent to recapture the city the previous Wednesday during the fighting along Northumberland Road and at Mount Street Bridge. Two Sherwood Forester Battalions – the 2/7th and 2/8th – had suffered a bloodbath in a battle that lasted for over nine hours.

Once they were inside the showgrounds, a British captain named Hitzen, who had accepted their surrender, ordered his infantrymen to sweep out the adjacent stables and place fresh straw in them. Once this was done, between twenty-five and thirty prisoners were herded into each one.

Not far away from where the 3rd Battalion men were getting some much-needed rest, one of its section commanders, 27-year-old Volunteer and former office clerk Séamus Grace was beginning to recover from the recent ordeal of spending three days on the run with no food or water. He had been captured by the enemy the previous day and brought to the showgrounds with some other prisoners. Grace had hidden in a shed on Haddington Road after defending against overwhelming odds a strategic corner house – 25 Northumberland Road – alongside Lieutenant Michael Malone during the intense fighting in the area. Lieutenant Malone, Grace's good friend, had died in a hail of bullets in the same action. Their own and their battalion's astonishingly tenacious resistance in this area had barred the entry into Dublin city of several enemy battalions, and, consequently, the entire 59th Midland Division, which waited to follow them.

Mercifully for Grace, his captors had fed him the previous night and again on Sunday. Now he took as much opportunity as he could to rest in the pen he was sharing with about twenty others. Three times during the previous night and early morning he had been summoned and interrogated. On each occasion he provided his name, his rank – section commander – and his battalion, but nothing more. At one point, an increasingly frustrated interrogator bellowed into his face from inches away that it was useless for the insurgents to be holding out, asserting that five artillery brigades had recently arrived via Kingstown port (Dún Laoghaire) from England to flatten the entire city if necessary. The officer's claim was correct – the military had been gearing up to pulverise rebel positions throughout the city. Grace's interrogators had eventually given up, however, and he was escorted back to his comrades. Now, the following evening, still exhausted from his recent ordeals, he could rest.

Grace's peace was soon shattered by the synchronised clicking of boots as the sentries stood to attention. An officer of the Royal Irish Rifles arrived with unwelcome news. He announced that the rest of their men had surrendered, and asked if they would like to be taken to them.[9] None of the prisoners took this bombshell well. The relative silence from the city since Saturday morning had suggested defeat, but there was also the faint hope that things had somehow gone according to plan, and that perhaps a truce had been negotiated – the terms of which would soon be revealed to the soldiers of the Irish Republic. Grace was the most deeply affected, however, and began to shake; he was afraid he would be sick. The officer disappeared, then returned with a flask of black tea. He handed Grace a mug of hot tea and apologised for not having any milk or sugar. He then told Grace not to let the British see how he felt, and suggested that he could still serve his country by keeping a brave face.[10] Grace pulled himself together, and he and the men with him were soon taken to the rest of their battalion. Moving across the grounds, they could still hear the distant cracks of rifle fire and the answering staccato of a machine gun. They thought that perhaps the fight was still on.

A surreal atmosphere hung over the city that Sunday night. Ambulances sped through the deserted city streets. Hundreds of homes were raided by the military and the police. North King Street was in a state of trauma following the massacre there, while rumours abounded about numerous atrocities carried out by the British military over the course of the week.

To the men of the Volunteers' 5th Battalion, Dublin seemed like a dead city[11] as their transportation trucks jolted towards Richmond Barracks from Swords. Here and there was the eerie glow of a fire, while at times the density of the hanging smoke made it difficult to breathe. The trucks were halted periodically at army checkpoints. When they eventually turned into Richmond Barracks, Joseph Lawless, who had been gripping the side of his vehicle for support, let out a shriek. The driver had misjudged the angle of the turn and the vehicle's near side had struck the gate pillar, crushing Lawless's little finger. The driver reversed out and attempted the turn again, getting it right the second time. An argument erupted between the driver and the guards manning the gate over who would take responsibility for the damage to the pillar. Lieutenant Lawless had more immediate concerns. He held his hand up to the light from the guardroom door. To his horror, his torn leather glove revealed a mangled bloody pulp where his little finger had been. Mick Fleming, who had been sitting between Lawless's legs for the journey, tried to help, but when he saw the extent of the damage he quickly called one of the soldiers on the truck. He refused to help. Bartle Weston, Lawless's comrade, reasoned with the soldier, protesting that Lawless had lost his finger, only to receive the reply, 'Pity he didn't lose his head.' When an officer stepped out of the guardroom, Weston seized his chance and called out to him. After taking one look at the wound the officer told Lawless to follow him inside. As they climbed down from the truck Lawless collapsed, overwhelmed by exhaustion and pain.

The energy-sapped men on the various vehicles were now ordered off, and once again the searches began. Then they were marched into a small barrack room on the ground floor, which contained a pile of blankets and a large iron tub in a corner to act as a latrine. Most of them were too tired to care about their overcrowded surroundings and suspect sanitation facilities and settled down as best they could. Shouts of: 'Stay away from the windows!' came from the sentries outside as some of the men tried to look around. Bartle Weston sat next to his brother Charles. Vice-Commandant Mulcahy sat nearby, pondering what lay in store for the men under Commandant Ashe. Ashe, a Kerryman from the village of Lispole, was an avid motorcyclist, and had spent a good deal of the previous week taking orders from place to place in north Dublin on his New Hudson motorbike. Dressed in leather motorbike trousers and boots, he stood out among his fellow Volunteers. Music, particularly pipe music, was another of his passions, and he began singing 'The Cottage by the Lee' to keep up his men's spirits.

Joseph Lawless revived and was taken to the medical station. He was met there by a friendly orderly who was quick to inform him and his escort what he thought of the barracks: 'Nice sort of kip to be stuck in; sweet Fanny Adams in the place.'[12] He then added, pointing at Lawless, 'A case like this and we have to search the town for a doctor.' As if to prove him wrong, a doctor soon arrived, quickly getting to work on the suffering Volunteer's hand, with the orderly's help. Lawless had also suffered a leg injury, but the dreadful pain of his hand wound had masked it. His leg was also seen to, however, and he was given a sleeping draught to get him through the night. Eventually Lieutenant Lawless was brought to the barrack room that held his comrades, to find three mattresses in the corner of the room laid out as his bed. The mattresses were each two feet square and six inches deep, earning them the nickname 'biscuit' mattresses. His pain abated when the sleeping draught took effect and he fell into a deep sleep.

Back in the Royal Dublin Showgrounds, at around 11 p.m. Vice-Commandant Joseph O'Connor was taken out of the stable he was sharing with his men and marched away. O'Connor, who was 35, had helped galvanise his 3rd Battalion comrades during the latter part of the previous week, showing continued composure while under incessant pressure from the enemy. He had been a member of the Irish Volunteers since its genesis, as well as an IRB member for many years.

When O'Connor showed no sign of returning, Volunteer Peadar O'Mara became concerned for him. He went over to the stable door and looked out. An enemy officer then called out to him. O'Mara stepped out as the stable's guards stood aside and was taken by the officer to the building opposite, where he found O'Connor speaking with two British officers. One of the officers turned suddenly to O'Mara, asking him about the numbers and the locations of his men still positioned on the nearby Dublin South-East railway line – a position that had been a thorn in the military's side for days. O'Mara was surprised by this, but replied nonetheless that he was unwilling to provide the enemy with such an answer unless ordered to do so by his superior officer – as was protocol. O'Connor ordered him to answer, adding that he had received instructions from Commandant de Valera to facilitate the British military.[13]

Facing O'Connor, O'Mara told him that the orders he had received that morning to call in all the battalion men had been carried out in full and that every man had reported. He emphasised that none had been left behind; they were now prisoners.[14] After conferring for several moments, the two British officers appeared satisfied. They dispatched O'Connor and O'Mara back to the stables. The unmistakable sound of rifle shots could still be heard from not far away. Some, it seemed, were still holding out.

Seán Byrne, meanwhile, had made himself as comfortable as possible and was talking about the events of the previous week with Séamus Grace, when one of his fellow prisoners whispered to him that three British officers were looking in on them.[15] Byrne leaned forward to have a look. Captain Hitzen, one of the officers, saw him and beckoned him over. Byrne complied, doing his best not to trip over his slumbering comrades. When he stepped outside the stable, Hitzen told him that some of his comrades had not yet surrendered, and added that it was utterly hopeless for them to hold out. He asked if Byrne could do something about it, stressing that he simply wished to prevent any further bloodshed. Byrne paused and then answered 'Yes.' The captain thanked him.

Byrne was then handed back the white flag that had been used earlier on, and escorted by one of the other two officers out of the showgrounds' Merrion Road exit. Pointing along the length of Serpentine Avenue, the officer instructed him to proceed there until met by a captain of the Leicester Regiment. Byrne then nervously entered Serpentine Avenue. Despite the darkness he could make out several dozen British soldiers skulking in positions of cover in the road's many gardens. Shadows danced under the flares sent up by the British. Local residents looked on from their open doorways as he pressed on, holding his white flag aloft. Eventually he came to the attention of the Leicester Regiment captain and two privates, who were taking cover in a garden ahead and to his right. The captain signalled Byrne to approach and then introduced himself. He pointed to a nearby house close to the road's level crossing, signalling that a sniper was on its roof somewhere. The two privates stood motionless and silent. The captain asked Byrne to enter the house and persuade the sniper to surrender. When Byrne appeared hesitant the officer suggested that the two privates, one of whom was carrying a satchel of hand grenades, would go with him as support. Byrne reluctantly agreed, but only under the condition that the grenades were left behind and that the soldiers would hold their fire. This was agreed to. Moments later, when they approached the house, they were greeted by the surreal sight of an elderly lady sitting listlessly in her armchair among a clutter of furniture strewn about the front garden.

The three men cautiously stepped inside the pitch-dark house. Once their eyes became accustomed to the dark and they had checked that the ground floor was clear, they warily ascended the staircase. Eventually, one of the soldiers pointed to an open window. Byrne apprehensively stuck his head out and started calling on his unknown comrade to surrender, but was met only with silence and the barking of dogs from nearby gardens. Returning minutes later to the British captain, he explained that he had been unable to make contact. The captain asked him to go down to another house in the area where rifle fire had been coming from; he assumed that the same sniper had redeployed there. Byrne had had enough. He refused. The captain paused for a moment before instructing him to report back to the showgrounds. Byrne departed, making sure that his white flag was raised. When he eventually arrived back, the officer who had earlier escorted him out brought him to see Captain Hitzen and the other officer who had made up the original trio. He informed them of the result of his sortie. The officer next to Hitzen said 'Hard luck' and took Byrne back to the stables, where he settled down once again next to Séamus Grace. Soon afterwards, hot tea with milk arrived for the rebels gathered in the stable, paid for by Captain Hitzen and the other two British officers, one of whom said philosophically, 'The same blood is in my veins as is in yours.'[16] The grateful prisoners savoured the unexpected luxury of tea, warm, sweet and milky, while they spoke quietly among themselves, prayed for the fallen and fell into a deep sleep.

Captain E. J. Hitzen of the 2/5th Lincolnshire Battalion, who displayed both respect and kindness to the surrendered Volunteers of the 3rd Battalion while they were in captivity in the Royal Dublin Showgrounds. COURTESY OF PETER AND ANNE HEARSEY

On board the *Slieve Bloom,* which was now being tossed about like a cork as it crossed the Irish Sea, the rebels in the cattle pens were enjoying no such comfort as their 3rd Battalion comrades. They were suffering terribly from seasickness. The already fetid stench was soon added to by the rank odour of vomit. In their cramped conditions with little or no room to move, the only option for many was to retch and heave where they sat or lay. Their comrades now suffered the indignation of being vomited on as they sat with their backsides immersed in filthy sludge. The luckier ones had been overcome with exhaustion and appeared blissfully unaware as they grunted and rolled their heads in fitful sleep. Those less fortunate were also desperately thirsty. Their rations of bully beef had added to their thirst. Some of them appealed to the guards on the far side of an open hatch for water. One of the soldiers looked down upon them and replied that the only kind of offering he had in mind was a bullet. Pity seemed to overcome his bravado, however, as he soon fetched a bucket of water. Frank Robbins managed to find an empty bucket in his part of the hold. He called out to a soldier outside and asked him to fill it. The response was: 'You dirty Irish pig, get back in the hold or you won't require any water.'[17] Robbins was taken aback. He had found during the day that the ordinary British infantrymen had been more affable to him. Eventually weariness overcame him and he fell asleep.

Back in Richmond Barracks, John MacDonagh sat down beside his 38-year-old brother and battalion commandant, Thomas. Commandant MacDonagh pulled a tin of concentrated food tablets from the pocket of his Volunteer overcoat and began sharing them among the half-dozing men in the barrack room. John beckoned 17-year-old William Stapleton over, asking if he was hungry. The answer from the pint-sized Volunteer was an immediate 'Yes'. John smiled at his young comrade and handed him the two food tablets his brother had given him moments earlier. Stapleton thanked him and devoured them. Thomas MacDonagh, originally from Tipperary, had been employed by Pádraig Pearse as a teacher in St Enda's, a career move that had ultimately led him to his current position. Before that, he had been a lecturer in English at University College Dublin (UCD). He was a writer, a playwright and a poet. Before the rebellion, he had been the Director of Training of the Irish Volunteers. Now that was all at an end. Nevertheless, he maintained a cheery disposition as he discussed the day's events with his brother and with Peadar McMahon. He recalled that before the Rising he had made up his mind never to surrender, adding that he had only agreed to it in order to save Dublin and its citizens.[18] Thomas then stood and removed his overcoat, placing it around the shoulders of Major MacBride, who only had his light suit overcoat and had been shivering with cold. Returning afterwards to his conversation with McMahon and his brother, MacDonagh assured them that the Volunteers would someday live to see the fruits of their efforts, but that he himself and the other leaders would 'be in heaven' by that time – at least he hoped so. McMahon was astonished at MacDonagh's philosophical acceptance of death, as well as his cheery disposition in the current circumstances. After their conversation, Commandant MacDonagh began walking around and speaking to each man in the room, ensuring that morale was in good shape.

Other men who had made up the Jacob's garrison just lay down on the floors of the various barrack rooms. Among some, the vitriolic response unleashed during the day by the civilians haunted them as they slept fitfully. John Kelly sang an old rebel song. Gerry Boland found the lack of beds and the sanitary conditions most disturbing. The foul odour from the latrine buckets did not help. The cold hard floor added to the prisoners' woes; they paced the room to keep warm and occupied.

In another room, Volunteer Michael Molloy, one of the printers of the Republican proclamation, checked his pockets to ensure that they contained nothing incriminating. He was horrified when he pulled out a folded piece of paper and discovered that it contained a list of actual signatures on a proclamation. Realising how dangerous such a piece of evidence was, he began to tear it up into tiny pieces, until a comrade sitting beside him suggested the best thing to do was to chew it up into small bits.[19] He did just that, before scattering them around the room.

Meanwhile, in the elegant Georgian setting of Dublin's Merrion Square, 35-year-old Lieutenant William Wylie had just retired for the night. Just after midnight there was a loud knock on his front door. The barrister and soldier dressed and opened the door to find an army dispatch rider standing at his doorstep. He handed him a letter saying that his presence was required immediately at General HQ in the Royal Hospital. Wylie had recently been on holiday in Killarney and had borrowed a Ford Model T motor car to get back to the capital as quickly as possible when he heard of the rebellion. He sped from checkpoint to checkpoint as he drove to Kilmainham. There, Wylie was ushered into a room where a high-ranking staff officer – Brigadier-General Joseph Byrne, General Maxwell's Deputy Adjutant – sat at a desk.

Wylie came to attention as the brigadier looked up, and in a distinctive Northern Irish accent, asked 'Are you Wylie?' 'Yes, Sir,' he replied. The general spoke again: 'Good; you will prosecute the courts martial.' He then added that Wylie was to start first thing in the morning. Wylie was taken aback. His training was in civil, not criminal or military, law. He asked, 'What will the charges be, Sir?' General Byrne said: 'That is for you to decide. Make out the charges and notify the accused. General Blackader will be president of the court.' He was referring to 46-year-old General Charles Guinand Blackader. There was to be little sleep for Lieutenant Wylie that night.

In Richmond Barracks, meanwhile, Volunteer Joseph Gleeson was in a room with Seán MacDermott, Tom Clarke and Michael Mallin. Their conversation focused on the Rising. Tom Clarke, now looking very drawn, mirrored nonetheless the optimism shown by Commandant MacDonagh to his own men. He reasoned that he was happy with the outcome, explaining, 'We have a minimum loss, which will result in a maximum gain,'[20] and adding, 'We will die, but it will be a different Ireland after us.'[21] Clarke had no fear of death. To him it was preferable to returning to prison. Clarke had been instrumental in reorganising the IRB, following his return from the United States with his wife Kathleen and his eldest son John in 1907. Before his time in America, he had spent 15 brutal years in Pentonville Prison in London (under the false name Henry Wilson) following his involvement in a bombing campaign on mainland Britain. Most of his sentence had been spent in solitary confinement. He was released in 1898. His entire adult life had been dedicated to overthrowing British rule in Ireland. He was also a founding member of the Irish Volunteers. A member of the IRB's Supreme Council, Clarke, along with MacDermott, a close friend, was the driving force behind the Rising.

MacDermott concurred with Clarke, suggesting with characteristic intensity that their executions would wipe out any remaining pro-English spirit in Ireland. Clarke and MacDermott then listened as Mallin recounted how he had got a bullet hole in his Citizen Army hat. He then spoke of the fighting in the Stephen's Green area, and each man contributed his own recollections of Easter Week. Mallin was, however, feeling far less enthusiastic about the prospect of imminent martyrdom than his two comrades.

When their conversation died down, Tom Clarke banged on the door and asked the sentry if he would deliver a letter in exchange for his wristwatch. The soldier eyed both him and the watch as he pondered the proposal, and then handed Clarke a page torn from a notebook and a pencil, telling him to address it to Mrs O'Toole, 32 King's Inn St, for Mrs T. Clarke.[22] He promised him that from there he would ensure it fell into the right hands. Clarke adjusted his narrow-rimmed spectacles and began writing a note to his wife. When he had finished, he handed it to MacDermott, who scribbled his own note on the other side. The letter and watch were handed over to the soldier, who promised he would deliver it. The promise was subsequently kept, several days later. Clarke

Thomas Clarke, the 59-year-old Fenian veteran and first signatory to the Proclamation of the Irish Republic, had suffered terribly at the hands of a deranged enemy officer prior to the march to Richmond Barracks. Clarke and Seán MacDermott were very close friends. COURTESY OF KILMAINHAM GAOL ARCHIVES

Seán MacDermott, Clarke's fellow-architect of the Easter Rising, and his good friend. MacDermott had also suffered at the hands of the British officer Captain Percival Lea Wilson when the Republican prisoners had been held in the Rotunda. NATIONAL LIBRARY OF IRELAND

soon settled down while MacDermott fell into a restless slumber with his head lying on Clarke's chest, periodically crying out in his sleep: 'The fire! The fire! Get the men out!' MacDermott had played a pivotal part in the evacuation of the burning GPO two nights earlier. He now appeared to be reliving the frantic escape in his nightmares. Clarke soothed his comrade with the words: 'Quiet, Seán, we're in the barracks now. We are prisoners now, Seán.'[23]

Not far away, in a room in which sat Éamonn Ceannt and several dozen of his men, the more ludicrous side of war was providing a welcome distraction. One man, whom none of them recognised, spent a great deal of time banging on the barrack room door to summon a guard. When a sentry eventually arrived, the man protested that he was not a rebel but a driver for Eason's bookshop. The sentry was entertained by his story, but summoned his sergeant. When he arrived he asked, 'What's the row?' Pointing over his shoulder, the hapless man protested that he had nothing to do with the men behind him. He then went on to explain that he had been drinking earlier that day with a friend and, under the influence, had joined their ranks as a prank in Marrowbone Lane when they marched past. The sergeant looked him up and down and said: 'You are not a soldier, so you must be a Sinn Feiner.[24] There are only soldiers or Sinn Feiners in this barracks.' The door was then slammed shut, leaving the man with two nagging concerns – where his drinking companion was and what would become of the pair of them.

Éamonn Ceannt, 35 years old, who was looking on in amusement, was, like Pádraig Pearse and Tom Clarke, one of the Irish Volunteers' founding members. He had been raised in County Galway but had settled with his family in Dublin, where he had worked as a bookkeeper. As an avowed nationalist, the Volunteers afforded him the opportunity to do something he was far more suited to than accounting – soldiery. He was hugely respected by his men. His tenacious defence of the South Dublin Union had impressed the British officer who had accepted his surrender, Major Rotherham, to the point that he had paid Ceannt the compliment of inspecting his men afterwards.

Ceannt now ordered the windows opened in an attempt to clear the foul air, but enemy sentries outside shouted at the men to get back any time they tried. Despite the limited space in the room, Ceannt got the Volunteers to perform some simple exercises, in spite of their exhaustion, to keep their minds off the smell. He then addressed them with characteristic sternness. He said that they must look to the future and regard the Rising as a success, not a failure. He considered the surrender to have been a mistake and would have preferred to have carried on the fight. Heads nodded in agreement. He then added: 'They will probably shoot us,'[25] referring to himself and the Rising's other leaders, before adding: 'But you will either be in prison or internment for a few months or until the end of the war.' The men sat, listening silently. Ceannt's words would prove prophetic.

Robert Holland was in another room with some other men from Commandant Ceannt's 4th Battalion. The room was so crowded that in order to get any rest, half of the men had to sit down, back to back, while the other half stood in shifts. Thomas Young was among the first group, sitting next to Holland, Mick Liston and 27-year-old Captain Con Colbert. When their conversation veered towards what would become of them, Young replied: 'The Lord only knows.' Martin Kavanagh, sitting nearby, suggested that they could all be sent to France to fight the Germans, considering they were so well trained and the British were so desperate for men. He added as an afterthought that they would be divided into smaller groups to represent less of a threat. Liston reckoned they would be shipped out to the colonies. Colbert, from Athea in County Limerick, drew a breath and said he would prefer to be executed.[26] His wish would soon be granted. His fatalistic assertion led to a momentary silence from those around him. Colbert reasoned that the response of the civilians to their rebellion had convinced him of this. 'We would be better off dead as life would be torture.'[27] A more prolonged silence descended among the small group. Colbert, a deeply religious man, then called for a rosary to be said for those who had died in the fight for Ireland's freedom. To the murmur of prayers Holland fell into a deep but brief sleep, until it was his turn to stand.

5

The Military Prepare to Make Their Next Move

'Like a rat in a trap'

On Monday morning, the women held overnight in Richmond Barracks' married quarters were ordered out onto the square and marched under a heavy escort the half mile or so to Kilmainham Gaol. As they went in, Annie Cooney noticed the inscription inside the prison's gates: 'Sin no more lest worse shall come to thee.'[1] Once they were inside, they were asked their names. They responded in Irish. The English soldiers struggled to understand the pronunciations and to spell the names. A while later a dozen or so female warders arrived from Mountjoy Prison. The female prisoners were then searched. No weapons were found, however; they had been left behind, still hidden up the chimneys in Richmond Barracks. The women were divided into groups of three and locked into cells.

Volunteer Gerald Doyle, also imprisoned at Kilmainham at that point, was, with some of his fellow prisoners, allowed outside after breakfast to wash and get some exercise. Doyle was 20 years old and had joined the Volunteers in 1914. He and about two dozen of his 4th Battalion comrades had been captured on Easter Monday in the South Dublin Union, fighting under their company commander, Captain George Irvine. They had held off several enemy assaults before being finally overwhelmed by vastly superior fire. At the time, a British officer

– incandescent at their tenacious resistance – had wanted to shoot Doyle and his comrades out of hand, but a more senior officer had arrived and, luckily for them, ruled otherwise. For a week since then, Doyle and his fellow captives had been subjected to repeated interrogations and beatings. One of the men captured with him, James Burke, had his Volunteer uniform torn to pieces by enemy bayonets while a prisoner in Kilmainham. Doyle was himself badly bruised from the seemingly endless beatings he had received during his repeated interrogations. Doyle was a keen footballer, however, and his fitness and strength had stood to him. He had divulged nothing. Nonetheless, he could see that more than a few of his comrades were rapidly becoming worn down by the repeated punishments.

When Doyle and his section members were being brought back inside the prison buildings following a few circuits of the yard, Captains Tannam and Staines were in another group being led out for exercise. Doyle knew both men. They exchanged warm greetings, delighted to find each other still alive and in one piece. That day, 1 May, was Captain Staines's 31st birthday. Good wishes were offered, accompanied with some friendly jibes. Then, luckily for Doyle, the soldier escorting Tannam and Staines' group outside mistook him for one of the second group and shoved him back out to the yard. The three rebels found this state of affairs most agreeable in the circumstances, particularly Doyle, now enjoying his second dose of fresh air.

The men exchanged stories. Doyle entertained the officers with an amusing anecdote of two men from Derry who had been rounded up in Dublin with about ten other men who had been mistaken for rebels. They had been put in Doyle's room overnight. When the pair heard several among their fellow prisoners reciting a rosary during the night they apparently feared for their lives and banged on the door to get the guard's attention. When he arrived they told him they were Protestants and loyalists and had nothing to do with the rebellion. The guard's response was to threaten to shoot them. They persevered, however, insisting that they were terrified. Astonishingly, they were convinced that the other men in the cell, being Roman Catholics, would kill them when they finished praying.[2] Their protests fell on deaf ears. They sat down to glares of disgust from their fellow captives who were appalled that they considered they were in danger from them simply because of their faith.

The three men discussed the fighting in Dublin; then their conversation became more ominous. Tannam and Staines told Doyle that he and his comrades must 'sit tight' and keep their mouths shut. They were to tell the enemy nothing, adding that if they did and were singled out they would be in real danger of facing a firing squad.

On the far side of Kilmainham crossroads, meanwhile, General Maxwell and his staff sat at their breakfast table in the Royal Hospital discussing what charges they could bring against the more prominent Republican prisoners. Maxwell had already ordered the army and police to co-operate in rounding up those who were known to be involved in the Volunteers, Sinn Féin and other similar groups – whether or not they had taken part in the insurrection. Ireland, in his opinion, would remain a dangerous place if these people were permitted to remain free. His main hurdle, however, was a legal one. Martial law had been declared on 25 April, the second day of the rebellion, but his political and military overseers wanted him to charge the insurgents under the Defence of the Realm Act (DORA). Maxwell's problem was that DORA would not permit executions of the Republicans unless there was tangible proof they had been colluding with an enemy of Great Britain – in this case, Germany; and he had no evidence to verify this. When he had insisted he be allowed to exercise his plenary powers and try the prisoners in military courts under martial law, his deputy adjutant, General Byrne, had contended that he must adhere to his original instructions in order to avoid political repercussions. He reassured Maxwell that it was a simple matter of time before the link between the Germans and the Republicans was established, and this would permit him to pass death sentences under DORA. Nevertheless, the German ship, the *Aud,* had since been scuttled and was now lying at the bottom of the ocean off the coast of County Cork. They needed something fast. With the round-ups about to begin, which would inevitably add to the number of prisoners already in custody, they would need to act quickly and expedite the daunting number of cases already waiting.

Maxwell made a quick decision. The rebels would be tried under field general courts martial (FGCMs). This process required only three officers to be present, while a general court martial required at least five officers and up to 15 men to staff and administer the court. The prisoners' guilt, as far as Maxwell was concerned, was a foregone conclusion. The question now was just how guilty they were. FGCMs were held for soldiers on active duty, normally close to the front line. They were officially open to the public, although it was practically unheard of for civilians to travel so close to a combat zone to observe them. Maxwell decreed that in the interest of public safety all forthcoming courts martial would be held in camera. No members of the public would be admitted.

At roughly 9 a.m. that Monday, the four infantry companies of the 2/6th Sherwood Forester Battalion formed into ranks on Great Britain Street. They had been in the area for the best part of four days. The nearby barricade that had fortified the street from attack from Moore Street the previous Friday and Saturday was stripped of its contents by civilians desperate for firewood. Within a short time barely a splinter remained of what had been a formidable structure. Then swarms of ravenous looters poured into the local shops through the broken doors and windows, desperate to pillage whatever food and other goods they could get for their starving and beleaguered families. The battalion was paraded and marched away to Sackville Street and from there to Trinity College, where it was joined by other units that had been engaged in combat in the city during the week, and had since been taken out of line duty.

Soon the troops stood together in the college's majestic Parliament Square. The four-storey enclosing stone walls echoed to the barks of sergeants and the stamping of boots, until General Maxwell arrived to address and congratulate the assembled men. He proclaimed that through the tireless efforts of the officers and soldiers all the surviving rebels had now surrendered unconditionally. He expressed gratitude to the Irish regiments for their role in helping to crush the rebellion. He then read a message from King George V, conveying the king's gratitude to the gallant soldiers of the British Army, RIC and DMP for their self-sacrifice. Maxwell had since been presented with the bloodstained letter removed from the body of Michael O'Rahilly in Sackville Lane. He read from it, mockingly describing its contents – poignant words of farewell to his family written as he lay dying – as 'high-falutin'.

Brigadier-General Lowe, 54 years old, was next to address the ranks. Lowe had overseen the troop deployments in Dublin city during the week, as well as taking Commandant Pearse's initial surrender two days earlier. On a strategic level, Lowe had performed exceptionally well as a commander, methodically employing his battalions to isolate enemy positions. On a tactical level, however, his attitude mirrored that of his colleagues overseeing the slaughter in the trenches of Western Europe: casualties among his men came a distant second to securing objectives, even when equally useful alternatives became available as battles evolved. The regimental comrades of the men standing rigidly before him – the 2/7th and 2/8th Battalions – had suffered appalling casualties as a direct result of Lowe's tactical intransigence.

Lowe now joined Maxwell in thanking the assembled ranks of troops for their efforts, adding that he himself would no doubt get the credit for their victory, but that he knew it had been down to the men and their officers. He added that he knew it was the long-suffering foot soldiers who got 'all the kicks and none of the praise'. Following this, the men were inspected by General Maxwell, Major-General Friend, General Lowe, and other senior members of Irish Command. The 2/6th Battalion then marched to the Royal Hospital, where the men rested on its lush green lawns. They were soon joined by the remnants of C and D companies from their recently decimated sister battalion, the 2/7th, when Major Raynor, acting in command, was ordered to withdraw from line duty in the Smithfield area to the Royal Hospital Kilmainham. Once there he was to dispatch a single company to Richmond Barracks to support the guard compliment already there.

Mid-morning on Monday, a small team of ambulances made its way from Sir Patrick Dunn's Hospital on Lower Grand Canal Street into the Royal Dublin Showgrounds. Some of the patched-up Volunteers transported included Seán O'Keefe, James Purfield and James Rattigan. As they arrived their comrades from 3rd Battalion were washing at a huge water trough set out in the open. The men alighted from the ambulances under guard soon after the gate was closed behind them and made their way to their comrades, eager for news. Gunfire could still be heard in the east and north of the city. Rumours abounded that their comrades were holding out, or at least some of them were.

Gunfire was heard again in Serpentine Avenue, where Seán Byrne had been unable to make contact with a rebel sniper the previous night. O'Keefe and the others spoke of rifle and machine-gun fire from Haddington Road as they passed earlier in the ambulances. Some spoke of heavy shooting coming from a considerable distance to their north-east, possibly from the Irishtown/Ringsend area. Inevitably the authorities began to close in. The Leicester Regiment placed a triangular

Major John MacBride, from Westport in County Mayo, who was something of a legend among the ranks of the Irish Volunteers as a result of his exploits during the second Boer War in South Africa. He had led the Irish Transvaal Brigade against the British, which made him a marked man in the eyes of the authorities following the Rising. NATIONAL LIBRARY OF IRELAND

Major MacBride being marched under escort in Richmond Barracks. SOUTH DUBLIN LIBRARIES

cordon from Ringsend Road to Baggot Street Bridge and from there to Sandymount. The noose was tightening. In some cases, houses were ransacked as arrests were made. But the sniper fire was unrelenting. As soon as a position was pinpointed by infantrymen it would come under fire, but when it was stormed the frustrated British soldiers would find, time and time again, that the sniper had slipped away to another position.

Shortly after 11 a.m., back in Richmond Barracks, the men of the South Dublin Union and Jacob's garrisons were ordered out of the barrack rooms to parade on the square. Volunteer Patrick Kelly lined up next to John MacBride, who was jingling some coins in his hand. Kelly leaned in, saying, 'I suppose that's some of the German gold.'[3] Both men laughed at the joke, having by now heard the rumours that the Rising had been financed by Germany. The men on the square were divided into smaller groups, then ordered to proceed to the gymnasium in fours, as their comrades had the previous day. This time, however, there were no bursts of machine-gun fire in the background to torment them. As the first four dashed under the archway they were met by the NCOs, who searched them thoroughly. Any documents that might be of interest were to be handed to Lieutenant Jackson, sitting once again at the same desk.

When MacBride approached and handed over his notebook, Jackson flicked through it and discovered a document proving MacBride's appointment to a position of command in the Irish Volunteers' 2nd Battalion. It also contained some half-torn pages and illegible writing. While MacBride had kept his notebook, he had removed any evidence that would incriminate his officer comrades. His discretion would ultimately save them. The surrender of the notebook to Jackson would, however, within days cement his own fate. Jackson kept it safely, correctly suspecting its importance. MacBride then passed through to his left and joined his men inside the gymnasium. Soon both battalions were gathered inside.

Peadar Doyle – BQM of the 4th Battalion – and his 15-year-old son Seán entered the gymnasium side by side, observing the detectives watching and taking notes behind glass panels. Robert Holland was also watching the detectives with keen interest, and he recognised some of them: Barton, Hoey, Bruton, Smyth, Inspector Barrett. There were also a few he had never seen before.

Volunteer Michael Lynch of the same battalion, who was sitting close by, noticed Major MacBride in front of him. Edging over, he introduced himself. MacBride smiled warmly when he realised he knew Lynch's father, but he had not set eyes on the man sitting before him since he was a boy. He grabbed his hand and shook it. The two men spoke of the fighting in their respective areas. MacBride lamented that he had not fired a shot during the week as he had been 'shut up like a rat in a trap' in Jacob's;[4] but it didn't matter any more now that it was all over. Lynch, alert to MacBride's resigned tone, asked him what he meant, but MacBride cut him off: 'I am for it, they have wanted me for many years,' alluding to his Boer War exploits, as he gestured at a British soldier standing guard with fixed bayonet. Lynch needed no explanation of MacBride's exploits, however; he already knew of them. Then the partition door opened. Heads turned in its direction. Detectives Hoey and Barton stood arrogantly in the doorway, sizing up their quarry once again; Barton with his ash walking stick, Hoey with his umbrella. They strutted up and down in front of the prisoners, sneering. Some British officers followed them into the gymnasium, the left-hand side of which was now empty, as if awaiting victims. Then, when everyone was in place, the selections began again. Detective Hoey stopped in front of MacBride and Lynch, pointing with his umbrella, and saying: 'Come on, MacBride.' The major stood and turned to Lynch, shaking his hand as he bade him farewell.

It went on: 'You, and you and you, get up and over the other side of the hall.'[5] The stick and umbrella were used to point towards the prisoners they could not reach. Those overlooked by Barton fell under Hoey's stare. More detectives entered in pairs. Robert Holland looked on as the detectives' victims were selected, thinking that these men were the scum of the earth, intent on keeping them in British bondage and revelling in their power. Éamonn Ceannt was picked. As he stood up, he called over one of the British officers, bringing his attention to one of his men, William Fogarty, who had become mentally unbalanced during the recent fighting. The British officer assured Ceannt that he would keep an eye on Fogarty. Ceannt moved across to the left.

Detective Barton stopped in front of Volunteer Dick Davy, a medic from Jacob's garrison, and asked: 'Don't I know you?' Davy stood up and answered back venomously: 'I know *you*!' The detective signalled him over to the left. Thomas MacDonagh warned Davy not to answer any more questions as he crossed the room, and then followed him over as his own turn came. Con Colbert and Vice-Commandant Tom Hunter were next. Soon afterwards, five DMP constables were brought in to pick out any men they could identify from their recent captivity in Jacob's. They strode slowly between the two groups, staring intently at each face. Many of the prisoners feared their time was up. They were mistaken. The policemen reported to a disgruntled Inspector Love that they recognised nobody. A little later, Peadar Doyle's turn came to move over to the left. His teenage son Seán instinctively clasped his arm. Doyle reassured him and implored him to be brave, before he apprehensively took his place. When there was a big enough gap among the unselected men it was filled with the remaining men from the 4th Battalion who had been waiting outside on the square.

In the barrack rooms containing the men selected the previous day, witnesses were now called to identify the prisoners. Captain Mahoney of the Royal Army Medical Corps (RAMC) was brought into each room for this purpose. Mahoney had been taken prisoner by the GPO garrison during Easter Week and, being a doctor, had tended to the wounded James Connolly, among others. When he had arrived at Richmond Barracks he had protested to the authorities at being asked to perform any identification, insisting that he was a doctor, not a policeman.[6] He had relented, agreeing that he would at least view the prisoners. Ultimately, however, he failed to identify a single one. Looking on, Jack Plunkett muttered to a comrade that he hoped the cigar he had given Captain Mahoney some days earlier in the GPO had been a good one – he was aware that the doctor would be able to identify a great many of them. When Mahoney had had enough, he turned to his escort, saying: 'I know nothing about combatants, my job was to care for British and Volunteer wounded impartially.'[7] With that, he turned and left.

Outside on the barracks square, the men who had been held captive at the Custom House since the previous Friday had now arrived on foot. Still among their ranks were Captains Frank Thornton and William J. Brennan-Whitmore. They were accompanied by a large group of civilians suspected of being Volunteers. Among the latter group was one of the leaders of the Irish Transport and General Workers' Union (ITGWU), 35-year-old William O'Brien, a long-standing associate of James Connolly. He was accompanied by Connolly's son, 15-year-old Roderick (Roddy). The two stood among approximately 150 fellow prisoners. O'Brien told Connolly to use the name Carney whenever he was asked. They waited for several hours in the unseasonal heat in the square, tormented by soldiers, as their fellow prisoners had been the previous day. Mugs of water were poured onto the ground in front of anyone who asked for a drink. The prisoners were then ordered into temporary holding rooms – 40 to each room – until their turn came to enter the gymnasium.

Captain Brennan-Whitmore had recognised some of the men of the Royal Irish Regiment when he entered the barracks earlier. He was a Wexford man, and the Royal Irish was the territorial unit for County Wexford.[8] One NCO from the regiment approached Brennan-Whitmore in the barracks room and quietly told him that many men from his own battalion – the 18th – were unhappy that they had not been given the chance to join the rebels at the outset of the Rising. Brennan-Whitmore replied that they could have taken over their barracks and joined regardless. The sergeant then said that several of them had considered the idea, but they had decided against it, fearing that the vastly superior number of English, Scottish and Welsh soldiers in the barracks would have made it near impossible to seize by force, and that their efforts would merely see them shot for mutiny. Many Irishmen in British Army units had also wanted to join the rebels, but were unable to. Some had deliberately aimed their weapons to miss during the fighting, not wanting to kill fellow Irishmen. Others, however, thought very differently and had fought aggressively against the Volunteers and Citizen Army.

Back in the gymnasium, at around 2 p.m. the order was shouted to clear out some of the men and make room for others. A group of prisoners from the right-hand side were hastily picked and lined up at the exit desk. John MacDonagh, brother of Thomas, stood in the line. When his turn came, one of the G-men called Superintendent Quinn over, telling him, 'This is MacDonagh's brother,'[9] implying that he should be sent over to the selected ranks simply by virtue of his relationship with his 38-year-old sibling. The superintendent just shrugged his shoulders. MacDonagh was allowed to pass through, but not before he turned to look at Thomas, who smiled and waved at him. He did not know it then, but it would be the last time he saw his brother.

As John MacDonagh walked out to the square he saw Joseph Plunkett being marched under escort towards the Medical Room. Plunkett was instantly recognisable in his rimmed spectacles, high-top boots, slouch hat and bandaged neck. He looked gravely ill, but his stoic demeanour drew great admiration from MacDonagh, as well as the 5th Battalion men who could also see him from their barrack rooms. Soon they too were ordered out into the square, and then the gymnasium. Once inside they were ordered to gather on the right-hand side. They recognised comrades across the room, including Con Colbert, looking as resolute as ever. On the other side, Joseph Lawless, his hand still throbbing with pain, watched as Commandant Ceannt, tall and upright, paced up and down among the selected men like a caged lion.[10]

While the detectives were giving the 5th Battalion men the once-over, a British officer entered, followed by three RIC sergeants. The officer pointed out to them the area containing the rebels they had come to identify – those who had fought at Ashbourne. The RIC men took a good look. Richard Mulcahy recognised the policeman who had driven him to Dublin from Kilsallaghan the previous day. Commandant Ashe – distinctive in his motorcyclist's gear – Richard Hayes, and Frank and Jim Lawless were selected. Then a staff officer arrived, recognised by Mulcahy as one of the men who had accompanied General Friend when they had spoken the previous afternoon. Mulcahy made himself as small as possible to avoid recognition, and hoped his growth of stubbly beard would also help disguise his lean, austere face. It did. The officer walked up and down a few times eyeballing the Volunteers, before turning once again to the officer who had brought him in. He shook his head before leaving the room.

On the opposite side of the River Liffey, in Arbour Hill detention barracks, Pádraig Pearse, having been confined to his cell for two days, had thrown himself into a frenzy of activity.[11] He wrote three poems and several letters, and put his financial affairs in order. He also wrote a letter to General Maxwell, appealing to him to spare the lives of his followers if he himself forfeited his life. These items were handed over to Sergeant Goodman, the same NCO who had provided him with the writing materials, who forwarded them to General Maxwell's staff for examination. The general considered them to be seditious, and sent them through channels that ultimately led to the British Prime Minster, Herbert Asquith.

Pearse then wrote a letter to his mother in which he described the events since the previous Friday, 28 April. He added a postscript to the letter before handing it to Sergeant Goodman. When Goodman read the postscript he immediately sought out his officer in charge. The letter was then dispatched in great haste to the Royal Hospital Kilmainham, where Lieutenant Brucknill took a quick look. He then rushed to General Maxwell. Maxwell's eyes widened when he read the postscript: 'I understood that the German expedition on which I had counted actually did set sail.' The general did not need to read any more. Lieutenant Brucknill explained that this was now adequate proof to tie Pearse to Germany, and charge him under Section 50 of DORA. Brucknill was concerned, however, that the same charges could not be used against the rebel commandant's fellow captives, but nonetheless concluded that if Pearse was found guilty, the other prisoners could also be assumed to be guilty – something that Pearse had not anticipated when he had in effect offered himself up to spare them. Maxwell ordered the charges to be drawn up immediately.

Both Brucknill and Lord James Campbell, the Irish Attorney-General, drew up the charges. Everything was now falling into place. The charge was framed: 'Did an act to wit did take part in an armed rebellion and in waging of war against His Majesty the King, such an act being of such a nature as to be calculated to be prejudicial to the Defence of the Realm and being done with the intention and purpose of assisting the enemy.'[12]

The trials could now begin.

All across Dublin, as Monday wore on, the military round-ups escalated. Truckloads of soldiers and policemen sped throughout the city, smashing their way into suspected Volunteer or sympathisers' homes. The continuous sound of small-arms fire from rebel snipers who still – even now – refused to surrender created an unforgiving sentiment among the soldiers, who continued to drag people out through their front doors, beating and shoving them with their rifle butts. Elsewhere, civilians had ventured out in crowds to see the destruction wrought on their city. Families of both insurgents and civilians searched for loved ones, often weeping with frustration and grief when their searches proved fruitless or – worse – ended with the discovery of a corpse. Dublin's Fire Brigade was tearing down unsafe, smouldering buildings on Sackville Street. The once-splendid GPO was a smoking, ghostly shell. Dublin's inhabitants stood in clusters looking on in shock. Others bent to pick up souvenirs such as empty shell casings or cooled molten glass. To the north-east of Sackville Street, a commandeered coal truck was loaded with dead bodies from the Mater Hospital. The ghastly scene was repeated throughout the city. The bodies, many of them children, needed to be interred as quickly as possible to prevent disease. In back gardens, yards and, in some cases, the rooms of homes, bodies were dug up or removed to be interred in cemeteries.

In the gymnasium in Richmond Barracks, the incessant selections continued. However, when a British Army officer entered and handed Colonel Fraser a note, the colonel ordered their immediate cessation. Those who had been selected were now ordered to their feet and marched out. Then another British officer and some detectives stood in front of the remaining Volunteers and, as had happened the previous day, separated out the younger among them. William Stapleton, 17 years old, was asked his age, and replied that he was 21. The officer moved on. Captain Dick McKee, sitting behind Stapleton, asked him why he had lied. Stapleton answered that he was staying with his comrades 'come what may'. When the more compliant younger Volunteers had been removed, the remainder were lined up, fingerprinted and marched back to their barrack rooms. The 5th Battalion men had now lost all their senior officers in the selections, with the exception of Vice-Commandant Mulcahy. Accordingly, they were particularly careful not to draw attention to the fact that Mulcahy remained among them.

At roughly 4 p.m., Major Rotherham, who had accepted the surrender of the South Dublin Union and Marrowbone Lane distillery garrisons the previous day, was brought into a waiting room that now contained the most recently selected men. The waiting room was beside an office where Major Armstrong – an acting Provost Marshal – sat at a desk. When Rotherham was asked if he could identify any of the Volunteers, he replied that he would not know them: he had never seen them before the surrender; and he would not feel justified in giving testimony.[13] He added that his eyesight was not what it used to be. Rotherham's respect for the enemy as fellow soldiers had clearly not diminished since the previous day. He was dismissed. Major Armstrong now began checking Lieutenant Wylie's unarmed prisoner list, put together in Bride Road the previous day, against the names of those now under guard in the waiting room. His rationale was as simple as that employed the previous day – if they were not on the unarmed list, they must have surrendered under arms and should therefore be listed as 'armed'.

Three hours later, the men whose names were now on Armstrong's 'armed' list were summoned one at a time into the major's office, where he read to each the summary of evidence. Thomas MacDonagh went first, followed by John MacBride. Éamonn Ceannt then entered and heard Armstrong read from a deposition stating: 'E. Ceannt was in a party which surrendered at St. Patrick's Park on April 30th at 5 o'clock p.m. which had come from Jacobs, from which shots had been fired at His Majesty's troops causing some casualties. That E. Ceannt was armed.'[14] Armstrong looked at Ceannt, eager to hear his response, but was taken aback when Ceannt asked whether or not this was a court and whether he was obliged to answer. Armstrong answered 'No' to both questions. Ceannt told the major that he wished to reserve his defence. By 9 p.m. all the men were marched back to the gymnasium, now empty apart from soldiers. Exhausted, the prisoners huddled down as best they could without bedding and with a cold night breeze blowing in through the open windows.

Throughout the barrack rooms that Monday night, prisoners lay down on cold, hard floors struggling to get comfortable. Those fortunate enough to have overcoats shared them. Others discovered that boots or empty bully beef cans wrapped in caps made reasonably effective pillows. Others shivered, unable to sleep, and listened to the nocturnal sounds of the barracks: boots in corridors as guards patrolled; snores of varying tones; coughs; and sudden frantic shouts from those tormented by nightmares, frequently followed by the protesting groans of those unlucky enough to be lying within earshot of them. Monday night in Richmond Barracks was a long one.

6

The First Courts Martial and the Second Deportations

'This is not the end of our fight'

Richmond Barracks came to life in the early morning of Tuesday 2 May with the raucous harmonies of barked orders and the changing of guards. In the cramped barrack rooms, prisoners again roused themselves and stretched their cold, stiff limbs. Following another breakfast of dog biscuits at 6 a.m., Seán Murphy, a Volunteer from the Jacob's garrison, was crossing the barracks square to the latrines when he spotted Seán MacDermott limping ahead of him. Murphy caught up and grabbed his arm to help support him. MacDermott thanked him, and Murphy asked what he thought would happen next. MacDermott said, 'The cause is lost if some of us are not shot.'[1] Shocked, Murphy replied: 'Surely you don't mean that? Are things not bad enough?' They walked on slowly in silence. MacDermott was acutely aware of the propaganda value of Irish martyrs. History would soon prove him right.

To the east, meanwhile, in the Royal Hospital Kilmainham, the men of the 2/6th Sherwood Foresters received fresh orders. Captain Edmunds and 50 men from A Company were dispatched to nearby Islandbridge Barracks to bolster their sister battalion – the 2/5th – already in position there. Major Heathcote and Captain Orr from B Company were simultaneously detailed to report to Colonel Fraser in Richmond Barracks, and then to take charge of the prisoners and their effects. Company Sergeant Major Lomas and 90 men of D Company were retained for duties in the Royal Hospital itself, pending a detail that few of them would ever forget. C Company and the remainder of D Company were told to await further orders.

At 7 a.m., General Maxwell and the 178th Brigade[2] Commander, Brigadier Colonel Ernest Maconchy, inspected the remaining men of the Sherwood Foresters 2/7th Battalion, who had now formed up in the grounds of the hospital. The General complimented them on their gallant behaviour on 26 April,[3] six days earlier, when they had endured a bloodbath by enemy fire along Northumberland Road and at Mount Street Bridge. The battalion's commander, Colonel Fane, himself wounded during that battle, issued the order: to proceed to Richmond Barracks, and once there, to provide escort for enemy prisoners on their route for deportation, as well as various other duties.

Back in the barracks itself, Joseph Lawless was among another prisoner group on a latrine run when he noticed Pádraig Pearse ahead of him. Pearse had only just been transported from Arbour Hill and was now being walked around in circles, guarded by three soldiers. Lawless's right arm was in a sling following his recent injury, so he threw up his left arm to salute his commander-in-chief. The prisoners nearby looked in the direction of the salute and followed with standard right-handed versions. Pearse stopped walking, stood erect, saluted back, and watched his men file past.

Lieutenant Brucknill had by now arrived at the barracks to make sure that everything was in place for the, thus far, thirty or so hastily prepared court martial cases. He was also there to deliver a reply to the letter received the previous day by General Maxwell from Commandant Pearse. He approached Pearse and handed him Maxwell's response. It simply read: 'I acknowledge receipt of your letter of 1st May, '16 which I have read. – J. G. Maxwell.'[4] Pearse thanked Brucknill, and carried on with his exercise.

Shortly afterwards, the detachment of prisoners who had arrived from the Custom House the previous day were marched out to the barracks square from their rooms. Frank Thornton, Séamus Daly, William O'Brien and several dozen others were lined up in separate groups before the order was eventually given to move towards the gymnasium, where the customary searches and name-taking were carried out before they entered. Thornton and Daly's uniforms were particularly tattered and burned. They had defended the burning Imperial Hotel positions in Sackville Street until the flames almost engulfed them. When Frank Thornton approached the entrance desk he told Lieutenant Jackson that his name was Proinsías Úa Droighneáin – an Irish name. Lieutenant Jackson simply wrote the name Frank Drennan. Thornton passed into the gymnasium with a furtive sigh of relief, knowing that if the military authorities ever found out his real name he could be conscripted into the British Army. Thornton was originally from Drogheda in County Louth, but had been living in Liverpool until recently, and was therefore liable for conscription.

As the others entered the gymnasium they were moved to the right-hand side and ordered to sit down. They immediately recognised some of the previous day's selected men still sitting on the left-hand side in the corner furthest from the entrance. They looked worn out. Séamus Daly managed to position himself directly opposite 39-year-old Michael O'Hanrahan, the Wexford-born 2nd Battalion Quartermaster, who had been at Jacob's biscuit factory, and who sat among the latter group. O'Hanrahan immediately spotted Daly and signalled across to him. He then put up his hand and, using his finger, spelled out the name Paddy, all the while looking around to make sure that no unwelcome eyes were looking on, before pointing at his arm. Daly quickly got the message – his brother Paddy had been shot in the arm. Lieutenant Paddy Daly had, in fact, been wounded in the arm at the Four Courts. Both O'Hanrahan and Séamus Daly then gave each other reassuring nods before the detectives descended like hawks and the selections began yet again.

Frank Thornton was selected, simply because he stood out in his Volunteer officer's uniform. William O'Brien then went across, having been sent initially to the desk near the exit to provide his name and address. O'Brien noticed a piece of paper on the desk on which were written the names and ranks of the leaders. He noticed his own name among them – a disconcerting discovery. He and the others were told to sit on the gymnasium's left but were also warned not to approach or speak to those under guard in the top left-hand corner. Meanwhile, Captain Brennan-Whitmore was put next to Gerald Crofts on the gymnasium's right-hand side. Crofts spotted a detective approaching them. He leaned over towards Brennan-Whitmore and assured him that they would be all right; this particular detective was a family friend and a very decent man. Brennan-Whitmore watched as the policeman came

Michael O'Hanrahan being led in to Richmond Barracks, flanked by guards. NATIONAL
LIBRARY OF IRELAND

closer, concluding that Crofts must have been right about the man. So far
he had not selected anyone. Once the detective faced Crofts, however,
he stopped and said, 'Oh Gerald, how did you get here? Step forward,
please.'[5] Crofts was staggered that a family friend had chosen him, of all
people. Family friendships, it appeared, meant nothing when the King's
work was to be done.

At Kilmainham Gaol on that Tuesday morning, a large detachment
of prisoners, including Captain George Irvine and James Burke, were
gathered to be transported the short distance to Richmond Barracks.
Some were scheduled to be court-martialled there; others were to be
deported. Also among the group was Tony Makapaltis, the Finnish
sailor, and the two hapless Derry men who had shared a cell with Gerald
Doyle following their accidental arrest. Marching towards the barracks,
however, the Derry men had a glimmer of hope. An onlooker, High
Court Judge John Ross, recognised them among the prisoners, his eyes
widening in disbelief when he saw the pair. He approached the officer
in charge of the escort, introduced himself and told the officer that two

of his charges could not be rebels as they were Derry Apprentice Boys and Orangemen[6] – in other words, staunch loyalists. The irony was not wasted on him as he pointed out the absurdity of the situation. The officer suggested he went to Richmond Barracks to clear the matter up, which he did. When the two men's identities were confirmed, they were released, much to their relief. They thanked Judge Ross and explained that they had been in Dublin on business when they were caught in a round-up.

Back inside the gymnasium, a guard of soldiers arrived, ordered Thomas MacDonagh to his feet and marched him out. As he left, the other men in the top left corner jumped to their feet and saluted him. All around the barracks men were being called out and marched from their holding rooms and cells. Joseph Gleeson watched on as Tom Clarke was called out of the room they were both being held in, followed by Seán McGarry, and others.

Soon afterwards, in another building in the barracks, which had been turned into a makeshift courthouse, General Blackader, Colonel German and Colonel Kent sat next to Lieutenant Wylie as the first of the men due to be tried that day, including MacDonagh and Clarke, were escorted in. Blackader then introduced each member of the court to the accused and informed them that they were about to be tried by court martial. He asked if any of them had an objection to any member of the court. Once this formality was out of the way, each prisoner was handed a charge sheet, taken out of the room and told to wait on a grassy area outside.

A short time later, a detachment of soldiers arrived and ordered those who had been selected the previous day out of the gymnasium. They included Major MacBride, Commandant Ceannt, brothers Harry and Michael O'Hanrahan, Lieutenant William Cosgrave and his younger brother Philip. They were paraded in front of Lieutenant O'Brien to confirm their identities, then taken to the same grassy area, where by now a number of other Volunteers – including Liam Tobin, Peadar Clancy and both Pearse brothers (Pádraig and William) – were sitting and awaiting developments, having been taken out of their own holding rooms moments earlier. They did not know what lay ahead, so word was quietly circulated with the instruction to plead ignorance of the Rising.[7] Commandant MacDonagh explained to 26-year-old James Burke that he and the other leaders wanted to ensure that they would not give the

Prisoners gathered under guard on a green area in Richmond Barracks. NATIONAL LIBRARY OF IRELAND

enemy an opportunity to 'do in' too many of them. Tom Clarke told Seán McGarry that the charge 'with intention to help the enemy' gave him the right to plead not guilty – they had had no such intention. The fact that the Volunteers had solicited the Germans for help was a simple matter of expediency. He then asked him to spread the word for all prisoners to plead accordingly.

Meanwhile, Gerald Doyle found himself in the yard of Kilmainham Gaol once again. This time, however, it was not for exercise. He now stood among a circle of prisoners while three British officers within the circle went from man to man, looking closely at each. Soldiers stood around the yard. One of the officers had a shillelagh decorated with a green ribbon in his Sam Browne belt. A prisoner made a half-muttering joke about the officer's flamboyancy, which prompted Doyle, unable to restrain himself, to erupt into laughter. The officer did not appreciate the funny side, however. A soldier grabbed Doyle by the shoulder and wrenched him out of the ranks. The officer asserted: 'This is our man.'[8] Doyle was handcuffed to the soldier and marched to Richmond Barracks.

Fifteen minutes later, Doyle entered the barracks. He was ordered to sit with the other prisoners on the grass. The three Plunkett brothers – Joseph, George and Jack – were also there, with Éamonn Ceannt and Con Colbert. Sitting closer to Doyle were Harry Boland and 33-year-old Jack Shouldice. Doyle sidled over to them. Boland and Shouldice explained that the block of buildings to their front was now being used as a temporary courthouse, and that Pearse, MacDonagh and Clarke, and three others recently summoned from among them, were now being tried inside. Commandant Ceannt asked Doyle why he was being treated as a special prisoner, curious as to why he had been escorted individually into the barracks. Doyle's tale of his recent encounter with the stuffy enemy officer and the shillelagh gave the men a brief respite of laughter.

Inside the building, Pádraig Pearse was the first to be tried, shortly before noon, followed by MacDonagh and Clarke. The first witness against Pearse was Lieutenant King. He testified to having seen Pearse from the direction of the Rotunda on 29 April. He saw him come from the same direction as the earlier rebel fire – Moore Street. He then recounted seeing Pearse surrender to General Lowe on Great Britain Street. King was briefly cross-examined by Pearse, who asked him about his treatment while he was a prisoner in the GPO. He answered that he had been treated well.

King was followed by Detective Daniel Coffey. The detective testified to having been present at Irish Command HQ at 5 p.m. on Saturday 29 April. He saw Pearse being held there under guard. Sergeant Goodman was the final witness. He recounted having seen Pearse write the letter to his mother the previous day. This was the letter that also contained the postscript referring to the German guns. The letter was presented to the court as evidence.

When Pearse's turn came to address the court he asserted that he had surrendered to prevent the further slaughter of Dublin's civilian population. He then stated that he would happily accept the consequences of the Volunteers' defeat, but requested an amnesty for his followers. He attested to having promised God as a young child that he would dedicate his life's work to freeing Ireland. As General Blackader listened intently, Pearse admitted to negotiating with Germany, adding that that country had subsequently kept its word and sent a ship with arms and ammunition. He then stated that he had never received any gold from Germany.

Pearse's trial concluded and he stepped out of the building. Flanked by British officers and soldiers, he faced the small green area. Every one of the men there sprang to his feet, stood to attention, and saluted his commander-in-chief. Startled by the abrupt movement, several dozen soldiers guarding the men readied their weapons. Lieutenant Brucknill, looking on, was impressed by the respect shown to this enemy officer. Blackader had been similarly impressed by the rebel leader. Pearse lingered there for a moment. He adopted a stoic demeanour, standing at attention as he looked towards his men, each of whom would soon face his own trial. Pearse was then marched away.

Back in the courtroom, Thomas MacDonagh was next to face Blackader. Major Armstrong was the only witness against him. Armstrong testified that he had seen MacDonagh make several trips through the British lines under a white flag. He added that MacDonagh had told him following the surrender that he held the rank of commandant. He also added that he had destroyed any paperwork he had. When MacDonagh cross-examined Armstrong he asked him if he knew that he had crossed the British lines on the invitation of General Lowe. The major answered 'No'. MacDonagh then attested that he had done everything within his power to assist in the surrender. He had informed the British officers where the Volunteers' weapons and ammunition were stored in Jacob's biscuit factory following the capitulation.

MacDonagh's trial ended and he left the court. He stood outside the building for a moment as the men gathered there again leaped to their feet and saluted. Shortly afterwards, Tom Clarke followed MacDonagh out, to a similar salute. Clarke's trial had been a short one. Lieutenant King had testified to seeing him in a position of authority in the GPO. Clarke had said nothing in his defence. Both MacDonagh and Clarke were then marched away under guard. The three others soon followed – Joseph McGuinness, selected erroneously on Sunday, Piaras Béaslaí and Edward Duggan. They too were led away. Meanwhile, the officers of the court took a recess.

By early afternoon, the detectives in the gymnasium had finished their work on the Custom House contingent of prisoners. They were promptly ordered up and out. Captain Brennan-Whitmore gave the name William Whitmore at the desk on his way out and said he was a farmer by trade. He was really a freelance writer. He placed the blame for his name and occupation differing from those on the original Custom House list on the colonel who had been in charge there, insisting that he had given him no other name or occupation. The officer eyed him for a few seconds and amended the original list. Brennan-Whitmore passed through, leaving only a handful of selected men, and some of the younger Volunteers, inside. Roddy Connolly also passed through, and was soon placed in a room with some of the other younger Volunteers, and those who had been selected much earlier, including Seán MacDermott. MacDermott and Connolly recognised each other but feigned otherwise. MacDermott was determined not to provide the enemy with such a valuable prisoner, and Connolly clearly understood.

The six men who had been led away following their courts martial were now taken to an empty hall in another area of the barracks. They were heavily guarded, but the officer in charge permitted them to mix freely. The men were in a surprisingly good humour, except for Pádraig Pearse. He appeared to be in deep thought, saying nothing except for a few derogatory comments regarding the conduct of some of the soldiers in the barracks. Tom Clarke seemed content, while Thomas MacDonagh was still surprisingly jovial and chatty. At one point MacDonagh suggested the judgments from their trials could take over a week. Vice-Commandant Béaslaí, aged 35, observed Pearse's reaction to that view – the look in his eyes suggested he thought very differently – and if so, he was correct. The judgments – and sentences – would be delivered far sooner.

On the other side of the city on the same afternoon, the 2/4th and 2/5th Leicester battalions were not having much luck silencing the rebel snipers still active in the Irishtown area. The sharpshooters were somehow managing to filter through the cordon that was now closing in from the north and south-west, and then open fire on the soldiers from positions that had been previously declared clear. The previous evening, one company captain ran his outposts right up to the sea wall along the Merrion Strand, assuming he had trapped any rebels by using the sea as a barrier, only to discover that the enemy had taken advantage of the extremely low tide during the night to slip past his positions far out in the sands. The soldiers increased the number of strongpoints to bolster the cordon.

Not far from this cat-and-mouse game, at the Royal Dublin Showgrounds, at 2 p.m. the 3rd Battalion Volunteers were hustled from their cattle pens. Then, as they lined up four deep, Vice-Commandant O'Connor saw ahead of them a lorry with a heavy machine gun mounted on its back, its engine ticking over and its three-man gun crew looking menacingly at them. Two lines of soldiers stood on either side. Then another truck with a machine gun flanked by a similar number of soldiers pulled up just behind them.

The British officer in charge of the prisoner escort warned them that if anyone tried to escape they would be shot. When the wounded had been loaded on, he mounted the lorry in front of the prisoners and called them to attention. Séamus Grace saw him point in the direction of the sniper fire and emphasise to them that if there was any attempt at escape or rescue, there would be 150 dead rebels on the streets of Dublin.[9] Once he was sure the prisoners understood he gave the order to move out.

Soon after the battalion left the showgrounds they were joined by Commandant de Valera, who towered over the guards flanking him. De Valera, a mathematics teacher by profession, had until now been segregated from the rest of them. They then set off towards Richmond Barracks. As intermittent gunfire continued to ring out to their south-east the guards escorting the prisoners became jumpy, while the machine gunners on the trucks curled their hands tightly around the grips on their guns, ready to mow down their prisoners on command.

During Tuesday afternoon, the officer in charge of the six court-martialled prisoners in Richmond Barracks received the order to move them. General Blackader had decided that no more trials would be scheduled for the rest of the day. The six men were ordered to their feet and marched under heavy guard to Kilmainham Gaol. Back on the green outside the temporary courthouse, meanwhile, the other men awaited developments, until they too were ordered to return to their barrack rooms. Éamonn Ceannt and the others who had been taken from the gymnasium earlier were returned there, once again to the top left-hand corner. Gerald Doyle was handcuffed and marched back to Kilmainham with the other small group of prisoners who had arrived in Richmond Barracks before him that day.

Shortly after 4 p.m., the marching men of the 3rd Battalion arrived at the barracks. They had run a gauntlet of abuse from the civilians in

Thomas Street as they passed on their way. Lieutenant O'Brien was now awaiting their arrival. Addressing the officer in charge of the escort, he asked for the list of prisoner names, only to discover that no lists had been taken. O'Brien was aghast at this apparent carelessness. He asked if there was even a list of officers. The reply was the same – there was no list. The escorting officer assured him, however, that he knew who their commandant was, pointing out de Valera, who was then separated and guarded. Without a list of names, however, the task of selecting and court-martialling any of these men had just become significantly more difficult.

Lieutenant O'Brien immediately ordered a list of names, addresses and occupations to be taken from the Volunteers. Then the men were divided into groups and taken to barrack rooms. Andrew McDonnell, 17 years old, wondered what purpose the bucket had in the completely bare room that he and 60 others, including Séamus Grace, were now packed into like sardines. To his disgust he soon found out. On the door of the room was painted '9 men', signifying the maximum number of prisoners it was supposed to hold. The wounded Volunteers who had arrived on the trucks were dumped into another room and left to themselves.

The noise of the trucks and marching feet had brought other Volunteer prisoners rushing to the windows of the barrack rooms overlooking the square. Word spread that the 3rd Battalion had arrived. Peadar McMahon, of the 2nd Battalion, watching from a window, let out a shout, drawing his fellow inmates to the windows, that Commandant de Valera was being taken away. De Valera was detained separately from his men.

By now, Gerald Doyle was back in his cell in Kilmainham Gaol with several other prisoners, including Tom Clarke, who sat alone on an upturned bucket.[10] In the half-darkness of the dank and gloomy cell Clarke looked haggard and spent. When the guard outside slid the bolt across the rusty metal door to lock it, and then stepped away, the men gathered around in the confined space and began asking about the court martial. Speaking from beneath his long, drooping moustache, Clarke repeated what he had said to Seán McGarry earlier about the charge of aiding the enemy, and his assertion that it had allowed him to plead not guilty. He added ominously, however, that the British had waited a long time for their chance and were not going to let it slip now. He was referring to himself and the other leaders. Clarke looked at the young men around him. All eyes were on him. They were aware of his desperate physical frailty, but hung on his every word: 'This is not the end of our fight for Irish freedom; it is only the beginning.'[11]

Meanwhile, at about 6 p.m., back in Richmond Barracks, the barking of orders outside drew the watchers back to the windows. They saw a large body of soldiers preparing weapons and equipment and fixing bayonets, just as they had done on Sunday. Something was about to happen. Then the doors were flung open. British officers came in and took one last look for underage Volunteers. The rooms were then emptied. Once again names were called out at the doors for more victims to join the selected prisoners. Heartfelt farewells were said as those who were summoned stepped out.

The main body of prisoners were then ordered out onto the barracks square, where desks had been set up. The men had to line up for their names to be checked against those on the lists now allocated for deportation. Seán Murphy noticed Seán MacDermott standing awkwardly among the men around him. Somehow, the rebel leader had made it out of his holding room, and then outside, unnoticed by the policemen. Murphy asked the Volunteer standing beside MacDermott if they could change places so that he could assist MacDermott if required. His comrade stepped out of the way. The prisoners then awaited their turn at the desk. Once again Detectives Barton and Hoey, among others, prowled along the lines, checking the men's faces to make sure that no one was there who should not have been. MacDermott stood by. Barton then stopped in front of him and sneered: 'Sorry, Seán, but you can't get away that easy.'[12] He pulled him out of the line, MacDermott stumbling and struggling to remain upright. Barton then gloated that there would be 'six for him in the morning' – referring to bullets. Murphy looked on angrily as his comrade was roughly manhandled over to a soldier and harried back inside the barracks.

Séamus Daly noticed that once a prisoner's name was taken he would form up with other prisoners in ranks of four on the far side of the table and then be handed a ration of bully beef and biscuits. Daly sneaked past the desk across to the same ranks when he thought no one was looking, hoping that his name would not be taken. A sudden shout – 'Daly, from Clontarf – don't you try any of your so-and-so tricks on us, get back in line!'[13] – stopped him in his tracks. He turned to see a captain by the name of Bruen watching him from near the table. When

Daly's turn came to provide his name at the desk Bruen approached him, saying: 'You are known, Daly. Where are your brothers? We know all about them.' Daly abruptly replied that he did not know where they were. The officer at the desk interrupted the impromptu interrogation and told Daly to move on. Every second man who had just joined the ranks was then handed a tin of bully beef with the instructions to share it with the man behind. The dog biscuits were then issued by a sergeant – once again, four per man. The sergeant looked intently at each man, as if he was taking stock of the enemy before him, but every now and then he stuck his hand back into the bucket and gave an extra biscuit or two to a prisoner who looked as if he needed it.

The G-men began circling again. This would be their last opportunity to select their quarry and they were determined not to waste it. The Volunteers scanned the faces of those around them, looking for comrades they knew, or for family members. The 5th Battalion men did their best to shield Richard Mulcahy from the attentions of the hated detectives. Then, as soon as the assembled men were ready, the order was given to the infantrymen of the 2/7th Sherwood Foresters, who were about to form their escort, to take their positions. The prisoners, of whom there were now 308 in total, found themselves preparing to march out of the barracks behind an advance guard, flanked on both sides and with another guard detachment taking up the rear. Many asked where they were being taken, and were generally ignored. Seán Murphy got an answer from the soldier next to him: England. Word quickly spread through the ranks as they marched out.

The hostile crowd of civilians was once again waiting. A barrage of vicious abuse flew at the marching prisoners. Captain Brennan-Whitmore and the group around him bore the brunt and had to duck their heads repeatedly as they were escorted along Emmet Road. Stones and bottles were hurled. The crowd attacked them incessantly for the half mile to Kilmainham cross, where a roadblock had been erected.[14] They turned left and proceeded, unmolested now, for another hundred yards until they passed underneath Richmond Tower at the entrance to the Royal Hospital. As they marched under its arch their guard detail was joined by a cordon of enemy riflemen on both sides lining the quarter-mile avenue leading to the hospital itself. Joseph Lawless suggested that this was an act of humiliation – as if someone in the hospital wanted to gloat as they passed. The Wellington Monument, a half mile to their left, was now almost an additional source of ridicule to these men, a symbol of the empire they had risen against and a testament to their apparent folly in even assuming they could be victorious against such might. Volunteers scanned the 200-year-old hospital's windows for onlookers as they skirted the building, but saw none. The men began singing in an act of defiance. This infuriated the officers among their escort, who gave orders to shoot any man who sang. The singing stopped.

They left the hospital, marching onto Military Road and then alongside Kingsbridge railway station. They then crossed to the north quays via the ornate bridge adjacent to the station. Their eyes widened when they saw a dozen horse-drawn artillery pieces to their left on Parkgate Street. This was part of the recently arrived British artillery brigade that was moving into camp in the Phoenix Park.[15] The brigade had landed in Kingstown the previous Friday, as Séamus Grace, himself still in Richmond Barracks at this point, had discovered from his interrogator on Saturday night. The prisoners then marched further along the quays, passing the Royal Barracks and the 'Croppy Acre' to its front, famed for its association with an earlier rebellion – 1798. Large crowds quickly assembled and the prisoners feared additional abuse was coming their way, but the hostility was more subdued here. Patrick Kelly noticed people crying as he passed, and Richard Mulcahy felt that their attitude was 'one of interest'[16] – as if they were searching for loved ones in the ranks. Passing Arran Quay, they saw on the opposite side of the river the smouldering ruins at the bottom of Lower Bridge Street. Volunteers Peadar Clancy and Thomas Smart, fighting around the Four Courts, had set fire to the buildings there the previous Wednesday and the fires had spread, ultimately resulting in the collapse of several buildings. They then passed the Four Courts to their left. Most of the huge building's windows were smashed, and its concrete façade was riddled with bullet holes.

When they arrived at O'Connell Bridge the men's jaws dropped. This was the first time most of them had seen the devastation wrought on the city centre. The majority had fought on the south side of the city, while a few had fought in the countryside to the north. Most had heard the noise of the artillery but were only now witness to its effect. Robert Holland now understood the source of the bright red glow over the city that he had observed from his elevated vantage point in Marrowbone Lane distillery towards the end of the previous week. It then started to rain heavily.

When eventually, at 8 p.m., they arrived at the North-Western Railway building on North Wall, the rain-soaked men were halted in its subway, like their comrades two days previously. Now, however, arc lights were suddenly shone into their faces, blinding many of them for a few seconds. Soldiers then ordered them forward towards the gangway of the ship docked before them. Standing at the top of the gangway was Captain Bruen. Thomas Pugh, an engineer with the Jacob's garrison, ascended the gangway, quickly reaching the top, where Bruen stopped him, looked at him suspiciously and shouted above the background noise of several hundred moving men: 'I know you! Where did I meet you?'[17] Pugh replied, 'In Nagle's pub.' Bruen appeared disgusted that he had drunk in the company of a rebel. He pushed Pugh onto the ship. As the other men piled onto the vessel, Kevin McCabe ended up next to the Finnish sailor, Makapaltis. The Finn beckoned a few others over to a big locker and signalled to them that they needed to get up on top. When they did they discovered a comfortable enough spot for their journey. McCabe soon fell asleep. Séamus Daly was placed in one of the ship's cattle pens, ankle deep in cow dung.[18] There was no option but to try to get comfortable in the disgusting conditions, as more men were coming on board.

When everyone was on the ship, a detachment of the Sherwood Foresters took positions around the numerous hold openings and on the decks. John MacDonagh was looking up through an opening when a drunken British officer appeared and came down into the hold. He began calling the prisoners dirty dogs and traitors, and boasted that he himself was a true Irishman. This prompted a salvo of sneers in reply, which seemed to jolt him back to reality. He asked: 'Why didn't you wait till the war was over, and we'd all be with you?'[19] No answer came. As he stood there several prisoners began singing a rebel song, which was quickly taken up by the others. Their defiance seemed to affect the officer. He began to weep. He then took out a packet of cigarettes and passed them around to those nearest him. Richard Mulcahy and some men who had fought alongside him at Ashbourne were sitting together in the filth. Above the singing, Charles Weston asked Mulcahy what his thoughts were. Mulcahy smiled and told him: 'I am happy as the day is long – everything is working out grand.'[20] Weston, reassured by Mulcahy's astonishingly optimistic words, tried to get his head down.

Soon the ship shuddered as its engines roared to life and it pulled away from the dock.

That same Tuesday evening, General Blackader visited the elegant residence of Elizabeth Burke-Plunkett, Countess of Fingall, on Elgin Road in Ballsbridge. Blackader appeared subdued as he and the countess spoke together over dinner. When she asked him what was wrong, Blackader told her that he had that day done one of the 'hardest things ever'. Referring to Pádraig Pearse, he spoke of having condemned to death one of the finest men he had ever come across. He went on to suggest that something must really be wrong in Ireland to make a man like that become a rebel. He said that he had been told that Pearse's students loved him, adding that he could now see why.

7

The First Executions in Kilmainham Gaol

'It is a lousy job, but you are only doing your duty'

By Tuesday evening, the six prisoners who had been court-martialled earlier that day had been found guilty and sentenced to death. At this point, however, none of them was aware of his sentence. Standard British military procedure following such cases was to refer the verdicts and sentences to a Deputy Judge Advocate General, who in turn would refer them to his superior – the Judge Advocate General (JAG) in London. This system was designed as a fail-safe against excessively punitive sentences, particularly when a person's judgment could be swayed by the myriad of challenges to the human mind that accompany warfare. In short, it was designed to function as an independent review of sentences. The JAG provided a vital restraint on army generals during martial law.

Crucially, however, no Deputy JAG was available in Dublin. Instead, the files of the six convicted men were sent to Irish Command HQ on Parkgate Street, where they eventually landed on General Maxwell's desk. It was now up to him to decide whether the six men were to be executed or to have their sentences commuted. Maxwell's problem, however, was that he was unaware of who these men were and what each man's position was in the grand scheme of things. The only personal contact he had had with any of them to date was with Pádraig Pearse.

He therefore relied principally on the DMP files he had on each man to make the decision whether he was to live or die. The files themselves had not been used as evidence in the courts martial but he opted to read them to see if there were any mitigating factors or, conversely, if any contained information that would underpin the justifications of the death sentences. He had earlier telegraphed Lord Kitchener – Britain's Secretary of State for War – at the War Office in London to inform him that some questions had been raised by the president of the courts martial regarding possible ambiguity in their legal foundation. He reassured Kitchener that he intended to overcome any such hurdles and intended to have three courts sitting by the week's end. He added: 'I hope the politicians will not interfere until I report normal conditions prevail ... there is still work to be done.'[1] Ultimately, he upheld the death sentences of three men: Pádraig Pearse, Thomas Clarke and Thomas MacDonagh. The other three convicted prisoners, Piaras Béaslaí, Joe McGuinness and Edward Duggan, had their sentences commuted to terms of imprisonment. Now that this was out of the way, each prisoner could be informed of the verdicts of the courts martial and the sentences to be carried out.

General Maxwell summoned Brigadier Maconchy and told him that to speed up the court martial process he was setting up an additional court, to commence the following morning, and that Maconchy was to be its president. Maconchy, however, protested that he was part Irish and that such a duty was therefore repugnant. Maxwell considered Maconchy's objection, but insisted that he accept the position. He reassured him that as soon as recently requested officers had arrived from England to administer the courts he would be replaced. Maconchy's fellow officers in the court would be Lieutenant-Colonel Arthur Milton Bent and Major Francis Willoughby. The prosecutor would be Lieutenant Ernest Longworth.

A short time later, in the grounds of the Royal Hospital Kilmainham, Lieutenant Rogers of C Company, 2/6th Battalion Sherwood Foresters, approached Company Sergeant Major Lomas, and informed him that he was to select 48 men and four sergeants for special duties at 3 a.m. the following morning at Kilmainham Gaol. Lomas immediately got to work. Lieutenant Rogers then instructed a sergeant from his own company to take a dozen men with shovels and report at once to Arbour Hill detention barracks.

Within half an hour, 13 infantrymen from C Company arrived in Arbour Hill and, as the sky darkened, began digging a large pit in some rough waste ground to the rear of the prison's north-eastern side. An old graveyard was situated nearby. Within the prison, having been held there since the previous Wednesday, were 22 Volunteers who had been captured following an intense battle at the Mendicity Institute. They were under the command of Captain Seán Heuston, a 25-year-old Dubliner. They had been joined by more surrendered Volunteers, as well as some civilians. Volunteer Thomas Peppard, alerted by the sound of the soldiers digging nearby, rushed to the window of the small gymnasium that held him and the others in the barracks. When he saw what the soldiers were doing he was horrified. Word was passed around among the prisoners that a large grave was being dug. He assumed it was for them.

In Dublin Castle, meanwhile, Lieutenant Wylie, deeply disconcerted by the secrecy of the trials he had prosecuted that day, was involved in a heated argument with the attorney general, Lord Campbell. Wylie insisted that the courts martial should take place in public. He feared that secrecy would draw suspicion on both the trials and their subsequent verdicts. He also contended that the prisoners should be allowed a defence counsel. Lord Campbell, however, was unimpressed by Wylie's protestations. He retorted angrily that he would give the prisoners no public advertising. He then asserted that he would not be satisfied unless 40 of them were shot.[2]

As the daylight faded, the cold, damp cells in Kilmainham Gaol were quick to darken. There was no gas to light the prison because during the Rising the Volunteers had seized the gasworks on South Lotts Road and disabled most of its plant and machinery. Tom Clarke, Gerald Doyle and the other men sharing a cell quietened as night fell. Their conversation slowed and became more hushed. Suddenly, they heard movement and talking on the far side of their cell door. A key turned in the lock, the bolt slid back and the door was opened. The men shielded their eyes as a flashlight was shone into each face. A guard called out: 'Tom Clarke! Where is Tom Clarke?'

Clarke stood. The other prisoners also rose to their feet, forming a circle around him. The guards were initially wary until they realised that the prisoners were saying their farewells. Doyle was the last to shake Clarke's hand before he was led away. The cell door was slammed shut

The main entrance to Kilmainham Gaol. The exterior wall of the Stonebreakers' Yard is to the right of picture. NATIONAL LIBRARY OF IRELAND

again. Doyle and the others stood in silence for a time, then began to pray quietly for the man they now suspected they would never see again.

At 9 p.m., Clarke was taken to a cell on his own in the damp and disused west wing of the gaol. The west wing had been closed since 1910, which rendered it particularly bleak. Commandants Pearse and MacDonagh had also been placed into one-man cells in the same comfortless wing. An army officer – Lieutenant Colonel Edward Bradbridge, accompanied by a guard holding a candle, had the dispiriting task of informing each prisoner of his fate. He soon stood in Clarke's door, and in the flickering candlelight told him, as he had already done to the other two men, that he had been found guilty of the charge set out against him and sentenced to death by firing squad. He allowed a pause for the prisoner to take in the judgment, and then informed him that the sentence would be carried out the following dawn.

An hour or so later, in the gaol's main office, its commandant, Major William Lennon of the Royal Dublin Fusiliers, looked over

a list a subaltern had given him. It contained the names and locations
of relations the three condemned prisoners wished to see before their
executions. Major Lennon had himself only recently been declared fit for
service, having been wounded fighting in the Dardanelles the previous
year. He prepared dispatches to be sent out to the listed people. Three
names stood out – Sister (Mary) Francesca (Thomas MacDonagh's
sister), Edward Daly and William Pearse. Having a nun in the gaol at
that time was not a particularly welcome prospect for the commandant,
but more disconcerting for him was the fact that the other two names
were those of prisoners in Richmond Barracks. Nonetheless, he sent a
request to Colonel Fraser there for the men to be brought to the gaol.
Also named on the list were two priests: Father Aloysius and Father
Columbus from the Capuchin Friary on Bow Street. Both priests would
soon have their mental and emotional constitutions put to a gruelling
test. They had been instrumental in brokering ceasefires between the
opposing sides at the end of the recent fighting. Their upcoming tasks,
however, would be far more unsettling. A dispatch was prepared for the
friary.

About 20 minutes later, a military car pulled up outside the wrought-
iron gate of the friary on Bow Street, only yards from where some of
the most intense street fighting of the entire Rising had taken place.
The driver kept the engine running as a soldier alighted and knocked
on the door. It was promptly answered by a monk, who was handed an
envelope. Father Aloysius was then roused from his bed and handed the
dispatch. Aloysius read that Pádraig Pearse had asked to see both him
and Father Columbus, who was then also woken, and soon the pair
joined the soldiers in the waiting car.

As the car set off the driver explained to the priests that they had two
more passengers to collect on the south side of the city whose names
were also on the list: Pádraig Pearse's 59-year-old mother, Margaret, and
Thomas MacDonagh's wife, Muriel. The car made its way through the
night, stopped every few hundred yards at checkpoints by edgy soldiers.
Gunshots still rang out sporadically in the distance. Their first port of call
was to be Oakley Road in Ranelagh – MacDonagh's home – but as the
car approached Charlemont Bridge they were stopped and forbidden to
proceed any further due to the increasing intensity of the shooting in the
area. A minor battle appeared to be taking place just beyond the Grand
Canal. The car's military occupants needed little persuasion to turn

Major William Sherlock Lennon, Commandant of Kilmainham Gaol. NATIONAL LIBRARY OF IRELAND

MAJOR W. SHERLOCK LENNON.

around and make their way back to Kilmainham. When they arrived back, almost 30 minutes later, at 11.30 p.m., having stopped at another series of checkpoints, the two soldiers explained to Major Lennon why they were short two passengers. Major Lennon then decided to allow MacDonagh's sister to be brought to the gaol. Father Columbus returned to the car with the two soldiers as they set off again – this time to Basin Lane Convent, just beyond the South Dublin Union.

Father Aloysius and Major Lennon entered the candlelit west wing of the gaol, where they were met by two other priests – Father Tom O'Ryan of Goldenbridge and Father Edward Morrissey of James's Street. Father Aloysius was directed first to Pearse's cell. When the guard opened the door, Aloysius stepped inside and Pearse stood up to greet him. The priest told Pearse that he had seen James Connolly at Dublin Castle that

Pádraig Pearse, pictured in uniform addressing a small crowd some time before the Rising. It was his flair for oratory, as much as his intelligence, that brought him to prominence in the Republican movement – a journey that was fated to end on May 3 1916. COURTESY OF THE MILITARY ARCHIVES

morning and had given him Holy Communion. Pearse replied: 'Thank God. It is the one thing I was anxious about.'³ The two men spoke for a while. Pearse told the priest that he was not in the least worried about dying; in fact, it would be his privilege to die for his country. Aloysius then handed Pearse a crucifix.

Pearse had earlier written a farewell letter to his mother, and he now asked the priest to present the letter to Major Lennon with the request that he see to its delivery. Aloysius then left. A short time later he gave the letter to Major Lennon, who assured him that he would safeguard and deliver it. Satisfied with this, Father Aloysius then entered Thomas MacDonagh's cell. The 2nd Battalion Commandant said that he too was happy to die. Aloysius gave him Communion and the pair spoke for a time. The priest then went between the cells of Pearse and MacDonagh providing as much comfort as he could to each man. Thomas Clarke remained alone for now.

Clarke's wife, 38-year-old Kathleen, had been arrested earlier that day at their home on Richmond Avenue, between Fairview and

Drumcondra. She and some other female detainees were now being held in a foul-smelling cell in Ship Street barracks. Arthur Griffith, the Sinn Féin founder, had been transported in the same car after his own arrest and had given Kathleen Clarke his overcoat. She now had it wrapped around her as she lay on the cold concrete floor trying to sleep. When a sergeant knocked on her cell door and opened it she stood up. He handed her a note from Major Lennon in Kilmainham. It read: 'I have to inform you that your husband is a prisoner here and wishes to see you. I am sending a motor car to bring you here. I am, Madam, your obedient servant.'[4] As she prepared herself, a fellow prisoner, Marie Perolz, a 40-year-old Citizen Army member who had been arrested that day, asked her what the note had said. Kathleen told her of its contents, but added ominously that it meant the imminent death of her husband. Perolz replied in dismay: 'Oh God no, surely not that.'[5] Kathleen asked her if she really thought that the British would allow her to see her husband if he was not about to depart to the next world. Perolz responded: 'God, you are stone.'[6] Mrs Clarke lowered her head. She felt she had to present herself as just that – as cold as the raw grey brickwork that surrounded them. She was determined to maintain a brave face in front of the soldiers and not to break down, despite her growing anguish. She then joined the sergeant who was waiting outside for her, who in turn handed her over to two soldiers to drive her to Kilmainham.

At around 1 a.m. on Wednesday, Father Columbus arrived back at Kilmainham with Sister Francesca. She had a chaperone – the convent's Mistress of Novices. Father Aloysius greeted them and Sister Francesca was directed to her brother's cell. MacDonagh embraced her as Father Aloysius returned to Pádraig Pearse. MacDonagh told his sister that he needed her to look after his wife and two children until their brother John was released from prison. He then took photographs of them from his pocket and kissed them.

One of the first people Kathleen Clarke met as she waited to be taken to her husband's cell was Father Columbus. He asked her to try to convince her husband to allow him in. Clarke was refusing to see any more priests, having angrily dismissed one earlier. Kathleen told him: 'I have never interfered with my husband in anything he thinks is right, and I am not going to begin now.'[7] A soldier led her up the stone staircase, the damp, musty smell of the disused prison becoming stronger until they came to a narrow passage. The soldier stopped outside a cell

The corridor in Kilmainham Gaol's west wing that housed Pádraig Pearse, Thomas MacDonagh, and Tom Clarke before they were executed. NATIONAL LIBRARY OF IRELAND

door and unlocked it. Kathleen stepped inside and saw Tom lying on the floor. Tom's eyes widened in disbelief, as he rose to his feet. She went over to him and asked, 'Why did you surrender? You said you would never surrender.' Tom replied in as comforting a tone as he could muster: 'I know, and I meant it. If it had been down to me there would have been no surrender.' She asked him what had led him to dismiss the priest. He told her the priest had warned him that he could not receive absolution unless he said he was sorry for what he had done. Clarke had said that he was not sorry – on the contrary, he was proud – before telling the priest to leave. He then told Kathleen that he was relieved to be getting a soldier's death, not a prison sentence. Having spent 15 years of misery and torment in an English prison, he had no wish to return to such a pitiless regime. He began to recount to her the events of Easter Week and the frenetic redeployment from the GPO into Moore Street. Behind Kathleen, the soldier who had led her to the cell stood silently in the doorway, holding a lit candle in a jam jar. Clarke warned his wife to be wary of Eoin MacNeill, the leader of the Irish Volunteers, accusing him of treachery because he had issued Easter Sunday's countermand order. He said it was imperative that MacNeill never again be allowed into the inner circles of the movement.

Thomas MacDonagh, Commandant 2nd Battalion Irish Volunteers, executed 3 May 1916. COURTESY OF KILMAINHAM GAOL ARCHIVES

IRISH REBELLION, MAY 1916.

THOMAS MacDONAGH
(Commandant of Bishop Street Area),
Executed May 3rd, 1916.
One of the signatories of the "Irish Republic Proclamation."

Clarke told Kathleen that she should remarry and not allow his death to cast a shadow over their three sons, but he added that he hoped they would follow in his Republican footsteps. Kathleen was pregnant with their fourth child, but had not told her husband. She thought now of their unborn child, but did not have the heart to inform Tom of her condition when he was just hours from death. Just then, a soldier appeared at the cell door and told them their time was up. Kathleen stood for a moment in the narrow doorway, catching a last glimpse of her husband as the door closed behind her. In the ensuing silence she heard acutely every turn of the key in the lock before she was led slowly away.

Time was also up for Thomas MacDonagh's visitor. Sister Francesca was stricken with grief when the same soldier solemnly told her she should go. She asked for a lock of her brother's hair. Soon afterwards, Major Lennon arrived with a small pair of scissors. In her grief, however, Sister Francesca's hand shook so much that she could not use them. The soldier standing guard intervened, cutting a lock of MacDonagh's dark, wavy hair for her. With shaking hands, she then placed a pair of rosary beads around her brother's neck. MacDonagh looked at them, shaking his head, and said: 'Ah no … they will shoot it to bits,'[8] but she insisted that he wore them. She was then led away.

Shortly before 3 a.m. on Wednesday 3 May, Sergeant Major Lomas paraded the hand-picked NCOs and privates he had been ordered to assemble the previous evening. Standing to attention in the still, cold air of the grounds of the Royal Hospital, they were informed of the duties that lay ahead of them. To the east the sky had just begun to brighten. The command was then given to move out. Lieutenant Brucknill was lying awake in his quarters listening to Sergeant Lomas barking his orders. He then heard the fading tramp of hobnailed boots as the firing squads left the hospital grounds for their short march to Kilmainham Gaol. Father Columbus, Sister Francesca and her chaperone noticed the soldiers on their way out of the gaol to their waiting car. They were not the only ones: from a window of the nearby DMP barracks Constable Michael Soughley could see them marching in step across the wide junction and towards the front of the gaol. When British Army staff cars began to arrive, Soughley wondered what was going on. Word quickly spread around the police barracks that something was afoot in Kilmainham. As soon as the car had departed for the convent, Father Columbus went back into the gaol.

By now, Tom Clarke had relented and allowed Father O'Ryan to visit him in his cell and to give him Holy Communion. When Father Aloysius returned to see Pearse in his cell for the final time, Pearse kissed and then handed him back the crucifix he had been given by the priest during their first encounter that night. The crucifix now had Pearse's initials carved into its back. As Aloysius left Pearse's cell he was joined by Father Columbus. Major Lennon then told the pair that all clergymen, apart from the prison chaplain, Father Morrissey, had to leave. They protested that their capacity as priests dictated otherwise. Lennon contended that his orders were for everyone to leave. Aloysius asked him to telephone his HQ to request that they be allowed to remain. Lennon made the call but returned to tell him that it was not possible. The order was confirmed and no exceptions would be made.[9] Fathers Aloysius and Columbus left the prison following a final request from Major Lennon: that they would not speak to anyone about the imminent executions.

A mile or so away in Aughrim Street, meanwhile, Father Francis Farrington, chaplain to the military at Arbour Hill,[10] was awoken by loud knocking on his front door. He found a soldier on his doorstep and a large military truck on the road with its engine running. The soldier informed him that his presence was required at Arbour Hill detention barracks. Within minutes the priest joined the soldiers in the truck.

After dawn had broken, the doors to the cells housing Pádraig Pearse, Thomas MacDonagh and Tom Clarke were once again opened. The three condemned men were told that the time had come. Each man walked out to a small corridor to meet his fate. Commandant MacDonagh looked at the young soldiers waiting for him there and said: 'It is a lousy job, but you are only doing your duty.' There was a short period of silence, then Pearse's name was called out. The President of the short-lived Irish Republic had his hands bound behind his back and was led out. It was 3.45 a.m.

Around Kilmainham the dawn chorus resonated in the still air as the sky brightened over the city – a sight that none of the three men would see again. As Pearse approached a set of steps leading from the prison to an exercise yard, he was stopped. He then stood dead straight as a blindfold was applied. Seconds later the medical officer, Captain Stanley, pinned a hand-sized piece of white card on his tunic in the centre of his chest. Two soldiers, each linking an arm, then led him briskly down the steps and across the yard past an unseen gauntlet of soldiers standing on either side – Sergeant Major Lomas and the execution squads for the two comrades he had just left behind. The soldiers' feet crunched on the gravel as they jostled the prisoner through an arched doorway and into the Stonebreakers' Yard, where, to their right, an Assistant Provost Marshal (APM), Major Rhodes, and the 12-man firing party waited at the ready, their hearts pounding and their mouths dry with apprehension. They had been given the word to take their positions as soon as the prisoner was on his way out. The firing party was formed into two ranks – the front kneeling and the rear standing, left legs forward. Pearse was quickly positioned, standing on a large canvas sheet spread on the ground, in front of a sandbagged wall to the yard's east, out of sight of any cell windows. Major Rhodes gave the subaltern in charge of the squad the order to proceed. The officer turned instantly to the men. 'Ready!' The soldiers raised their rifles to their right shoulders, their trigger fingers resting on the trigger guards. 'Present!' Each man pulled the stock of his rifle firmly into his shoulder and lined up his rifle-sights on the white card ten paces to his front, doing his best to hold his weapon steady. Safety catches were switched off. Fingers moved to triggers. 'Fire!' Twelve rifles fired in unison as eleven .303 bullets smashed into Pearse's chest at twice the speed of sound, shattering his breastbone, heart, spine and upper torso, and hurling his pulverised body backwards, killing him instantly. He collapsed on the blanket spread on the ground. The men lowered their rifles and averted their eyes.

Echoes of the shots reverberated within the 30-foot walls of the yard, the air stinking of cordite, as the medical officer stepped forward to check that the victim was dead. The shots had been true. One had been a blank – a 'conscience round' – standard procedure to ensure that no member of a British Army firing party could definitively say that he had killed the victim and suffer the guilt of shooting a defenceless man. Such was the vicious recoil of the Lee-Enfield rifle, however, that the lesser recoil of a blank cartridge was easily identifiable to a seasoned infantryman.

Constable Soughley, still in the nearby police barracks, saw another 12-man squad of British soldiers marching quickly towards the gaol from the Richmond Barracks direction, a Volunteer officer in the centre of them. Soughley guessed that this must be an important man, considering the number of soldiers escorting him. He was correct. The officer was Commandant Edward Daly. Colonel Fraser had granted Daly permission to see Tom Clarke before he was shot. By the time they arrived at the gaol, however, Major Lennon informed Daly that Clarke was to be executed imminently and it would be impossible to see him. Daly replied that he would like to see him, dead or alive.[11] His request was granted. He was brought into a guarded room to wait.

Back in the Stonebreakers' Yard, as Pádraig Pearse's limp body was wrapped in the canvas blanket and carried off to a nearby wooden shed, the subaltern in charge of the firing squad waited for the order from Major Rhodes to dismiss the men – which was standard procedure. The order never came. Instead, the 12-man squad, each infantryman now standing, waited at attention as Rhodes ordered the subaltern to reload the men's rifles. The officer knew this was a breach of protocol. Nevertheless, he ordered the firing party's NCO to tell the men to place their weapons against a nearby wall. Then, unseen by the firing party, he unloaded and reloaded each rifle, pulling the bolt rearward and forward, and making sure the safety catch was on. Once again, a 'conscience' round was inserted into the chamber of a single weapon, the blank round identifiable from the crimping of the cartridge where the projectile would normally be. He then switched some of the rifles round and ordered the NCO to tell the men to retrieve them and re-form into the same standing and kneeling positions as before.

When Thomas MacDonagh's name was called in the prison he whistled as he was led to his fate. Sergeant Major Lomas's eyes were drawn momentarily to the doorway from where the tune came. The deathly quiet in the yard seemed to amplify its absurdity. Lomas, however, had more pressing concerns than the irony of a man whistling on the way to his execution. He knew that by now a new firing squad should have been called to replace the first. Instead, the group of khaki-clad infantrymen he had detailed as the second firing squad stood uncomfortably next to him as, moments later, MacDonagh – his hands tied behind him and a white card pinned to his chest – was hustled past them into the Stonebreakers' Yard. At 4 a.m. they heard the second volley. MacDonagh was killed instantly, his heart shot to pieces by the same men who had executed Pearse 15 minutes earlier.

Willie Pearse had followed the same route to the gaol from Richmond Barracks as Edward Daly. He was briskly escorted by a dozen or so soldiers to see his beloved brother. He mistakenly assumed that Pádraig was still alive. The sound of the shots that had just slain Commandant MacDonagh, however, suggested to his escorting officer that it was now too late. He ordered his men to turn around and march the prisoner back to Inchicore.

Yet again, Major Rhodes, contrary to protocol, made no attempt to replace the firing party in the Stonebreakers' Yard. Again he ordered the same subaltern to reload the same dozen rifles. The young subaltern's hands shook as he ejected the spent cartridges and slowly inserted the new ones before swapping the weapons around once again. Then the same 12 soldiers were ordered to collect their rifles and reassume their positions. They followed their orders, suppressing their revulsion. A few yards away, MacDonagh's remains were wrapped in another canvas sheet that had been placed on the ground for him to stand on, and carried into the same wooden shed as Pearse's body. The rosary beads he had worn around his hands, now stained by his blood, were removed and returned to Major Lennon.

Tom Clarke stood in the dark, dreary corridor that led to the exercise yard. He had waited almost 30 minutes after leaving his cell for his turn to face the firing squad. The soldier who approached him to tie the blindfold around his head greatly respected the fortitude displayed by the frail-looking man, knowing that it must have been incomprehensibly dreadful to stand in place for that length of time listening to the executions of comrades and friends, knowing that the same gruesome fate awaited him. Then Clarke, to the soldier's incredulity, said he would go before the firing party without a blindfold.[12] The soldier replied that he was sorry, but he had his orders. He removed Clarke's glasses and placed the blindfold around his eyes. The purpose of the blindfold was not only to lessen the unbearable trauma of the man to be executed, but to prevent the firing party having to make eye contact with the man they were about to kill. In this case the ghastly mosaic of blood, bone splinters and tissue that already adorned the sandbagged structure in the Stonebreakers' Yard from the first two executions was repulsive enough to shatter the strongest disposition. Assuaging the distressing effects of such circumstances was one of the reasons for the protocol of replacing each squad after each execution – completely ignored on this occasion by Major Rhodes. The purpose of rushing and jostling the prisoner, once blindfolded, was to remove his cognitive awareness, and consequently, to deny him the possibility of focusing on his fate. In short, the procedure was considered humane for both the condemned and the executioners. Once the blindfold went on it was all but over.

When the white card had been pinned to Clarke's chest it was his turn to be hurried down the steps and into the Stonebreakers' Yard. Major Rhodes once again gave the order to proceed, but now, as the increasingly sickened firing squad brought their rifles into the 'present' position, they were unable to hold them steady. Clarke, unlike his two comrades, would not receive a quick death. His life as an unflinching advocate of Irish independence was about to meet a tragic and horrific end at the hands of a firing squad who were so jittery they could not aim their rifles properly.

Thomas Clarke pictured here standing outside his tobacconist shop in Great Britain
Street *c.*1916. NATIONAL LIBRARY OF IRELAND

'Fire!' Another deafening volley of gunshots. Clarke was hurled back by the force of the bullets. He collapsed in a heap on the groundsheet that had been replaced after the previous execution, but he had not been killed outright. He twitched and groaned faintly where he lay, his bloodied, smashed torso riddled with rounds that had completely missed the white card. The horrified subaltern ran forward, drawing his pistol, to end his suffering with a single shot to the head. The groaning and twitching stopped. It was 4.15 a.m.

Commandant Daly had heard the two volleys that had shot MacDonagh and Clarke. After Clarke's body had been wrapped and placed in the old wooden shed, and the firing party finally dismissed, Daly was escorted out to the Stonebreakers' Yard and directed to the shed. His escort held back and stood in silence as he then strode slowly towards it. At the shed door he looked down at the three bodies. Daly then stood to attention and saluted the remains[13] before removing his cap and kneeling to pray. There had been a long-standing association between Clarke and the Daly family. Three decades before, Clarke had shared an English prison cell with Daly's uncle, John Daly, following the Fenian bombing campaign on mainland Britain. Since then, as well as marrying Daly's sister, Clarke had employed Daly in his tobacco shop on Great Britain Street as the planning for the Rising intensified. The two men had great admiration for one another. When Daly finished praying, he stood to attention, saluted, turned, and made his way back to the waiting escort. They left the prison to return to Richmond Barracks. As soon as they were out of sight the three blood-soaked corpses were carried by pairs of men to a waiting horse-drawn military ambulance, which then began its melancholy mile-and-a-half journey to Arbour Hill prison.

Roughly 30 minutes later, Father Farrington, who had been waiting at the recently dug pit in Arbour Hill, which was now lined with quicklime, watched in the early morning light as the ambulance, its red cross painted on a circular white background, came into view from the road outside. It passed between an old church and the prison itself. Moments later its driver called the horses to a halt. Father Farrington stepped closer as the back of the ambulance was opened and he saw that large pools of blood had congealed around the three bodies, each still wearing a blindfold. It was a horrific sight. The priest reached out and touched the remains as they were slowly removed from the ambulance. The bodies were still warm. Then, as they were placed into the pit, a soldier told him, 'They all died well – like soldiers.' Father Farrington prayed as quicklime was shovelled on top of the bodies, followed by earth. Soon all that marked the place was disturbed earth and a large, albeit smaller, open pit.

In the cells at Kilmainham, Rose MacNamara and some of the other female prisoners had been woken by the rifle fire, but, unaware of what it meant, had returned to their uncomfortable slumbers. Gerald Doyle, however, knew precisely what had happened. He had remained awake, watching as light came into the sky.[14] He knew that Tom Clarke was no more, but wondered now who the other victims had been.

Meanwhile, Sergeant Major Lomas marched the firing parties back to the Royal Hospital. They hardly spoke a word on their return. A few among the 48 infantrymen appeared to be absorbed in their own thoughts. Many of their comrades glanced uncomfortably at them. At 5 a.m. they were informed that they were excused duties until noon. Most went back to their bunks for a few hours of rest, but for the men who had taken part in the firing squads sleep would not come easily.

8

Courts Martial in Richmond Barracks Gather Steam

'Blow his brains out'

Kathleen Clarke had been driven from Kilmainham Gaol to Dublin Castle after bidding her husband farewell before his botched and bloody execution. Then she was taken to the guardhouse, where she sat for several tortuous hours. She was physically and emotionally drained from lack of sleep, grief and being pregnant. The British military policeman (MP) who had been placed in charge of her showed some empathy, making her as comfortable as he could, even making her tea as he struck up a conversation. Their discussion led eventually to an unexpected question from the MP: 'Why start a revolution?' Kathleen replied, 'If the Germans win the war and conquer England, and subjugate the people ... If this happened; don't you think, as an Englishman, you would rebel?' He answered, 'I am damn well sure I would.'[1] Kathleen added: 'Then you have our point of view.' The MP looked away momentarily before nodding in agreement. He then made to shake her hand. Kathleen hesitated, uneasy about the prospect of shaking the hand of someone wearing the khaki uniform of the army that had no doubt, by now, shot her husband. Nevertheless, the handshake followed.

The MP said he did not see the need to detain her any longer. He told Mrs Clarke that he would fetch her a permit to travel home, as the curfew was still in force within the city. A short time later he escorted her out of the castle and across Cork Hill, as far as the battle-scarred

Kathleen Clarke pictured with her three sons (*l–r*: Tom, John and Emmet) following the death of their father Tom Clarke. Her brother, Ned Daly, was executed the day after her husband. NATIONAL LIBRARY OF IRELAND

Evening Mail offices at the junction of Parliament Street. Silence hung over the city, broken intermittently by the periodic cracks of distant small-arms fire. As they parted company and shook hands a second time, the MP told Mrs Clarke that he had the deepest respect for her. She then solemnly walked away.

Warily she made her way along Dame Street, watching for the military, her curfew pass at the ready. The only soldiers she encountered, however, were several dozen slumbering infantrymen wrapped in blankets, lying on the pavements underneath the portico of the old parliament building at the junction of Westmoreland Street. They were guarded by NCOs who sat against the nearby walls smoking cigarettes, barely awake themselves. As she passed them, an infantryman shuffled in his sleep, trying to get comfortable on the hard ground. Soon afterwards, when she crossed O'Connell Bridge into Sackville Street, she moved into the middle of the road for safety. All around her, parts of buildings were still falling and the pavements to her left and right were covered in debris.

Ahead of her, by the bullet- and shrapnel-riddled Nelson's Pillar, she noticed the tall figure of a DMP constable, who approached her. She handed him her curfew permit and gave her name and intended destination – Richmond Avenue – adding that she had planned on turning right at the top of Sackville Street onto Great Britain Street. The policeman advised her not to, however: 'there's some soldiers up at Parnell's monument and they are not very nice.'[2] He suggested it would be best to go instead via Fairview. She thanked him, then climbed over the remains of the barricade to her right on North Earl Street, briefly reflecting that her late husband would have watched the same barricade being erected just over a week earlier. She then continued alone for the two-mile journey to her home as the city slowly awoke.

Liam Tannam had endured a restless night in the room he had been packed into with 30 others in Kilmainham. Any chance of sleep had finally been shattered by the volleys of rifle fire and the single pistol shot from the Stonebreakers' Yard. Since then he had listened to the sounds of the prison as it came to life. The door of his room was opened at 7 a.m. by a red-haired Royal Irish Regiment NCO, who stood aside as some privates brought in buckets of tea and hard biscuits. Then, as the soldiers left the room, he gloated that he had been at the earlier shootings and had seen the victims' brains splattered all over the wall. He sneered to the prisoners that their turn would come very soon.[3] Moving on to the other cells under his charge, he took similar relish in describing his version of what had happened to their leaders. Diarmuid Lynch had been placed in a cell under the charge of a different sergeant, whose demeanour was considerably less obnoxious. When Lynch asked him what the earlier noises had been the NCO replied that three of his leaders were gone, but added that he did not know which ones.

In one of the prison yards a young soldier was on fatigue duties chopping wood. He stopped what he was doing and glanced around to make sure no one was watching him, then pulled a small piece of brown paper from his tunic and slipped it discreetly through a nearby cell window. Annie Cooney was incarcerated with several other women in the cell. As soon as the paper fell to the floor she rushed to pick it up. She unfurled it while the other women gathered round. The note said that three of their men had been shot that morning. The women sat silently for a time, wondering who had been killed. Outside the cell, the chopping resumed.

In the adjacent police barracks, at 8 a.m. Constable Soughley was wrapping up his shift in the police barracks. As he left for home he spoke with a military NCO who had been on duty in the gaol during the three executions. The NCO told Soughley, ominously, that there were 35 blindfolds and white cards already prepared for those expected to be executed. Both men became concerned that the men earmarked for the firing squads would have no chance of receiving final visits from priests or relations. This was because the English soldiers now detailed to driving duties had a very poor knowledge of the city[4] and, consequently, would not know where to find them. This presented an additional conundrum. On the one hand, they wanted to help; on the other, they wanted nothing to do with the shootings. Soughley assured the NCO that, in any case, he would discuss it with his colleagues that night when he was back on duty at 10 p.m. He then made his way home.

Séamus Grace had also heard the shots that morning, as had many others held at Richmond Barracks. On that Wednesday morning, the barracks gymnasium teemed with more Volunteers and civilians from the incessant round-ups both in Dublin and in the numerous nationalist hot-spots in the surrounding counties. The more prominent figures were still corralled together in the gymnasium's top left corner. William O'Brien and several others moved surreptitiously towards this group and began speaking with them. Then a British officer appeared with an escort. He ordered the men O'Brien had just engaged with to be marched out of the gymnasium. Meanwhile, the same procedure was happening elsewhere in the barracks as the courts martial now began in earnest. Down the road in Kilmainham, meanwhile, Gerald Doyle was on the move once again towards Richmond Barracks with his 4th Battalion comrade James Burke, and his captain, George Irvine. They too were on the list of prisoners to be court-martialled.

When Doyle and the others arrived in the barracks they were taken to the blacksmith's shop and held there along with the leaders recently taken from the gymnasium, among several other groups of prisoners. When Éamonn Ceannt saw Doyle he walked over to him. Doyle told his commandant about the developments in Kilmainham. Ceannt drew a deep breath and looked momentarily distant, but half-smiling, when Doyle recounted what Tom Clarke had said to him before being taken away the previous evening.

Soon after 9 a.m., the men began to be ushered into the two separate courts that were now sitting. Once inside, they were told by the president of the court – General Blackader and the reluctant Colonel Maconchy – that they were about to be tried by field general courts martial, and added that it was the right of each prisoner to object to any member of the court. The British officers conducting the proceedings in each court then introduced themselves. Lieutenant Wylie, to his continuing resentment, remained the prosecutor under Blackader; Longworth prosecuted under Maconchy. One plucky Volunteer asked General Blackader if he could object to the court itself. The general answered impatiently, 'No – not to the Court, only individuals.' A question was then posed in Blackader's court as to whether or not legal representation was allowed. This threw the court into a quandary, before Lieutenant Wylie addressed the issue. He stated that the prisoners did have a right to a 'friend', whether legally trained or not, but added that this person would not be permitted to address the court directly on behalf of the prisoner – he could only provide advice. The prisoners were then sent to wait outside on the green while the finer points of the 'soldier's friend' as a means of legal assistance were clarified behind closed doors. It was decided that external assistance could be sought, but that the 'soldier's friend' would not be allowed to speak for the prisoners. Word was then passed on to the prisoners. A Dublin-based barrister named Ronayne was sent for to advise any prisoners who requested this.

Meanwhile, in London, Prime Minister Asquith, having being notified of the first three executions, summoned the Commander-in-Chief of the British Home Forces, Lord John French, who was stationed nearby, to see him in 10 Downing Street. When the 63-year-old French arrived, Asquith asked him why the trials in Dublin had been so swift, expressing concern that some of the executions had already taken place. Lord French replied that General Maxwell was simply doing the job that he (Asquith) had given him. Maxwell was carrying out his instructions in strict accordance with military and martial law.[5] He then pointed out that only three of the men tried the previous day had been executed, and that the other three had instead been given reduced sentences. Satisfied with this, Asquith decided to leave Maxwell to his own devices. French then asked Asquith what they should do with Countess Markievicz. She was due to be court-martialled imminently and her senior position in the enemy command would justify a sentence of death. However, Asquith considered that executing a woman by firing squad was a step too far in propaganda terms. He would need more time to deliberate the potential public relations pitfalls of such a sentence. Lord French arranged for a dispatch to be sent to General Maxwell confirming that he had the full confidence of the government, but that, nonetheless, he was to ensure that not all 'Sinn Féiners' would suffer death.[6] The position regarding Countess Markievicz remained ambiguous, but he assured Maxwell that he would be notified as soon as a decision was reached on her suitability – or lack of – for execution by firing squad.

Back in Dublin, Major Rhodes had by now made his way from Kilmainham to his APM office in Kingstown, where he wrote his report on the duties he had carried out shortly after dawn that morning. Word had, however, already reached both Irish Command HQ in Parkgate Street and 59th Division's staff offices on the North Circular Road of exactly what had happened during the executions. Brigadier Young, in Parkgate Street, was deeply disturbed by what he had heard. He had stated earlier in a memorandum to Major General Sandbach – the General Officer Commanding (GOC) of the 59th Division – precisely how the executions were to take place, and had emphasised that a separate firing party was to be used for each execution. Brigadier Young quickly concluded that a new officer was needed to oversee matters. Word was soon sent to Major Charles Heathcote to act as Rhodes' replacement. He was to be assisted by Captain Whitehead of the 2/7th Sherwood

Foresters. Major Rhodes was henceforth to continue his duties as APM back at Kingstown.

By late morning, Father Aloysius was back at Kilmainham. A guard brought him to Major Lennon's office, where he told Lennon that he had come to collect the rosary beads Sister Francesca had given to Thomas MacDonagh before his execution. He also complained that neither he nor Father Columbus had been permitted to remain to the end and to minister to the condemned men. Lennon reminded him that he had simply been acting under orders, but conceded that he would pass on to the relevant authorities his request to be present at any further executions.

Aloysius then left the prison with the bloodstained rosary beads and made his way to the convent in Basin Lane to give them to MacDonagh's grieving sister. When that sombre task was accomplished he went to see MacDonagh's wife, Muriel, in Oakley Road. Following an equally subdued meeting there he made his way to St Enda's School in Rathfarnam to see Pádraig Pearse's mother. Naturally, she was upset, but the news of her eldest son's execution came as no surprise.

When General Maxwell read the dispatch received from Lord French in London, he felt increasingly confident. With Dublin now virtually under complete military control, apart from some isolated snipers, he could now free up large detachments of soldiers to deal with the rest of the country. He decided now that all known 'Sinn Féiners' were to be arrested, whether or not they had taken part in the rebellion. Military columns would now be deployed from the capital to reinforce soldiers already combing the Irish countryside for rebels at large. The local police would be seconded to the columns as a source of intelligence. A show of force would encourage loyal subjects and overawe disaffected nationalists.[7] However, Maxwell warned General Lowe not to confuse nationalists with 'Sinn Féiners', and to exercise caution if in doubt about any particular suspect. Lowe set about his task.

James Connolly's daughter, 19-year-old Ina, spent the early afternoon of Wednesday in Dublin Castle, rushing from building to building searching fruitlessly for her father. Having being sent on several wild goose chases, she began to lose hope. When she spotted a nurse coming out of a doorway, she ran to her, beckoning to her to wait. Having introduced herself, she asked if the nurse knew of her father. The nurse knew him, but did not know where he was. She did, however, take Ina to a building that had been converted into a Red Cross hospital and

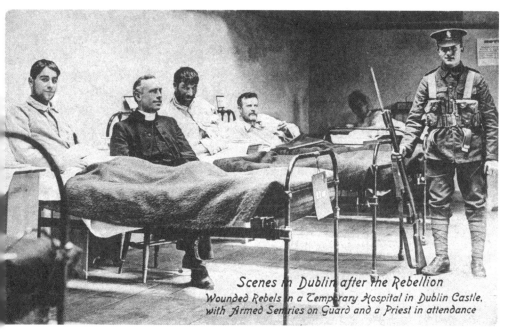

Scenes in Dublin after the Rebellion
Wounded Rebels in a Temporary Hospital in Dublin Castle,
with Armed Sentries on Guard and a Priest in attendance

Wounded Republican prisoners in Dublin Castle, most likely under the care of Captain Stanley. COURTESY OF KILMAINHAM GAOL ARCHIVES

suggested that she seek out a captain of the Medical Corps named Stanley, who had been in charge of Mr Connolly. The nurse then warned her that as far as she knew her father was very weak from loss of blood and was not improving.[8] Ina thanked her. She soon found Captain Stanley. He was exhausted after a sleepless night overseeing the executions. He told her that her father was not permitted to receive visitors, but he would tell him that she had come. He then took her address and reassured her that as soon as visitors were allowed he would send for her and her family. Ina was grateful but downhearted. Then, as she was leaving the castle, she bumped into the well-known suffragette Hanna Sheehy Skeffington, whose husband, Francis, had been brutally murdered by the military a week earlier at Portobello Barracks. Hanna was now at the castle to demand answers.

At 2 p.m., back in Richmond Barracks, British infantry Lieutenant Louis Barron stood in front of a growing group of prisoners who had been steadily assembling under guard on the green outside the courtrooms, and read out a list of names, instructing those named to stand up. Those in question were then marched under guard to their courts martial.

Willie Pearse was first to stand in front of Brigadier Colonel Maconchy, next to three other Volunteers: Seán McGarry, J.J. Walsh and John Dougherty. Word had been circulated among the prisoners to defend themselves as best they could. This made Pearse's later guilty plea something of a shock to his three comrades. Lieutenant King, the former GPO prisoner who had testified the previous day, testified against each of them. He was the only witness to do so. He claimed at one point that Dougherty had threatened to 'blow his brains out'. It was then the turn of each prisoner to offer their testimonies. Pearse, a genial man, a sculptor by trade and a teacher by profession, affirmed that he had no authority or direct command, while McGarry protested that he had no intention of 'assisting the enemy'. Walsh insisted that he never even shot his weapon during the entire week, while Dougherty argued that he had said no such thing to Lieutenant King.

When Commandant Daly's turn came to face his court martial, two enemy lieutenants named Halpin and Lindsay – from the Sherwood Foresters and the Inniskilling Fusiliers respectively – testified against him. Daly told the court, presided over by General Blackader, that he was not guilty, having had no dealings whatsoever with external forces, and added that he had had no knowledge of the insurrection until Monday morning, 24 April.[9] He declared that the Volunteer officers assembled in his battalion area on the morning in question had concluded that the mobilisation order was foolhardy, but that nonetheless, they had to carry out orders. Daly was taken from the court and led away.

Michael O'Hanrahan then stood before Blackader. O'Hanrahan, a former cork-cutter from a family business based in Carlow, was a hugely productive Volunteer quartermaster, and a member from the outset. He was known for his meticulous attention to detail and his boundless capacity for organisation. He was also a writer and novelist. He had spent the previous months under constant police surveillance as a priority target, regularly being followed to and from Volunteer HQ on his almost daily visits. Major Armstrong was the only witness against him, testifying that the accused had been in uniform and armed when he surrendered. O'Hanrahan then cross-examined Armstrong, homing in on the point that the major had not actually seen him with a weapon. Armstrong's response was that he could not say definitively whether O'Hanrahan had been armed or not, but explained that all the unarmed prisoners had been placed on a specific list, and that the

Michael O'Hanrahan, writer, novelist and quartermaster of the Irish Volunteers, who was court-martialled on 3 May. He was sentenced to death. COURTESY OF KILMAINHAM GAOL ARCHIVES

accused – not being on that list – must, by simple elimination, have been armed. Concluding his defence, Michael O'Hanrahan, wearing a characteristically posed and sincere expression, stood erect and told the court that he was a soldier of the Republican Army acting under orders from the Provisional Government, as was his duty.

The first accused men may have been dirty and fatigued, but that was as nothing compared to the physical state of Joseph Plunkett. The bandage wrapped around his neck to protect the wound from his recent operation was filthy. His uniform, pristine at the Rising's outset, was now soiled and dishevelled. He was a dying man.

Plunkett's military expertise in planning the strategic deployment of the Volunteers during the Rising had been key to their tenacious defence of Dublin. Unbeknownst to Colonel Maconchy, presiding over Plunkett's court martial, it had contributed in no small part to the horrific casualties suffered by the forward elements of the forces under the colonel's command. Maconchy listened attentively to Police Sergeant John Bruton as he recounted observing Plunkett entering the Volunteer HQ – at number 2 Dawson Street – on at least two occasions. Plunkett had been a member of the Volunteers from the off, and of the IRB since the previous year. Bruton then stated that the name of the same man now standing before the court had appeared on the proclamation issued by the Volunteers at the outset of the rebellion. Plunkett, summoning what meagre strength he still had, cross-examined Bruton: 'How do you know the Proclamation was issued by the Irish Volunteers?'[10] Bruton looked at Plunkett disdainfully, then turned to face the court again, asserting that he knew that all those named in the proclamation were associated with the Volunteers. Plunkett contested, however, that the proclamation had nothing to do with the Irish Volunteers, and added that he had nothing further to say regarding the proclamation itself.

When Commandant Plunkett's joust with Sergeant Bruton ended, he was taken outside under guard. John MacBride, Éamonn Ceannt and William Cosgrave stood nearby taking legal advice from the recently arrived barrister, Mr Ronayne. After exchanging salutes with Plunkett, they watched as he was marched to the barracks square. Suddenly he stopped, looking up at a nearby window, where his recently arrested father – 64-year-old Count George Noble Plunkett – caught his gaze. Both men stood motionless for a time, their eyes locked on one another. The four-man guard stood by.

With the courts martial now in full flow, more men were summoned and had their cases dealt with expeditiously: Liam Tobin, Peadar Clancy, Paddy McNestry and George Irvine soon joined the stream of those marched out from the courtroom to a holding area following their trials, pending their transfer to Kilmainham Gaol. Gerald Doyle and James Burke, still outside on the green awaiting their own trials, looked on as they assembled. Soon Joseph Plunkett joined those gathered there.

Liam Tobin spoke with Plunkett of his own court martial, recounting that when his prosecutor read out the charges he had said that the penalty for the offences was death. The court president, apparently annoyed by such an assumption from a man with no actual executive power – in front of those who had – looked up and interrupted the prosecutor, saying: 'Maybe death'.[11] As Tobin looked on, prosecutor and president began consulting papers and books to determine who was correct. Tobin then spoke of the president's unforgiving demeanour when a lieutenant named Halpin, testifying against him, had removed his officer's cap on entering the court. The president, disgusted at this, had glared at him and asked did he not know how to conduct himself at a court martial.[12] Halpin had apologised before giving his evidence, while Tobin had prayed quietly to himself.

Tobin then asked Plunkett what he thought their sentences would be. Plunkett answered that he was sure that they would live. He himself, however, would be shot. He would soon be proved right.

Soon afterwards, Commandant Ceannt took his turn to stand before General Blackader, next to whom sat Lieutenant Colonels German and Kent. He pleaded not guilty to the charges against him. As in the case against Michael O'Hanrahan, Major Armstrong was the prosecution's first and only witness. Armstrong explained to the court that British troops had been fired on from the Jacob's factory and that he himself had been present when its contingent of rebels surrendered. He explained, once again, that he had instructed another officer to compile a list of unarmed prisoners. He then elucidated that the accused's name was not on that particular list, but was now at the top of the more recently completed 'armed' list.

Ceannt seized on the ambiguity of the armed and unarmed lists. Armstrong was adamant, however, that his list was correct, adding: 'I had a list of unarmed men made before disarming took place. I arrived at the list of armed men by a process of elimination only, and recollection of men seen with arms.[13] The accused either had a revolver or automatic pistol.' General Blackader interrupted, asking Armstrong, 'Did you take the particulars yourself?'[14] Armstrong replied that he himself had not, but a reliable officer had. The 'reliable officer' referred to – Lieutenant Wylie – was present in court. He, however, remained silent. He could have cleared the matter up there and then by confirming that Ceannt had been armed, but chose not to. His rationale was that he could act as either a prosecutor or a witness – but not both – and he would certainly not add anything that could strengthen the case against a man who struck him as an honourable adversary and who he felt was being denied a proper trial.

When the prosecution concluded, it was then Ceannt's turn to call his witnesses. Ceannt initially set out to prove that he had not been a part of the Jacob's garrison, first calling Major MacBride. The major confirmed that this was the case. Ceannt then called Thomas MacDonagh as a witness. The court's response was simply, 'He is not available.' Blackader adjourned the proceedings to facilitate a search for additional witnesses. Ceannt had provided names and descriptions, but had been unable to provide reliable addresses.

As Wednesday evening drew in, General Maxwell was handed another dispatch from Prime Minister Asquith. It read: 'No sentence of death on any woman without referring to the Commander-in-chief and myself first, and the extreme sentence is not to carried out except on proved ringleaders or persons found to have committed murder.'[15] When he had read it Maxwell handed it to Lieutenant Brucknill.

Meanwhile, new orders were issued to some of the battalions within the Royal Hospital. The remaining infantrymen from the 2/7th Sherwood Foresters were now to form part of a southern cordon within the city, holding a south-eastward line from Kilmainham to Portobello Bridge. The battalion HQ would be at nearby Portobello Barracks. One company was, however, to remain in Richmond Barracks. Two companies, C and D, from the 2/6th Battalion – of which the former had supplied the firing squads that morning – with an additional platoon of 50 men of A Company received orders to deploy to Longford the following morning under Colonel Hodgkin. From Longford they would form part of Number One Flying Column, and would be deployed throughout the west of Ireland to round up suspected rebels. Accordingly, Sergeant Major Lomas issued orders to the men under his command to prepare for departure.

As the Sherwood Foresters got ready to move out, the 2/4th and 2/5th Leicester Battalions continued to close in around Irishtown. The occasional crack of a sniper's rifle still echoed in the area, but far less frequently than in the previous days since the surrender. The Leicester Battalions' constricting cordon appeared at last to be paying off. Its infantrymen could move more easily and the haul of captured arms and ammunition was growing. They looked on as trains once again began to enter and leave the city along the Dublin South-East railway line. Normality, it appeared, was slowly returning.

9

An Unexpected Wedding and Four More Firing Squads

'It will be over soon, lads. Shoot straight'

By 6 p.m. on Wednesday 3 May, when the courts martial concluded for the day, 22 men had stood before the judges. Orders were now sent out to transport these men to Kilmainham to await verdicts and sentencing. Soon, they were collected from their holding cells and marched away under guard.

In Kilmainham, Liam Tobin was placed in a cell with Joseph Plunkett, Peadar Clancy and Paddy McNestry. Plunkett was then separated from them and the remaining three were allowed out to the exercise yard with some other prisoners. Tobin struck up a conversation with one of them. Seeing this, an English soldier approached him and warned him that some of the Irish soldiers stationed in the gaol were a bad lot,[1] and that they would not react kindly to hearing them speak to one another. After their exercise, Tobin, Clancy and McNestry were segregated in different cells.

Soon afterwards, Michael Staines, Diarmuid Lynch and Liam Tannam were also brought out for exercise. At the same time, a sergeant named Smith escorted Joseph Plunkett outside but kept him apart from the others. Staines caught Plunkett's attention and saluted him. This resulted in an angry command from Sergeant Smith to 'Get back inside!' Just then, another sergeant named Doyle approached his fellow

NCO, demanding to know what the problem was. Smith replied that Staines had broken prison regulations by communicating with Plunkett. Doyle replied forcefully, 'I am in charge of him!' (pointing at Staines), 'And he is not going inside. In any case, I am senior to you, Smith.' Then, ignoring Smith's continued protests about prison regulations having been breached, Doyle addressed Staines: 'Go and talk to him'[2], referring to Plunkett. Sergeant Smith stood by, fuming with anger.

Diarmuid Lynch and Staines both joined Plunkett. Lynch asked him if he knew his sentence. Plunkett's resigned response was to imply that in spite of having heard nothing through official channels, 'What it would be was not far to seek.'[3] In other words, there was little mystery – he would be shot. Soon their time was up and Sergeant Doyle recalled his charges, leaving Plunkett in the yard with Sergeant Smith.

Seán O'Hegarty was among the next group brought out to the yard for exercise. He noticed Plunkett walking around in circles and coughing continuously. O'Hegarty collected any handkerchiefs his comrades had, went across to Plunkett and handed them to him. The others followed. This was too much for Sergeant Smith. He shouted at them to back off and then escorted Plunkett back inside the prison.

Back at the green outside the courtrooms in Richmond Barracks, the men who had been awaiting their own courts martial, or who had had their cases adjourned, were now split into different groups. James Burke was brought back to Kilmainham, while Gerald Doyle was put into a room with Con Colbert and others. Éamonn Ceannt and John MacBride were marched up a barrack staircase and locked into a room with William and Philip Cosgrave, Vincent Poole, Jack Shouldice and Con O'Donovan. Ceannt spoke to William Cosgrave. He was exasperated about the credence given to the flimsy evidence against him, particularly regarding Major Armstrong's lists. Cosgrave, looking characteristically dour, suggested that they should have been struck from the proceedings. He then agreed to act as Ceannt's 'soldier's friend' when his case reconvened the following day. Ceannt referred to the proclamation that bore his name, and said that he had not actually signed it[4] but had given his permission for his name to be added in his absence. Cosgrave suggested this did not matter as it had not been introduced in his particular case.

Earlier in the day, Joseph Plunkett's fiancée, 28-year-old Grace Gifford, had heard of the three executions on Wednesday morning.

Grace was a sister of Muriel Gifford, who was married to Thomas MacDonagh. MacDonagh and Plunkett had been very close friends, which is how Grace and Joseph had met, and they ultimately became lovers. During Wednesday afternoon, Grace had felt an inexplicable, almost supernatural sense that her fiancé would imminently face a firing squad, and was determined to marry him first, regardless of the circumstances.

After leaving her home in fashionable Rathmines, Grace's first port of call was to the small red-brick University Church on St Stephen's Green – which had been a British machine-gun post during the Rising. There she met with Father Sherwin, the same priest who had converted her from Protestantism to Catholicism several weeks earlier to facilitate her planned wedding to Plunkett. The Plunkett family's religious connections reached as far as the Pope, and their lineage included the Irish Catholic martyr Oliver Plunkett. Father Sherwin saw to it that the relevant paperwork was produced. Gifford then sped off to contact the British Army authorities to seek permission for the wedding. She then hurried to Stoker's jewellers at 22 Grafton Street, close to the Duke Street junction, fearing that it would be closed, but her luck held – the shop had reopened since the fighting. She stepped inside, by now completely overwhelmed, and burst into tears as she said that she needed a wedding ring. Mr Stoker, the proprietor, asked why she was crying – weddings were supposed to be joyous occasions. Grace told him the name of her fiancé, as well as his suspected fate. Stoker consoled her as best he could. She then chose two expensive rings, paid and left. Stoker rang the newspapers as soon as she had gone.[5]

At 6 p.m., Grace arrived at Kilmainham Gaol and was taken to see Major Lennon. He was surprised both to see her and at her reason for being there. After all, none of the prisoners' sentences had been announced, so Plunkett's fate was still unconfirmed. Nonetheless, Lennon sent a runner to Colonel Owens at Richmond Barracks, hoping he might clear the matter up. Grace, while she waited, noticed on Lennon's desk the letter written the previous night from Pádraig Pearse to his mother. She considered taking it but changed her mind. When Lennon returned he had her taken to one of the prison courtyards. Colonel Owens, meanwhile, was similarly perplexed by the news of her arrival in Kilmainham. He told Major Lennon's runner that as soon as he received further instructions he would inform him.

Grace Plunkett, pictured here at Joseph Plunkett's home, Larkfield House, Kimmage – Dublin. COURTESY OF KILMAINHAM GAOL ARCHIVES

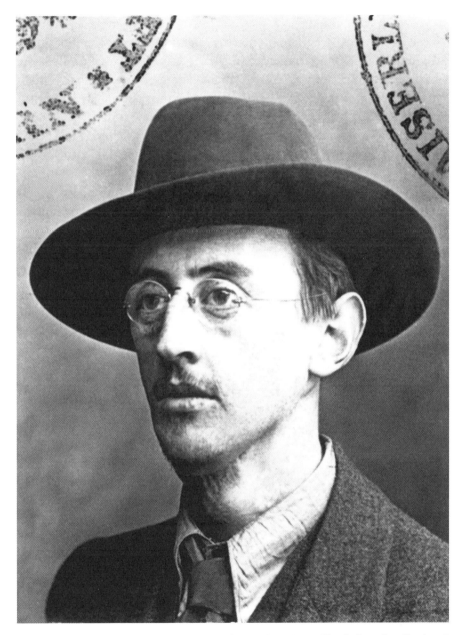

Joseph Plunkett, the 28-year-old signatory to the proclamation, Gifford's short-lived husband. They married in Kilmainham Gaol just hours before he was executed. COURTESY OF THE MILITARY ARCHIVES

After making inquiries at General HQ, Colonel Owens eventually received his answer. He summoned his valet into his office, emphasising the importance of the urgent message he was now to take to Major Lennon. The message was: 'Yes – tonight. The lady in question may take her own priest, and he *must* be recognised by the Prison Chaplain, who must assist.'[6] When Lennon received the message he replied: 'Tell your Colonel, all is understood.'[7] Lennon then contacted Father McCarthy, the prison chaplain, to explain what was to happen. McCarthy had, however, already been informed of Grace's plans by Father Sherwin, and agreed that he would perform the ceremony.

As the day faded, Fathers Albert and Augustine made their way from the Friary on Bow Street to the 59th Divisional HQ on the North Circular Road. They enquired of one officer present if there were to be executions the following morning,[8] so that they might be prepared. The officer answered, 'Yes, there are to be four.' He added, however, that no names would be divulged at this time. The monks returned to the friary and readied themselves.

Throughout the day, accounts had spread like wildfire among the enlisted infantrymen at the Royal Hospital Kilmainham of Major Rhodes' disastrous handling of the morning's firing parties. When senior NCOs were ordered to select an additional 48 men for special duties to be carried out the following morning they sensed their task would not be an easy one. They were correct. When their initial requests for volunteers yielded not a single man they took to offering bribes in the form of extra pay or leave.[9] Still no one came forward. They then reminded the young infantrymen of the recent decimation by enemy fire of two battalions from their brigade on Northumberland Road. Still no one volunteered. The NCOs had no option but to pick men out. Soldiers known for their good marksmanship were taken aside. Others with known misdemeanours were offered a 'clean slate' in return for their participation. Despite this, some of the chosen infantrymen implored their sergeants to excuse them; others cursed profusely when singled out. Eventually, slowly but surely, enough men were chosen for four firing parties.

As night fell, Grace Gifford was still pacing up and down Kilmainham Gaol's cold courtyard, where she had been left earlier by Major Lennon. She was shivering, having been outside for over two hours. Lennon eventually appeared and beckoned her over. He explained that her request to marry Plunkett was to be granted, then led her through a dark labyrinth to the prison's Catholic chapel. Father McCarthy stood by the tiny altar set back in an alcove. By the flickering light of a candle held by a soldier, Grace could make out the shapes of other soldiers standing guard around the chapel, their bayonets catching the candlelight. Grace was told to stand in front of the altar. As she stood, she heard footsteps approaching and turned. The handcuffed figure of Joseph Plunkett stepped inside the chapel, flanked on one side by Sergeant Smith and on the other by a sergeant named Carberry. Plunkett and his bride-to-be looked at one another, struggling to remain silent. The two sergeants agreed to witness the wedding. Father McCarthy began. The witnesses shifted their rifles from hand to hand as they assisted in the ceremony.[10] Then, a short time later, when it was concluded, Smith and Carberry replaced Plunkett's handcuffs and led him away. The only words the married couple had spoken to each other were: 'I do'.

Mrs Plunkett watched her husband disappear up the steps and into the darkness. Major Lennon then led her out of the chapel. Due to the continuing curfew Grace was unable to get to her home four miles away on Palmerston Road, or to her sister Muriel's home on similarly distant Oakley Road. Father McCarthy managed eventually to find her lodgings for the night in James's Street. From there she telephoned her parents' neighbours, and asked them to tell her parents that she would be staying in town for the night.

At 10 p.m., Constable Soughley was back on duty at Kilmainham police barracks. His first act was to relay to his fellow policemen the conversation he had had that morning with the NCO, during which they had expressed concern that none of the condemned prisoners' relations and clergymen would be located by English soldiers unfamiliar with the city. As he expected, none of his colleagues was keen to have anything to do with the work that was going on in Kilmainham.[11] Eventually, however, after much deliberation, they agreed to help. At 11 p.m., they were led to a waiting room in the gaol, while a staff officer set off to inform the relevant prisoners of their sentences. A list of relations and clergy was to be gathered afterwards.

Minutes later, Staff Captain Staniforth, and some aides, stood in front of Commandant Daly's cell door, which stood ajar. Staniforth asked Daly to confirm his name. Then, in the half-light of a kerosene lantern, Staniforth read from the sheet of paper: 'You, Edward Daly have been found guilty, and have been sentenced to suffer death by being shot.' After a momentary pause he added, 'Sentence has been confirmed.' Staniforth then moved to the cells of Willie Pearse, Michael O'Hanrahan and, finally, Joseph Plunkett. An NCO took a list of relations from each of the condemned men as soon as the captain had given them the grim news.

Liam Tobin had fallen asleep in his cell, finally overwhelmed by a week and a half laced with trauma and lacking in rest. He was jolted awake by another officer who stood over him and forcefully shook his shoulder. Tobin had barely opened his eyes when the soldiers accompanying the officer hoisted him to his feet. The officer addressed him: 'What is your name?' When he answered he was told: 'You, Liam Tobin have been sentenced to death.' The cell door was then banged behind the officer and soldiers. Tobin took a few minutes to take in the cold-blooded bombshell. Then the door was opened again, revealing the same officer, who now informed him, 'The sentence of the court has been commuted to ten years' penal servitude.'[12] The officer left. Tobin breathed a huge sigh of relief, but quietly cursed the officer.

When the condemned men's lists of relations had been gathered, and the requisite curfew permits signed by Major Lennon, an NCO took them to the policemen gathered in the waiting room. Constable Soughley noticed Edward Daly's name on a list, and volunteered to fetch his relations. The other policemen were instructed that all relations were to be brought to Kilmainham before any clergymen were collected. Soon afterwards, a cavalcade of military motor cars made their way into the city.

Within ten minutes of leaving Kilmainham Gaol the car carrying Constable Soughley arrived at the Capuchin Friary in Bow Street. Leaving the driver waiting, Soughley went inside and told a monk named Father Albert that some of the friary's priests would be required later during the night, and that a car would return at some point to collect them. He then went back to the car and directed the driver to go to Richmond Avenue.

The Clarkes' home was at the end of a cul-de-sac there. Kathleen Clarke heard the car approach and told her sisters, Madge and Laura, both recently arrived from Limerick, to get dressed. Kathleen was already wearing her clothes under her nightdress, having anticipated such a visit. She then heard a knock on the door and opened it. Soughley handed her the letter from Major Lennon. She told Soughley that two of Ned's sisters were with her, and that he would want to see them too. Kathleen and the constable explained this development to the soldiers. The driver kindly assured her that he would take any member of the family.[13] They were soon on their way.

Meanwhile, another car pulled up outside 97 Palmerston Road in Rathmines. When Isabella Gifford, mother of the recently married Grace Plunkett, answered the door, a British officer addressed her: 'I have an important letter for Mrs Plunkett.' Isabella was perplexed, replying that the Plunketts did not live there, unaware that her daughter had married Joseph Plunkett earlier. The officer conferred with the police driver. Realising now what the problem was, he returned, apologised and asked to speak instead with Miss Grace Gifford. Isabella told him that she had recently received a message from a neighbour that Grace was staying somewhere in town. The car left.

Back in Kilmainham, the four condemned men sat in their bleak cells, reflecting on their lives and their years as Volunteers, and wondering how their relations would react to the news that they were to be executed. They thought about what to say during their final meetings with their loved ones. Commandant Daly was able to communicate with a captain from his battalion – Dinny O'Callaghan – in the cell next door to him. The clock ticked relentlessly on towards dawn.

Two miles away, another military vehicle came to a stop outside 67 Connaught Street in Phibsboro, the O'Hanrahans' red-brick residence. The ringing and banging at the door woke everyone inside, as well as most of the neighbours. Eily O'Hanrahan answered to a soldier who, suspecting nosiness, shouted at the Greens living opposite that if they did not shut their windows and put out their lights they would do it for them.[14] A policeman then handed Eily a sealed envelope. The letter inside stated – erroneously – that 'Michael O'Hanrahan would like to see his mother and sisters before his deportation to England.' Eily, who was in the dark about her brother's situation, assumed that this was a plot hatched by the authorities to arrest Michael's entire family, so she and her sister, Anna, accompanied them to the prison, leaving their mother and their other sister, Máire, behind in the house. The policeman, knowing better, but unaware of what the letter had said, suggested that they would be sorry for not bringing their mother. They ignored him.

When Margaret Pearse, the Pearse brothers' sister, who shared her mother's forename, heard the knock on the door at St Enda's in

Kilmainham Gaol's concourse. It was in these cells that the majority of the Republican prisoners were held. NATIONAL LIBRARY OF IRELAND

Rathfarnam, the news that she was about to lose another brother hit her like a sledgehammer. She went to her mother's bedroom and sobbed: 'More bad news. Willie wants to see us, so he is going too.'[15] They quickly dressed and went in silence to the soldiers waiting outside to take them to Kilmainham.

The first relations to arrive at the prison were Ned Daly's three sisters. They entered a hallway to hear a soldier call out: 'Relatives of Daly, to be shot in the morning!'[16] Major Lennon was initially hesitant about allowing all three of them to see their brother at the same time, but relented. They were then escorted by soldiers into the main three-storey concourse, and from there up the iron staircase to Daly's cell. An NCO shouted 'Daly!' as he unlocked the cell door. Daly, half asleep, roused himself as Madge and Laura rushed forward and embraced him. A private stood in the doorway with a lit candle. Kathleen Clarke recognised him – he had stood with her in her husband's cell the previous night. She used her body to block the doorway and allow her family some privacy.

As the Dalys embraced, the military transport carrying Eily and Anna O'Hanrahan was making good time despite the numerous army checkpoints on the way. Like every other motor vehicle driving through Dublin, it was stopped. Torches were shone into faces. Rifles and bayonets were pointed. The words 'King's Messenger' brought forward officers to check permits.

The same expeditiousness could not be said of the Pearse family's transport – it broke down in Terenure. Soldiers struggled to repair the vehicle while Willie Pearse's sister and mother counted the minutes as if they were hours. Elsewhere in the dark and silent city, the hunt for Grace Plunkett continued.

Ned Daly assured his sisters, 'I have done my best.' Madge said that he would be remembered with the highest honour; he would attain 'A place with Tone and Emmet and all the others'.[17] Daly spoke of the gallantry of the men and women under his command. He said his only regret was their surrender, adding that he had not expected to survive the fight, and therefore did not fear his fate. Laura asked why he had not ordered their British prisoners to be shot, considering what was about to happen now that the shoe was on the other foot. 'No Laura, that wouldn't be playing the game,'[18] Daly replied. 'Anyway, our orders were to treat them as prisoners of war.' He mentioned the charges he had faced at his court martial. They then spoke of Tom Clarke, Pádraig Pearse and Thomas MacDonagh. Daly expressed great admiration for MacDonagh.

Kathleen Clarke remained in the doorway, until, to her horror, one of the soldiers called out, 'Time's up!' She protested vigorously, but to no avail. Laura and Madge kissed their brother farewell and left the cell. Kathleen rushed to him and they embraced for the final time as he whispered, 'Have you got Tom's body?'[19] She answered no, but told him she had requested it, just as Madge would request his. An officer now insisted that she left. The cell door slammed behind her. Once again Kathleen heard the slow, agonising turn of a cell key. As the three women descended the iron staircase, Laura began to falter, but Madge encouraged her: 'Keep up. You mustn't break down here.'[20] Laura reassured her sister, insisting she would be all right.

When the two O'Hanrahan sisters arrived at the gaol they were taken to the same room close to the main concourse and told to wait. Only one family was permitted to visit a condemned prisoner at any one time. A lantern lit the room. Moments later Kathleen Clarke came in, followed by her two sisters. The look of anguish on Kathleen's face greatly perturbed Eily O'Hanrahan. She asked her, 'Is there anything you want to tell us?'[21] Kathleen, straining to overcome her fatigue, drew a long breath and replied: 'They are executing the men.[22] This is your chance to say goodbye.' She then recounted her visit the previous night to her husband Tom and confirmed that her brother Ned would soon share his fate. Eily now realised that her own brother too would be shot, the sudden revelation draining her strength momentarily. The Daly family members then departed. On their way home they passed another car transporting Grace Plunkett to the prison to see her new husband. She had finally been located in James's Street.

Eily and Anna O'Hanrahan were escorted into the prison's main concourse, then slowly climbed the iron staircase, guided by six soldiers and two officers, to their brother's cell. The upper section of the staircase was surrounded by a circular iron grid – a standard feature in prisons to prevent suicides. Soldiers stood around the lower and upper balconies that completely encircled the concourse. Both balconies were enclosed by horizontal and vertical metal bars. They were in effect large cages. Candles and lamps provided light. A soldier confirmed the sisters' fears as they climbed the steps – their brother was indeed to be shot. Moments later they were in his cell embracing him. Michael asked them if they knew why they were there. They paused, and, sounding resigned, answered: 'Yes.' He then looked towards the ajar cell door, asking: 'Where is Mother?' The women explained their reasons for having left their mother and their other sister behind in Phibsboro. O'Hanrahan said, 'It was better after all Mother had not come.'[23] When asked about his brother Harry, he replied that he did not know where he was. At this point several soldiers and officers entered and lined the cell.

O'Hanrahan then spoke of the other prisoners, prompting one of the officers to interrupt: 'You must speak of nothing but personal matters.' Nevertheless, Eily managed to tell him that Ned Daly was to be shot with him. She then asked the same officer if they could stay with their brother until the end. He apologised and said, 'That would be out of the question.'[24]

The other officer in the cell told O'Hanrahan to settle his affairs – time was running out. A small table, a chair and a candle were procured. O'Hanrahan sat and wrote his will. He bequeathed the rights of his novel *A Swordsman of the Brigade* to his mother. Two of his guards acted as witnesses. O'Hanrahan and his two sisters then embraced once more. He appeared briefly despondent, voicing his fears for his mother and sisters, and fearing that his brother Harry would also be shot, but then collected himself. 'Remember, girls, this is God's will, and it is for Ireland.'[25] He kissed each of them as they left. They then slowly descended the candlelit staircase. A soldier with an Irish accent standing on a nearby balcony gloated about the executions. This was the last straw for Eily. She fainted at the bottom of the stairs. A stretcher was fetched and she was laid on it. When she revived a minute or so later she was taken back to the waiting room. Anna recognised a young woman sitting in the hallway, who, when asked by a soldier to identify herself, answered: 'I am Mrs Plunkett.' The soldier then led her away. Eily and Anna were surprised at the name she had given, knowing her as Miss Gifford and unaware of her wedding earlier that day. A soldier then brought Eily some water and tried to console her: 'After all, ladies, your brother is getting the death he would have wished for.'[26] The same young soldier then drove the despondent sisters home, shaking their hands as he saw them to their front door. Their mother was waiting just inside, watching their arrival from a ground-floor bay window. She ran to the door, asking, 'When will I hear from my boy?'[27] They did not have the stomach to tell her the tragic news.

When Grace Plunkett's turn came to visit her husband in his candlelit cell – referred to as the 'hospital cell' – she was lost for words. She noticed dirt on the bandage wrapped around Joseph's neck, which she had not been aware of during their wedding. A soldier looking on kept glancing at his watch. Plunkett broke the silence by telling Grace about his comrades' bravery during the fight. He appeared to feel no fear of his imminent execution. Then the soldier addressed them abruptly: 'Your ten minutes are up.'[28] Grace took a lock of Joseph's hair and they parted for the final time.

Willie Pearse's mother and sister then arrived at the prison, thanks to the mechanical skills of the vehicle's driver who had finally managed to restart it in Terenure. On entering his gloomy cell Mrs Pearse asked her son: 'Well, Willie, what did they say to you?' He replied: 'They asked me if I was guilty and I said yes.'[29] Both women then told him how proud they were of both him and his brother, adding that they were satisfied that the brothers had done right.[30] His sister asked if he had seen a priest yet, mentioning Father Aloysius, but before he could answer, an officer in

Clockwise from top left: Fathers Aloysius, Albert, Columbus, Sebastian and Augustine of the Capuchin Friary, Bow Street, who ministered to the condemned Republican prisoners in Kilmainham Gaol. COURTESY OF THE CAPUCHIN ARCHIVES, DUBLIN

the cell interjected: 'Yes, that clergyman is coming.'[31] Their conversation turned briefly to more personal matters. Then another soldier called out: 'Time's up!' Following a final embrace the two women stood for a moment outside the cell and looked at Willie for the last time. His eyes appeared sad as the cell door was slammed shut and locked. Then, as they left the prison, Major Lennon handed Mrs Pearse the letter from her other son – Pádraig – that he had promised the previous night to deliver to her.

At approximately 3 a.m. on Thursday 4 May, a military car pulled up outside St Mary's Church on Lower Church Street. A couple of soldiers alighted and knocked on the wooden front door. When no answer came they began to pound on it. They were in a hurry. The executions of the four prisoners were now imminent. These were not the same soldiers who had called earlier during the night, and they were unaware that the friary itself was on Bow Street, a hundred yards to the church's rear. Dawn was rapidly approaching. Luckily, a local civilian, alerted by the pounding, took a chance, risking arrest – or, worse, a bullet – and ventured over to the soldiers to explain that they were at the wrong door. They leapt back into the car and sped to Bow Street. Soon they were face to face with Father Augustine. They handed him a written request from Major Lennon, pleading, 'You've got to hurry, Sir, as we have but little time.'[32] The note said that four priests were needed. Fathers Albert and Augustine woke two other priests, Fathers Sebastian and Columbus. Within minutes they packed into the car with the soldiers and it was on its way to Kimainham.

At the same time, Father Farrington was again summoned to Arbour Hill. As on the previous day, a burial party was standing by.

At 3.20 a.m., the car containing the priests pulled up at Kilmainham Gaol. Major Lennon, now highly agitated, greeted the four priests and told them that there was not much time left[33] to attend to the condemned men. He added, however, that this time they would be permitted to remain until the end. He then said that three of the condemned men had been brought down from their concourse cells and were now being held in cells closer to the Stonebreakers' Yard. Father Columbus was taken to Ned Daly, who was in an empty cell that was to be used to hear the men's last confessions. Father Albert was assigned to Michael O'Hanrahan, and Father Augustine to Willie Pearse. Father Sebastian was taken to the more distant hospital cell containing Joseph Plunkett.

When Ned Daly saw Father Columbus, a look of tremendous relief crossed his face, and he knelt for confession. A soldier appeared at the cell door and, understanding what was happening, stepped in and released the binds around Daly's wrists. After hearing his confession and administering Holy Communion, the priest then explained to Daly that he had to go to Joseph Plunkett's cell with the same Communion habiliments, as his colleague had neglected to bring his own. He promised to return immediately. Daly prepared alone for death.

Outside in the Stonebreakers' Yard, under a brightening sky, Major Heathcote and his staff got ready. Captain Whitehead made sure that the junior officers knew precisely how to proceed. The young lieutenants and captains shuffled nervously from foot to foot, anticipating what they knew would be a ghastly business. They checked their revolvers over and over, hoping they would not need to use them. A 22-year-old captain named Kenneth O'Morchoe, an Irishman, had been charged with overseeing the fourth firing party. He prayed for a last-minute reprieve for the man who would face his squad – his childhood friend Joseph Plunkett. In the adjacent yard, infantrymen and NCOs sat or stood silently, fidgeting to ease their nerves, their faces ashen.

Just before 3.45 a.m., the order to begin was given. The first 12-man firing squad stepped into the yard, encouraged by their sergeant with the words: 'It will be over soon, lads. Shoot straight – it's the humane thing to do.' The soldiers left their rifles against a wall. Then, with the men's backs to him, the officer in charge loaded the rifles. Once again, a 'conscience round' was loaded. Captain Whitehead looked on as safety catches were checked. The weapons were then mixed around. At the order 'About face!', the soldiers collected the guns and held them at attention. Some of them knew straight away that their rifles had been switched – infantrymen became very familiar with their own weapons. Thoughts flashed through their minds about the efficacy of the Lee-Enfields they held, and whether they were properly maintained and sighted. They were then ordered into position, as before – six men kneeling and six standing.

Inside the prison, Major Lennon called, 'Edward Daly!' Daly's hands had been tied again. He and the others were standing in a corridor. Two soldiers then took position on either side of Daly as he was blindfolded. The soldiers guided him to the outside door where, once again, a white card was pinned over the condemned man's heart. Captain Stanley led the way into the Stonebreakers' Yard, past lines of waiting soldiers who were smoking cigarettes and pipes.

Commandant Daly was positioned in front of the firing party, facing west, with his back to the sandbagged wall, and standing on a similar sheet to those used the previous morning. The officer gave the firing squad a silent signal. Rifles were raised to the 'present' position. Their safety catches were clicked off instantaneously and almost silently. The officer raised his cane as he looked along the line of the half-dozen rifles of the men standing. As soon as they were aimed steadily he lowered his cane.

Twelve deafening shots rang out. Daly was blown backwards with the force of the fusillade. He died instantly, his heart shot to pieces. His bloody body collapsed onto the canvas sheet. The firing squad looked on momentarily in horror. Flocks of birds took flight, squawking loudly as if protesting at the coarse echoes.

Another three orders were barked: 'Slope arms – about turn – quick march!' as Captain Stanley hurried to the crumpled figure on the groundsheet to check for signs of life. The *coup de grâce* would not be necessary. He then collected the spent cartridges from the soldiers' rifles. Once again, the air reeked of cordite.

Father Columbus had rushed outside, seeking Daly, seconds after returning from Joseph Plunkett's cell. When he heard the shots he knew it was too late. He then stepped back inside the building where Joseph Plunkett now stood in the short corridor next to Michael O'Hanrahan.

Willie Pearse had by now taken his place in the confession cell with Father Augustine. An officer appeared, saying he was sorry but their time was up. Pearse left the cell and stood in the corridor next to his comrades and a few soldiers, speaking with both. Outside, the next firing squad marched into the Stonebreakers' Yard. The same procedure was repeated.

Moments before 3.55 a.m., Major Lennon was given a signal that all was ready. He called out: 'William Pearse!' Pearse's wrists were still bound. He did his best to shake hands with his two comrades, before he too was blindfolded and jostled away, preceded by Captain Stanley and manhandled by two soldiers. Within a minute another dozen Lee-Enfield rifles barked. Willie Pearse joined his brother in death. He was killed instantly. Small grains of sand and gravel cascaded from the closely concentrated holes in the bloodied sandbags the bullets had ripped into

Commandant Edward (Ned) Daly, Commandant 1st Battalion Irish Volunteers, executed at dawn by firing squad on 4 May 1916. NATIONAL LIBRARY OF IRELAND

William Pearse, brother of Patrick, who was executed on the morning of 4 May 1916. NATIONAL LIBRARY OF IRELAND

The Stonebreakers' Yard, Kilmainham Gaol. The photo shows the remnants of the sheds the executed men's bodies were kept in before their removal to Arbour Hill. Courtesy of Kilmainham Gaol Archives

after they had shattered the upper torsos of Pearse, and Daly before him. The air again reeked of gunpowder. Once again, the 'slope arms' order was given. Pearse's remains were wrapped in the groundsheet and carried to the wooden shed where Daly's warm remains also lay – the very same spot where Daly himself had stood and saluted the bodies of the three leaders executed 24 hours earlier. Both bodies were labelled for identification.

In the prison, the men and women confined to the frigid cells, having had their fitful slumbers shattered by the first volley, now spoke with growing trepidation following the second. Some prayed; others sat huddled on the bare floor wondering who was now gone. Michael Staines and Diarmuid Lynch assumed that Joseph Plunkett was among them. Meanwhile, back outside, Captain O'Morchoe grew more agitated by the minute. His turn to take charge of a firing party was rapidly approaching. Then, suddenly, the next squad were ordered to their feet. Soldiers stubbed out cigarettes and tapped out pipes, all the while avoiding eye contact with one another.

Michael O'Hanrahan now stood in the small, dark corridor. His hands had been tied behind his back. Nevertheless, he managed to clasp the hand of Father Augustine, telling him: 'Father, I'd like if you saw my mother and sisters and consoled them.'[34] Augustine assured him that he would. O'Hanrahan then squeezed the priest's hand as the blindfold was applied. Joseph Plunkett stood nearby, looking on and awaiting his own turn to die.

Father Augustine led the way to the yard, stopping momentarily for Captain Stanley to attach the white marker over O'Hanrahan's breastbone and heart. Stanley then led them to the Stonebreakers' Yard, passing the final firing squad, who were waiting for the next man. Most of its members stared at the ground as O'Hanrahan was led quickly past. Another firing squad waited at the ready, another young officer next to them. Around the yard behind the 12-man squad stood several more officers, each looking sombre and subdued. Captain Stanley took position next to Major Heathcote and signalled to the priest to stand next to him.

At precisely 4.05 a.m., O'Hanrahan was turned to face his executioners. Within seconds, another silent signal was succeeded by another deafening crack of rifles. O'Hanrahan convulsed backwards under the storm of bullets, which killed him instantly. The firing squad was dismissed, their duty done. Prisoners in Kilmainham's cells knelt together in prayer.

Joseph Plunkett turned to Father Sebastian. 'Father, I am very happy. I am dying for the glory of God and the honour of Ireland.'[35] Sebastian told him he understood. Father Augustine, returning from the Stonebreakers' Yard, was astounded at the tranquil expression on the condemned man's face. Plunkett then handed his glasses and ring to Father Sebastian to be given to his mother and to his bride. His hands were then bound.

In the Stonebreakers' Yard Michael O'Hanrahan's body was wrapped in a sheet and carried away to the shed. Captain O'Morchoe looked on in despair when, moments before 4.15 a.m., he heard Plunkett's name being called. He approached Major Heathcote and Captain Whitehead, and told them that Plunkett had been his childhood friend. He asked to be removed from the detail.[36] He was relieved, and another officer took his place.

O'Morchoe marched out of the Stonebreakers' Yard just as Plunkett was being led in. He stood sharply to attention and saluted his blindfolded old friend. He then hurried away, eager to distance himself from what was to come. The cold dawn air hung heavy with the smell of tobacco, cordite and blood. Plunkett stood before the firing party, his back to the grisly wall of perforated sandbags, now wet with blood. Another dozen shots rang out simultaneously and he buckled backwards and collapsed, dead. His father, transferred to Kilmainham only hours earlier, in erroneous anticipation that his son would ask to see him, heard the shots that killed him. Joseph Plunkett's body was rolled in a sheet, labelled, and placed with the other three fresh corpses from the morning's grim work. They were collected from the wooden shed by a military ambulance and brought to Arbour Hill.

As the sun rose over the silent city, Father Farrington stood waiting in Arbour Hill as the same horse-drawn ambulance as the previous morning approached and lumbered to a halt. The four limp, heavy bodies, still wrapped in their blood-soaked sheets, were then unloaded and placed in the pit. An officer oversaw the interment and drew a rough sketch for his superiors. Ned Daly was placed beside Thomas Clarke. Next came Michael O'Hanrahan, Willie Pearse and then Joseph Plunkett – the same order in which they had been executed. Soon, the rhythmic sound of loose earth being shovelled onto the quicklime-covered bodies punctured the silence.

Back in Kilmainham, Captain Whitehead wrote his report: 'That the rebel prisoners had been duly executed.' The report was forwarded to Major-General Sandbach at Divisional HQ.

10

Courts Martial Continue and Another Volley at Dawn in Kilmainham

'You have won, I have lost. Do your worst'

Later that same Thursday morning, six miles to the south of Dublin, the Royal Navy cruiser HMS *Adventure* was tied up at Kingstown Harbour, having docked shortly after dawn. The impressive warship contained 21 prisoners from County Galway. They had mobilised in Galway, with varying degrees of confusion, under Commandant Liam Mellows, before being captured at different times during the previous week. They had since been transferred from ship to ship, first in Galway Bay and then at Queenstown (Cobh) in Cork. When they disembarked, they were relieved to find their feet planted again on solid ground. Their relief would be short-lived, however, as it began raining heavily.

The prisoners were marched under escort to the town's police barracks. There they were left standing in the barracks yard waiting for a military escort and lorry to transport them to Richmond Barracks. They were soon soaked to the skin. News of their arrival had spread quickly, and despite the rain, many locals had followed them to the police barracks. At 9 a.m., when the prisoners were finally led out to the lorry, the locals ran to them with gifts of tobacco, cigarettes and sweets. Captain Peter Howley, who had driven Commandant Mellows to a safe house following the disbandment of the Galway Volunteers the previous Saturday, went to take his place on the transport, but he was pulled aside by detectives and detained for interrogation. He then watched his 20 companions depart to the cheers of the growing crowd of locals.

Seán Heuston and the 22 other men who had been captured and detained in Arbour Hill with him were taken to Richmond Barracks on the same Thursday morning. A British officer had told them the charges laid against each of them. When they arrived at the barracks they were placed among the other prisoners awaiting trial. They spread the word of the digging they had witnessed at Arbour Hill.

Roughly fifty Volunteers from Wexford had also arrived at the barracks that morning, having been transported to Dublin by boat from Arklow the previous evening. When they arrived they were packed into barrack rooms with other prisoners, and had their first taste of the repulsive dog biscuits.

Elsewhere in the barracks, as the morning wore on, the G-men made several swoops on the men of Commandant de Valera's 3rd Battalion. Each time, however, they walked away with nothing to show for their efforts. The detectives were finding it far more arduous to make their selections from this cohort of potential victims; they only had the prisoner list taken at the barracks itself to work with, which contained no details of rank. In addition, apart from a few fresher-looking teenage faces, most of the unkempt and foul-smelling men crowded together were now sporting beards. The detectives recognised nobody. The previous day had also seen them ramp up their efforts on the same contingent of enemy prisoners. The Volunteers played on their growing frustration by feigning cheerfulness. When they noticed that their tactic was proving effective, they escalated it. Their forced good humour grew proportionately with the ire and frustration of the guards and the hated detectives.

At 10 a.m., the military truck carrying the Galway Volunteers from Kingstown rolled into the barracks. The 20 men on board were shivering from their earlier soaking. The rain had become so heavy on their way into the city that it had cascaded through the many perforations in the waxed canvas sheet covering the truck's human cargo, making it impossible even to light a cigarette. The sweets provided by Kingstown's civilians had provided some welcome distraction from their misery. When Frank Hardiman, from Galway city, stepped down from the lorry he immediately spotted the friendly face of Seán T. O'Kelly in a barrack room window. The two men knew each other from numerous Volunteer

Some of the Volunteers from Galway, pictured in Richmond Barracks. COURTESY OF SOUTH DUBLIN LIBRARIES

meetings in the town of Athenry in Galway. O'Kelly – the late Pádraig Pearse's aide-de-camp – had been at the GPO during Easter Week. The Galway men's names were then taken before they were sent to a barrack room and locked inside. Captain Howley eventually arrived from Kingstown and was taken away for further interrogation before being sent into the gymnasium. He too was still drenched from the earlier rain.

By now, Seán Heuston had been placed in a room with, among others, Éamonn Ceannt, Gerald Doyle and Con Colbert, awaiting the day's courts martial. Colbert warned a pair of Volunteers speaking near the door to move to the centre of the room, telling them, 'The doors, walls and windows in the place have ears.'[1] He then complained to his comrades that they could not even go to the toilet without a soldier asking questions about men still to be tried. Gerald Doyle recounted being asked in the latrine if it was true that 'Willie' Cosgrave was in charge in the South Dublin Union instead of Ceannt.[2] He had said that he did not know. The men were also wary of men in civilian clothes pretending to be Volunteers and asking similar questions. When the orders came to move out, some of them were sent to the blacksmith's forge, others escorted to the green.

James Burke was again transported to Richmond Barracks from Kilmainham the same morning. He was followed by Countess Markievicz, who had been held at the gaol since Monday. She was transported in a horse-drawn army ambulance, accompanied by a female warder and a complement of guards.

Soon the trials reconvened. Seán Heuston and three of the men under his command – William O'Dea, Patrick Kelly and 16-year-old James Crenigan – stood before Colonel Maconchy. They pleaded not guilty to the charges. A Dublin Fusiliers captain named MacDermott was first to testify against them. When prompted by Lieutenant Longworth to present his testimony, he stated that the prisoners had worn revolvers when they surrendered, and that a search of the Mendicity Institute had revealed bombs, small arms and thousands of rounds of ammunition. An order from Commandant James Connolly addressed to 'Captain Houston' to 'seize the Mendicity at all costs'[3] was also found, as well as two notebooks signed by Captain Heuston. One of the notebooks contained a message dated 23 April reading, 'I hope we do better next time', which more than likely referred to the aftermath of Easter Sunday's countermand order. Maconchy then asked who had been in command of the men who surrendered at the Mendicity. MacDermott answered, 'Heuston commanded the party of men who surrendered.'[4] A lieutenant named Connolly, also from the Dublin Fusiliers, was next to testify, and confirmed MacDermott's prior testimony.

Captain Seán Heuston had been a railway clerk in civilian life. As an officer of the Fianna, he had served as a drill and musketry instructor. He had originally been detailed to hold the outpost at the Mendicity Institute for three hours. Then, having seen the situation on his arrival there, he had suggested to James Connolly – via a runner – that he could hold it for longer. When this was agreed, he held it for more than two days. The enemy had paid dearly in men to dislodge him.

When Captain Heuston's turn came to cross-examine, he asked Lieutenant Connolly precisely where the notebooks had been found. Connolly simply replied that they were in the Mendicity building. Heuston then seized on the aforementioned order from Connolly, insisting that it was addressed to Captain 'Houston' – suggesting another individual – and emphasising that his own name was spelled differently. O'Dea, Kelly and Crenigan insisted to the court when their turns came that they had been unaware of the planned rebellion, and had assumed they were going out on route marches or manoeuvres on Easter Monday. Crenigan protested that he was only 16 years old. The cases then closed, pending the verdicts.

By early on Thursday afternoon, a temporary third court had been set up in the barracks under a colonel named Sapte, who had arrived in Dublin that morning, having been summoned by General Maxwell to ease the burden on Brigadier Colonel Maconchy. Three courts would now remain in place until Maconchy dispensed with his current allocation of cases; then two courts would once again sit, under Blackader and Sapte. Sapte was accompanied on the bench by two majors, named James and Frew. In conjunction with the new court an additional charge was added to be applied henceforth to all defendants: 'Attempting to cause disaffection among the civilian population of His Majesty.'[5] Brothers Jack and George Plunkett soon faced Colonel Sapte, one after the other. When Jack asked Colonel Sapte to define the King's enemies,[6] the court fell silent. Sapte drew a breath and replied arrogantly, 'Well if you can't understand the King's English, there is no use talking. Do you plead guilty or not guilty?'[7] Both brothers pleaded not guilty to both charges. Members of both the military and the DMP gave evidence against them. George employed a simple defence: 'I have nothing to say. I merely carried out my orders.'[8] Jack said that he was only fighting for Ireland, adding, 'I had no intention of helping any enemy of England, unless Ireland is an enemy.'[9]

When Éamonn Ceannt's trial reconvened in front of General Blackader, Ceannt asked if he could now employ William Cosgrave as his soldier's friend. Blackader dismissed the request, on the grounds that he had not availed of it on the first day.[10] Ceannt paused for a moment to gather himself, then called his first witness of the day – Richard Davies, a medic from the Jacob's garrison. Davies had been tried the previous day. He now testified that if Ceannt had been at Jacob's, or had surrendered with the Jacob's garrison, he himself would have been aware of it, and he was not. Ceannt then called his next witness – Patrick Sweeney, who was awaiting trial. He also testified to having not seen the accused in Jacob's.

Ceannt then stood at attention and addressed the court. 'I have produced three witnesses who have sworn that I was not in the Jacob's factory,' referring to MacBride, Davies and Sweeney. 'Another witness who was not available would have been able to corroborate these 3.'[11] This sarcastic comment referred to the recently executed Commandant MacDonagh. He then refuted the reliability of Major Armstrong's 'armed list'. He protested further that an additional witness who could prove conclusively that he was not in Jacob's had not yet been found, despite a detailed description having been provided to the police. He insisted that he had given away his automatic pistol and carried no weapon on the day of surrender. Regarding his Volunteer uniform, he claimed that the uniform did not necessarily indicate that the person wearing it held a senior rank. He then concluded, 'I came at the head of 2 bodies of men but was only connected with one body.'[12] The trial ended.

Following a short recess, General Blackader asked Lieutenant Wylie which prisoner was due to be court-martialled next. Wylie replied: 'Constance Markievicz'. Hearing this, the general took out his revolver and placed it within easy reach on the desk. Markievicz had a reputation among the military for volatility and Blackader was not taking any chances. She entered the room. When the two charges were listed she pleaded not guilty to assisting the enemy, but guilty to the charge of causing disaffection.

The first witness to testify against Markievicz was a pageboy from the University Club on the northern side of St Stephen's Green. He recounted that he had seen the countess arrive at the green by motor car on Easter Monday and then issue orders to the men there to close the gate. He added that he had spotted her shooting at the University Club from a position close to a monument. The second witness against her was Major Henry de Courcy-Wheeler, who had accepted the surrender of the College of Surgeons garrison. He testified that Markievicz had surrendered her arms to him. He added that when she was offered a motor car to take her to Dublin Castle, 'She preferred to march with her men as she was second in command.'[13] When Markievicz was asked if she would like to cross-examine the witness, she replied, 'No, this officer has spoken the truth.'[14] Then, in her closing statement, she affirmed that she had gone out to fight for Ireland's freedom and that it did not matter now what happened to her. When her trial concluded, she was returned to Kilmainham in the same horse-drawn ambulance.

During the next recess Lieutenant Wylie approached John MacBride and asked the major how he planned to conduct his defence. MacBride replied that he had no defence but wished to make a statement.[15] Wylie, still greatly perturbed at the general lack of due process being afforded the defendants, offered to make the statement on his behalf, but MacBride declined. When Wylie asked why, MacBride said that he wished to keep his reasons to himself, but thanked him nonetheless.

Major MacBride strode into the court and stood at attention before General Blackader. The two men had fought on opposing sides in the Boer War. They stared at each other for a few moments, like two generals probing each other's defences before unleashing their armies.

Major Armstrong was the first witness. He testified that he recognised the accused, and that he had presented himself as having an officer's rank at the surrender. He then referred again to the 'unarmed' list and added that MacBride's name was not on it. Glaring at Armstrong, MacBride pounced on the list's vagueness as credible evidence. Armstrong simply responded: 'I identify the accused as one of the party that surrendered. I do not produce a list with the accused's name on it.'[16] Lieutenant Jackson was next. He told the court that he had overseen the searching parties at the gymnasium the previous Monday when the accused gave his name as Major John MacBride. He added: 'The accused handed me his notebook,[17] which is marked X before the court.' The members of the court examined the notebook and the papers it contained. On the reverse side of two pages of Jacob's headed notepaper were two commissions, each signed by Commandant Thomas MacDonagh. The first had listed three men as having attained the rank of lieutenant, and Major MacBride as commandant. The second named their three command posts. MacBride, however, had torn the names of the other officers and their posts from the notepaper before handing it to Lieutenant Jackson on Monday. His was now the only name and command detail on it.

The final witness for the prosecution was Police Inspector Richard Boyne. He testified to raiding the accused's lodgings on 2 May. He then produced evidence collected during that raid that the court had not yet been informed about. Lieutenant Wylie, despite being the prosecutor, objected to this and had the detective's evidence and testimony struck out.

MacBride then called his only defence witness – his landlady, Mrs Clara Allan. She had arrived accompanied by her sister. She

apprehensively entered the small but intimidating room, unsure what to
expect. MacBride immediately offered her his seat. Blackader, observing
this, ordered another chair to be brought in for MacBride. After being
sworn in, Mrs Allan told the court that she had known MacBride for 25
years and trusted him implicitly. She testified that he had left her house
in Glenageary on Easter Monday to meet his brother in the Wicklow
Hotel. His brother, who was travelling to Dublin from Castlebar, was
due to be married the following Wednesday, and Major MacBride was to
be his best man. MacBride confirmed his landlady's statement. Referring
to his arrival in the Stephen's Green area on Easter Monday – which
coincided with the marshalling of the 2nd Battalion – he went on, 'I saw
a band of Irish Volunteers. I knew some of the members personally. I
was informed by their commandant that an Irish Republic was virtually
proclaimed ... I considered it my duty to join them.'[18] At the surrender I
thought it dishonourable to escape – which I could have.'

When his trial ended MacBride asked to speak with Mrs Allan
concerning a private matter. The request was granted. The major asked
her to forward his brother's wedding ring, which – as best man – he had
been keeping, to him, and to pay the bill for the wedding suit he had
ordered. 'Surely that can wait till you get back,' she replied. MacBride
then said goodbye. Covering his mouth with his hand, he whispered,
'Mind the flag.'[19] This referred to his most treasured possession – the flag
of the Irish Transvaal Brigade. He then smiled, turned to Mrs Allan's
sister, and said, 'I might not be back.'[20]

As MacBride was marched across the barracks square, Seán T. O'Kelly
spotted him from the barrack window. O'Kelly asked him how the trial
had gone. MacBride replied: 'You know yourself, my case is a forgone
conclusion.' He added that he would be shot in the morning. O'Kelly
retorted in alarm: 'Don't be saying that, Major,' but the major replied
in a resigned tone: 'I have sinned against them before.' A British officer
then told O'Kelly to close the window, but not before O'Kelly and
several comrades who had now gathered around shouted a final farewell.
MacBride clasped his hands together and raised them above his head,
shouting back, 'Goodbye, men, success to you. I will see you no more!'
He then lined up with the other tried prisoners to be marched to a
holding room. A nearby British officer, recognising him from the Boer
War, asked the two leading soldiers to stand aside for a moment while he
took a photograph of MacBride.

John MacBride marching under escort with Éamonn Ceannt and William Cosgrave across the barracks square in Richmond Barracks. NATIONAL LIBRARY OF IRELAND

Back in front of Colonel Sapte, Con Colbert was next to face the same two charges. He pleaded not guilty to both. Yet again Major Armstrong was the only witness, informing the court that Colbert had been dressed in a Volunteer captain's uniform and had been armed.[21] When Colbert was asked what he had to say in his defence, he replied: 'I have nothing to say.'[22] He was taken out and placed with the other men who had been tried that day.

By early evening, when the courts martial had finished for another day, the day's defendants were taken to Kilmainham, flanked by guards. William Cosgrave, among them, spotted Father Augustine in the barracks as they were setting off. Cosgrave asked the priest to come to them in Kilmainham and see to their spiritual needs when the time came – he too expected to be shot. Éamonn Ceannt and Con Colbert remained in the barracks for the time being until some uncertainties in their cases could be ironed out.

General Blackader, seeking some much-needed refreshment, made his way to the officers' mess. Inside the mess, the 'Irish Republic' flag that had fallen from the roof of the GPO, and had later been taken from the ruins of Sackville Street, now hung between two poles – inverted. Blackader, pressed by his curious fellow officers as to the calibre of the men he had tried, responded: 'All the men behaved well, but one who stands out as the most soldierly was John MacBride. He, on entering, stood to attention facing us and in his eyes I could read: "You are soldiers, I am one. You have won. I have lost. Do your worst."[23] He then spoke of the Boer War, during which he had thought of MacBride as about the lowest thing that crawled, but now confessed: 'I will never think of him now without taking my hat off to a brave man.'[24]

By 6 p.m., General Maxwell had received the details of 36 court martial cases heard that day, as well as the recommendations of the court president as to which death sentences should be commuted to terms of imprisonment. Maxwell had been summoned to London that afternoon by Prime Minister Asquith. He was to appear before the cabinet to give an account of his actions. He dealt with three cases before leaving. Thomas Hunter and William Cosgrave – both tried that day – had their sentences commuted. MacBride, however, was to be shot.

Soon afterwards, Father Augustine reached 59th Divisional HQ on the North Circular Road, having walked from Kilmainham Gaol, where he had spent time with Harry O'Hanrahan, brother of the late Michael. Harry had been court-martialled that day and sent to the prison. When Augustine entered the HQ building he asked a staff officer whether there were any pending executions. The officer told him, 'There will be one in the morning.'

At around midnight, John MacBride was standing alone in his candlelit cell in Kilmainham when he heard the approach of footsteps followed by a key turning in his cell door. The door swung outwards. Captain Staniforth stepped inside and read out the court verdict and sentence. Two guards stood behind him, one carrying a lantern. Staniforth then asked MacBride if he had a list of visitors. Recalling what William Cosgrave had asked of the priest when they had left Richmond Barracks earlier that day, MacBride asked for Father Augustine and no one else.

MacBride had lived a turbulent and adventurous life. In addition to his recent revolutionary activities and less recent Boer War exploits he had travelled far and wide, married the beautiful actress and political activist Maud Gonne, only to endure a crushing and vicious separation. His child from the marriage, Seán, now lived in Paris. Major MacBride was a long-standing friend of both Tom Clarke and the Sinn Féin leader Arthur Griffith. He had been Clarke's best man at his marriage to Kathleen, and he had travelled with Griffith across the harsh plains of the Transvaal many years before.

Shortly after 2 a.m. on Friday 5 May, Father Augustine was roused from sleep by the increasingly familiar sound of urgent knocking on the Capuchin Friary's Bow Street gate. He had expected such a visit and quickly collected himself. When he opened the gate he was told by a young soldier that he had been asked for by one of the prisoners at Kilmainham.[25] Once again a car waited nearby with its engine running.

When he arrived at the gaol, Augustine climbed the prison's concourse staircase and was directed to MacBride's cell. As soon as the door creaked open MacBride strode forward and gripped his hand. The two men spoke quietly. MacBride told of the sorrow he had felt at the surrender the previous Sunday. At one point he reached into his pockets and handed the priest his last silver and copper coins, asking him to give them to the poor. He then smiled and pointed to a small cup of water in the cell, explaining that he had requested water to wash with, and that this was the result. He then took out a set of rosary beads, placing them in Father Augustine's hands and asking him to give them to his mother. Augustine assured him that he would be at his side until the very last moment and would anoint his body when he fell. Then, in the flickering candlelight, they knelt on the hard floor and prayed together.

William Cosgrave was in the next cell. Shortly before 3.45 a.m., he heard movement and whispering in the major's cell.[26] Through the adjoining wall the 36-year-old heard someone say commandingly: 'Sergeant', as an officer ordered his NCO to proceed. The sergeant told MacBride and the priest, 'Time's up.' Cosgrave rushed over to his cell door, straining to see through a tiny gap. He could just about make out the shapes of slowly receding figures in the half-darkness as MacBride, the priest and several soldiers descended the central staircase.

When the small party of men reached the ground floor a soldier went to bind MacBride's hands. The major protested at this, assuring the soldier that he would remain perfectly still if left unbound. The infantryman sombrely answered, 'Sorry, Sir, but these are my orders.'[27] MacBride nodded and his wrists were bound.

In the Stonebreakers' Yard Captain Whitehead issued the order to the assembled subalterns and NCOs to proceed, while inside the gaol Major Lennon gave a signal to two soldiers standing on either side of Major MacBride. The small procession moved forward as if choreographed, until they were stopped at the exit to the yard that connected with the Stonebreakers' Yard.

MacBride looked up at the lightening sky for the final time and muttered to Father Augustine, 'It's a fine morning, Father.'[28] A soldier stepped forward to blindfold him. MacBride asked not to be blindfolded, but was again told, 'It is orders.' Lieutenant Thomas Kettle of the Dublin Fusiliers, positioned nearby, heard MacBride saying to Augustine as the blindfold was tied on: 'I have been looking down the barrels of rifles all my life.'[29]

Captain Stanley stepped forward and pinned the white card on MacBride's breast. The two soldiers on either side then grabbed the major's elbows and the small group moved rapidly into the execution yard. MacBride was turned to face the firing party, his back to the sandbagged wall. The two soldiers stepped briskly away. Father Augustine, however, stayed at MacBride's side.

The assembled British officers appeared unsure of what to do with Father Augustine, expecting him to have moved away. Their eyes darted for a moment between the priest and the officer in charge, until he stepped forward and led him aside. MacBride stood motionless. The officer then signalled silently to the firing party. Rifles were presented. Detecting this from the faint clicking of rifle safety catches ten yards in from of him, MacBride stood erect, sticking out his chest.[30] Twelve muzzles flashed. The ear-splitting cracks reverberated around the yard walls as Major MacBride was thrown back and collapsed. His chest imploded under the force of the bullets. Blood poured from his face. He died instantly. Captain Stanley confirmed that he was dead. Father Augustine hurried over to the shattered body and anointed it. A gaping mess of exit wounds was visible on the major's back at chest height. Once again, the sandbagged wall presented an obscene patchwork of tissue, bone and blood. As on the previous morning, the firing party was dismissed and the body was wrapped, labelled and transported to Arbour Hill – now the resting place for eight victims of the executioners, whose work, however, was still far from done.

William Cosgrave heard the volley of shots from his cell. In the long silence that followed, he expected he would soon descend the concourse stairway to face the same fate. He waited apprehensively in the darkness for enemy soldiers to come and get him. He watched the cell door, his heart hammering, listening for the approaching footsteps that would signal his end, but they never came.

11

Changing Sentiment in Dublin and Further Deportations

'I wish you had the decency to shoot me'

Following John MacBride's execution on the morning of Friday 5 May, the authorities undertook a clear-out of both the male prisoners in Kilmainham Gaol who were yet to be court-martialled and the remaining prisoners in Arbour Hill detention barracks. The prisoners were transferred to Richmond Barracks. Liam Tannam, Diarmuid Lynch and Michael Staines were among them. When they arrived, their names were checked and then they were sent to various barrack rooms. Among the few left behind in Kilmainham was William Cosgrave, still palpitating at the imminent prospect of facing a firing squad. Father McCarthy relieved him of his anguish, however, with a visit to his cell during the late morning, informing him, unofficially, that his death sentence had now been commuted, and assuring him that he would hear the news officially later. Cosgrave breathed a huge sigh of relief. McCarthy later gave the same news to Tom Hunter.

Towards noon, the infantrymen of the 2/5th Sherwood Forester battalion received orders to deploy to the Guinness Brewery on St James's Street. Meanwhile, the remaining two companies of its sister battalion – the 2/6th – was ordered to deploy its 400 men to Richmond Barracks for escort duty that afternoon. Another deportation was scheduled.

Commandant Éamon de Valera under guard in Richmond Barracks. Courtesy of Kilmainham Gaol Archives

During the early afternoon, Commandant de Valera was taken to the Richmond Barracks gymnasium. After quickly scanning the room he made his way to Commandant Ashe, who was sitting next to William O'Brien, and sat down on the floor next to them. Ashe and de Valera were soon engrossed in a hushed conversation about their predicament. De Valera claimed to Ashe that he had had no responsibility for deciding anything, and that he had 'simply obeyed orders' by going out on Easter Monday.[1] He also spoke of having met Eoin MacNeill in passing on the staircase of Irish Volunteers HQ on Dawson Street, on Saturday 22 April, the day before the insurrection was originally set to commence. De Valera recalled that MacNeill had said to him in Irish: 'God speed the good work to-morrow.'[2] O'Brien, having introduced himself, told de Valera quietly that there were likely to be spies among the sixty-odd prisoners in the gymnasium. Several men had by now been brought in on their own, and no one knew who they were. Commandant Ashe singled out one such man to de Valera and the two men caught his attention and summoned him. It was Galwayman Peter Howley.

Howley told them of the dramatic events that had taken place during the rebellion in east Galway. De Valera and Ashe were tremendously impressed by his account, having been unaware that Galway had risen. Satisfied by Howley's credentials, they warned him that there were detectives among the prisoners.[3]

Not far away, Gerald Doyle and another Volunteer, Lieutenant William Corrigan, a 27-year-old Dublin-based solicitor, were marched into the court martial building together. Corrigan's head had been bandaged following a recent wound. Doyle was the first to go in. A middle-aged Sherwood Forester ushered him inside with the words, 'This is it, son, and I wish you luck.'[4] Doyle was met by the intimidating sight of three high-ranking enemy officers sitting sternly in front of him behind their desk, General Blackader at the centre. Military police, wearing their characteristic scarlet caps, flanked Doyle on both sides as the door was banged shut behind him. He felt powerless.

When Lieutenant Wylie stepped outside the court for a moment, William Corrigan was still awaiting his turn to face the three officers. The men came face to face and immediately recognised one another. Wylie was shocked at the sight of Corrigan. He asked, half stuttering in surprise: 'My God, Corrigan, what are you doing here?' Corrigan's answer was simple – he shrugged his shoulders and replied, 'Next to be tried.'[5] Wylie, still flabbergasted, returned to the courtroom.

When Doyle's trial concluded, Corrigan was called into the courtroom for his own trial. Wylie had by now collected himself and soon, albeit reluctantly, prosecuted the case against his former colleague. After Corrigan left the court, Wylie made an unexpected speech in his defence. Blackader was surprised at this and asked Wylie if he knew the prisoner. Wylie explained that Corrigan was a solicitor and had recently sent a few cases his way, one of which he had yet to cash the payment cheque for. He then told them that if Corrigan was executed the cheque would be worthless. The three judges sat open-mouthed until Blackader erupted into laughter: 'All right, Wylie, your five guineas are safe. We will recommend a reprieve.'[6]

Soon afterwards, Doyle and Corrigan were sitting on the green outside the courtroom building with the other tried men. Éamonn Ceannt and Con Colbert were also there. They had been notified that their cases had concluded and that they would soon be moved to Kilmainham to await the verdicts and sentences. When the soldiers guarding them received their rations of bully beef, bread and tea, the sergeant in charge asked one of the prisoners when they had last had anything to eat.[7] 'Eight o'clock this morning.' The sergeant went away and returned promptly with two soldiers, each carrying a bucket of tea and the same rations that the soldiers had just received, which they handed out to the grateful prisoners.

Outside the barracks, in the city itself, movement was becoming easier as the days passed. The military curfew remained in place between 7 p.m. and 5.30 a.m., but civilians were no longer required to carry a military pass to travel during daytime. Round-ups and searches continued, the British soldiers becoming more frustrated by the hour by having to carry out what they felt was police work. The Leicestershire Regiment continued to comb Irishtown for rebel snipers who, incredibly, were still evading capture.

General Friend had now taken responsibility for the courts martial and their accompanying documentation while General Maxwell was away in London. The confirmation or reduction of sentences was, however, to remain solely in Maxwell's hands.

When Maxwell stood before the cabinet in London that same Friday afternoon, he outlined as best he could the position in Ireland and explained the actions that he had carried out since his arrival there the previous week. The cabinet reaffirmed that he was not to execute any women. Maxwell assured them that in Countess Markievicz's case the court had recommended mercy and that he would apply it accordingly. The gathered politicians then advised him to execute prisoners only where he felt it to be absolutely necessary, such as in the cases of ringleaders and murderers, and to bring the matter to a swift, but not unnecessarily hasty, conclusion.

At this stage, as far as the authorities were concerned, things were indeed progressing towards a conclusion. Each man – with one notable exception – who had signed the proclamation was now either in custody or had already been court-martialled and sentenced. A niggling issue remained, however, in the form of Seán MacDiarmada – the name on both the proclamation and, equally important, the mobilisation order handed to Colonel Fraser in the gymnasium the previous Sunday. They had a 'John MacDermott' in custody – the name given to Lieutenant Jackson by Seán MacDermott. They were reasonably certain that this was their man. However, this man had been unarmed when the GPO garrison surrendered. He was also dressed in civilian clothing, and was lame – hardly a formidable revolutionary. And they had no known address for him. They were convinced nonetheless that MacDermott was indeed their man. The police were adamant that he was, but since they had little or no actual evidence they felt that, at this point at least, they could not reasonably prosecute.

When James Burke, the next Volunteer to be court-martialled, stood before Blackader, the general wanted to know why he was covered in coagulated blood, and why his uniform was in such a desperately ragged state. Burke spoke up, not realising that the question had been directed at Blackader's fellow officers. He began to explain that while he was in custody he had been set upon by drunken Dublin Fusiliers armed with bayonets, but he was interrupted mid-sentence by Blackader, who frowned at the prisoner's apparent impetuousness in speaking up without a prompt from the court, and told dismissively that he himself had not been asked to explain anything. The issue passed and the case proceeded. Afterwards, Burke joined his comrades outside on the green.

Detective Smyth and another G-man approached the green and began hurling abuse at Con Colbert and some other men. Smyth then vented his spleen at William Corrigan: 'Well, Corrigan, I am seeing the last of you; you are going to get what you deserve.'[8] One prisoner shouted back at Smyth that he shouldn't be so sure of himself. Some army officers then told the detectives to clear off. It began to rain heavily.

Down the road in Kilmainham, at roughly the same time, William Cosgrave received the expected official visit to inform him of his verdict and sentence. The officer charged with the task had no idea of what Father McCarthy had told the prisoner earlier. When Cosgrave confirmed his name he was told from his cell door: 'You have been found guilty and have been sentenced to death.' The officer paused, almost sadistically, watching for Cosgrave's reaction. Cosgrave said nothing. The officer eventually continued: 'The sentence has been commuted to penal servitude for life.' Cosgrave, looking completely unmoved, but secure in the knowledge that in this instance he had the upper hand, asked the frustrated officer, 'When can I see my solicitor?' There was no answer.

Back in Richmond Barracks, Michael Mallin's turn came to stand before Colonel Maconchy. Mallin pleaded not guilty when the charges against him were read. The first witness introduced by Lieutenant

Commandant
Michael Mallin,
Irish Citizen
Army. COURTESY
OF KILMAINHAM
GAOL ARCHIVES

Longworth for the prosecution was Constable John O'Connell, who
testified to having seen Mallin marching with the Citizen Army alongside
'Markievicz and Connolly'. He then added that the newspaper *Workers'
Republic* had stated at least once that he was Chief of Staff of the Citizen
Army.[9] When cross-examined, however, Constable O'Connell said
that he personally did not know for certain if in fact Mallin held such a
command, adding that he had never seen him drill or make a speech. A
policeman named Butler then testified that he had seen Mallin marching
with the Citizen Army in the same uniform he was wearing now before
the court, and wearing a revolver on his belt. He had seen him at Liberty
Hall on Easter Monday, and he had seemed 'busy organising the Citizen
Army'.[10] He added, however, that he had never known Mallin to be
anything other than cordial towards the police.

Major de Courcy-Wheeler appeared next for the prosecution. He
testified that Mallin had been unarmed when the College of Surgeons

garrison surrendered, and had informed him at the time that he was its commandant. Maconchy then asked Mallin if he wished to cross-examine the witness. Mallin declined, but turned unexpectedly instead towards the enemy officer, and said emphatically, 'I would wish it placed on record, how grateful my comrades and myself are for the kindness and consideration which Captain Wheeler has shown us.'[11] Both Mallin and de Courcy-Wheeler had shown great respect to one another during the surrender. Mallin had even presented his officer's cane to the enemy officer as a memento. Maconchy paused, then assured Mallin that, as he wished, his comment would be placed on record.

Before calling his only witness, Commandant Mallin told the court that he was a silk weaver by trade and worked for the Transport Union as a band instructor. This had eventually led him into the ranks of the Citizen Army, where he became a drill instructor. He insisted that he had received no commission in the Citizen Army. He contended that on Easter Monday he had been ordered to take 36 men and report to the Volunteer officer at St Stephen's Green, and that when the firing started Countess Markievicz had ordered him to take command of the men.[12] He then said: 'I felt I could not leave them and from that time I joined the rebellion.[13] I gave orders to make no offensive moves and I stopped them attacking the Shelbourne Hotel.' He then called his witness, Laurence Kettle, the brother of fellow Dublin Fusilier Thomas Kettle, who had been present at John MacBride's execution. Laurence Kettle had been a prisoner of the Citizen Army in St Stephen's Green and subsequently in the College of Surgeons. While recounting his imprisonment, he testified that Mallin had at one point saved him from being shot. When Kettle had finished speaking, Mallin concluded his testimony with the assertion: 'I indignantly repudiate any idea of assisting Germany.'[14]

While Mallin's case was being wound up that evening, elsewhere in the barracks British officers and NCOs began clearing out the barrack rooms. They would soon need the space to accommodate several trainloads of captured Volunteers from beyond Dublin. Just as before, the occupants who had avoided selection were now ordered out into the barracks square. They were handed extra rations on the way out. It was now raining heavily, almost as if nature was trying to correct itself following the recent unseasonably warm, sunny days, often described as 'rebellion weather' by those involved. When they formed into ranks on the square, Vice-Commandant Joe O'Connor sought out the men from his 3rd Battalion, many of whom he had not seen since their arrival and separation at the barracks on Tuesday, three days earlier – Séamus Grace, Andrew McDonnell, Peadar O'Mara, William Christian, Seamus Kavanagh, and others. Soon the entire battalion was assembled – minus its commandant and a few others – in the pouring rain, the men cursing at the deluge. The British officer in charge then began checking the names on a list, which he struggled to keep dry. He was removing the underage rebels, including 17-year-old Andrew McDonnell. Some of the recently arrived prisoners from Arbour Hill, apart from Seán Heuston's Mendicity garrison, were next to form ranks in the square. The G-men then arrived, scrutinising the men's faces to make sure for one last time that no one important would get away. They were still fuming that no list of names had been taken when the 3rd Battalion initially surrendered. Joe O'Connor, on the other hand, could barely believe his luck at having escaped their attentions so far – simply through the same lack of clerical foresight. Now he waited with bated breath.

Some of the prisoners transported from Kilmainham earlier were next to be marshalled on the square. Detective Hoey quickly zeroed in on Diarmuid Lynch. As far as he was concerned, he was far from finished with Lynch. He had him pulled out of the line and marched back inside the barracks. Michael Staines expected to follow Lynch, but he was overlooked. Liam Tannam, on the other hand, never even made it out to the square. The G-men were determined that he would be court-martialled and had held him separately under close guard. Almost as soon as Frank Thornton set foot in the square, he too was ordered back inside. Meanwhile, the gathered men were beginning to shiver in the cold and rain. Another officer addressed them and told them that they were being deported to England. Then the NCOs, their commands competing with the noise of the rain lashing the square and surrounding rooftops and windows, began ordering the grumbling Sherwood Foresters into escorting columns. The G-men stepped away and the order was given to march. Vice-Commandant O'Connor had escaped their clutches.

Minutes later, when the tail end of the column had marched out of the barracks gate, Andrew McDonnell and the dozen or so teenagers separated earlier were approached by an NCO and four soldiers, demanding back the bully beef and dog biscuits they had earlier been issued with. The prisoners reluctantly complied. They were then returned to the barrack room that McDonnell had originally shared with 60 others. Now it contained a dozen soaked, hungry adolescents huddling together in a corner.

Even before the tramp of the marching column's feet had faded from Richmond Barracks, word appeared to have reached the locals on Emmet Road, just outside, of its imminent departure. That evening, however, the prisoners were not attacked. Instead, the assembled civilians looked on silently from beneath umbrellas and coats held over their heads. About 15 minutes later the huge column crossed the River Liffey at Islandbridge, and turned right onto Conyngham Road. The rain was particularly heavy here, doing little to improve the men's morale. The nine-foot-high walls of the Phoenix Park on their left suggested to some Volunteers a bleak picture of what lay ahead – the dreary grey granite blocks of prison walls.

When they reached the River Liffey's quays, clutches of civilians lined their route, seeking shelter where they could while their number grew as the column approached the city centre. Once again, many prisoners glanced from face to face looking for relations. Many of those in the growing crowds had tears streaming down their faces. Women and girls grabbed at the Volunteers' hands and wished them good luck. The taunts and jeers from some of the civilians that had initially plagued the surrendered men days earlier were now completely gone. The number of onlookers increased even further as they approached the North Wall, as did the cheers and good wishes, giving the prisoners' morale a much-needed boost. Soon they were crammed aboard the TSS *Slieve Bloom*, in dripping wet clothes, and left in stinking filth. Finally, the steamer's engines came to life, its twin propellers spun and at 8.30 p.m. it was on its way to Holyhead. This trip would be even more arduous than the previous two. A strong wind whipped up huge swells and the ship was thrown about. When one of its engines suddenly stopped, Joe O'Connor thought they were under attack from the German Navy. In the end, the crossing took 12 miserable hours.

When the courts martial concluded that Friday evening, Gerald Doyle and the other court-martialled men in Richmond Barracks were marched to Kilmainham under a heavy guard. They included James Burke, Éamonn Ceannt, Con Colbert, Seán Heuston and Michael Mallin. It had now stopped raining. A crowd of several dozen looked on as they made their way eastward along Emmet Road.

Michael Mallin lived at 122 Emmet Road. The red-brick two-storey building stood on his right as he marched, a mere 200 yards from the barracks. Mallin looked out for his family as he passed the building, but the only familiar face he saw on that day was his dog's, standing guard by the building's front door. His family were in Drumcondra, staying with relations.

Further along Emmet Road, at the Turvey Avenue junction, a crowd of about a hundred civilians gazed on in silence. A crowd twice that size awaited the Volunteers on the roads and footpaths of Kilmainham. They too were silent, but the prisoners sensed that these people were now with them. The sentiment was confirmed when they heard shouts of 'Up the rebels!'[15] Commandant Ceannt began singing 'A Nation Once Again' as they waited for the gaol's gate to open. The other prisoners and the crowd quickly joined in.

Gerald Doyle's spirits had been lifted by the unexpected gestures of support from the local civilians, as had those of William Corrigan and James Burke. They nodded to one another in encouragement when they stepped into their adjoining cells a few minutes after re-entering the prison. When Doyle heard the key turn in the lock he sat down on what looked like an old tree stump and thought of the events of the previous two weeks. As his mind began to drift he recalled the smiling faces of Commandants Pearse and MacDonagh when they came out of their courts martial. He then remembered Tom Clarke calmly sitting on an upturned bucket and reassuring him and his comrades before he was taken away to be shot. He pondered Major MacBride's attitude and bearing at the end of his trial, and hoped that when his own time came he would meet death with the same courage.[16]

In the eerie silence of the cells and concourse of Kilmainham Gaol that Friday night, a sentry quietly unlocked Countess Markievicz's cell door. He lit two cigarettes and handed her one. The two sat and smoked in the dreary cell, saying nothing for a time, but smiling and nodding as they glanced at one another in the candlelight. The stillness was broken when Markievicz asked the young soldier 'who had gone'. He told her the names of the executed men. She chatted with him for a time, asking as many probing questions as the soldier dared answer, before he stood up, bade the countess goodnight, and took his place out on the landing.

At 7 a.m. the following morning – Saturday 6 May – the dozen or so teenage Volunteers in Richmond Barracks were ordered out of their holding rooms and brought individually before the police and the military to be interrogated. Plagued with hunger, they had spent a cold, sleepless night in wet clothes and looked the worse for it. The authorities wanted to know who had ordered them to fight, how long each of them had been in the Volunteers, and who had provided their supplies. More questions followed: where were their parents? Wouldn't they despair at their recent antics? When they had been fingerprinted and their descriptions recorded, they were brought back to the holding room. There they noticed that the Cockney NCO who had been guarding them had since been replaced by a corporal from the Dublin Fusiliers who had a very thick Dublin accent. He began handing out cigarettes to them. They also noticed, to their surprise, a bucket of strong hot tea and several large hunks of bread. They tucked in. The corporal closed and locked the door, but spoke to them the other side of the door, explaining that he had been home on leave from the front and how angry he had been at getting rounded up for duty because of the Rising. He then laughed, telling them they had been 'bloody fools', but at the same time, he liked the way they had 'put the wind up the so-and-so British regiments.'[17] The reviving youngsters smiled at his words as the tea warmed them up and they devoured the bread and smoked the cigarettes.

Soon afterwards, the barracks gymnasium was cleared of the 60 prisoners who had huddled on its floor overnight, sleeping as best they could. They too were separated into barrack rooms. Éamon de Valera and William O'Brien were put into a room with Count Plunkett. The count had been brought to Richmond Barracks the previous day with the contingent of prisoners from Kilmainham. Count Plunkett's mood had fluctuated between sadness and anger following his son's execution two days earlier. The same room now also contained Seán T. O'Kelly, Diarmuid Lynch, Frank Thornton and several others who had been selected for court martial. They did their best to lift Count Plunkett's spirits.

That Saturday morning, a mile to the north of the city centre in Dublin's North Strand, several detectives pulled up in a taxi at the home of Molly Reynolds. The engine was left running. When Reynolds, a teenager, answered the door and confirmed her identity to the officers, she was told she was wanted straight away in Richmond Barracks.

Molly's father, John Reynolds, had been court-martialled the previous day. During his trial, he had testified to having gone to the GPO during the fighting to look for his daughter, Molly, who had been sent there earlier to buy stamps. The DMP had no file on Reynolds: he belonged to a Volunteer company who did not have to drill or route march because of their advancing age and, accordingly, had kept a low profile. He was subsequently acquitted and sent home.

Molly, a Cumann na mBan member, had in fact served alongside her father in the GPO. A week before the Rising she had raised the Citizen Army flag outside Liberty Hall, standing on a chair to reach the halyard. The DMP had their suspicions about her, but for now the military needed her as a witness. When the taxi arrived at Richmond Barracks at around 10 a.m., Colonel Maconchy was back in his courtroom dealing with his last cases – the trials of Jack Shouldice and Con O'Donovan, both from the late Commandant Daly's 1st Battalion that had served in the Four Courts area. Maconchy was eager to finish up and hand over his unpalatable duties to Colonel Sapte. When Molly was brought in, Maconchy thanked her for coming. Then, after several general questions about her 'imprisonment' in the GPO, he asked her if she would be able to recognise any of the rebels from there.

Private Murray, who had so eagerly identified his captors in the gymnasium the previous Sunday, testified that while he was held in the GPO he had seen both Shouldice and O'Donovan on several occasions, carrying arms. This was untrue. Lieutenant Longworth eventually asked Molly if she recognised the same men. She answered no. When Private Murray argued the contrary she insisted that she was correct, and had been held in the same part of the GPO where Murray claimed to have seen them. Shouldice and O'Donovan both knew Molly, and that she could be trusted to stand her ground. A short time later, when Jack Shouldice had his turn to speak, he asked Molly if she had seen him in the post office, knowing what the answer would be. As he expected, she insisted to the court that she had not.

When she had given her evidence, Molly Reynolds was asked to wait outside. A detective sat down next to her and told her that they had a man in the barracks who was lame, who had been in the GPO, and who was anxious to send a message to some relations.[18] The man he referred to was Seán MacDermott. He asked if she would go and see him, hoping she might perhaps offer to take such a message, prompting MacDermott – he hoped – to write it and then sign it as Seán MacDiarmada – the same name on the mobilisation order, thus trapping himself. Molly, suspecting foul play, told the policeman that she knew no one in the GPO.[19] Moments later, Shouldice and O'Donovan were escorted from the courtroom. Knowing that the military would no longer need Molly, the policemen took her to another room and photographed her. She was then sent home, but this time not by taxi – she walked.

By late afternoon, General Maxwell had arrived back in Dublin from London. He immediately set to work on the pile of court martial files that had been accumulated by General Friend since his departure. Maxwell now thought about his recent meeting with the British cabinet. He commuted most of the death sentences that had been handed out by the court presidents, including that of Countess Markievicz. Most of the sentences handed down to prisoners tried earlier in the week that had not already been carried out were commuted. The relevant files would now be sent out so that the prisoners could be informed.

However, he confirmed the death sentences of Michael Mallin, Éamonn Ceannt, Con Colbert, Seán Heuston and Thomas Kent. Kent, from County Cork, who was 50 years old, had taken part in a three-hour gun battle with the RIC at his home, Bawnard House, outside Fermoy, on 2 May, during which a head constable was killed. Kent had since been tried by court martial in Cork detention barracks and sentenced to death there. He would be executed by firing squad on 9 May. Maxwell left these five files to one side, opting not to send them out yet to allow the prisoners to be informed. The general did not wish to risk being accused by the politicians of unnecessary haste.

At 5 p.m. on Saturday, the 2/5th Sherwood Foresters were ordered from the Guinness brewery to the Royal Hospital Kilmainham to relieve a cavalry detachment there. The men were disappointed with the redeployment. Their brief detail in the brewery had been a pleasant one for most. At the same time, the battalion's front-line transport and personal kits began to arrive in Dublin, as well as the officers and men who had been left behind in the hurried move from Watford.[20] The regiment had been forced to mobilise at short notice when the rebellion broke out. The Sherwood Foresters were not the only units on the move. Across Ireland, heavily guarded trains filled with rounded-up Volunteers left stations and steamed to the same destination – Dublin.

On South Anne Street on the same evening, teenager Vinny Byrne's luck ran out. Having escaped the attentions of the enemy rifleman gunned down in front of him the previous Sunday, he was arrested at home by a British officer accompanied by a sergeant and a dozen infantrymen. With the words 'Come along with me, boy,'[21] the youngster was grabbed by the collar and shoved into the back of an army truck. The sergeant was placed in charge of him. The truck was driven to Ballsbridge fire station, close to Anglesea Road. On the way, the sergeant, curious about the motivations of one so young, spoke with Byrne about his Republican aspirations and how far he was prepared to go to further them. At one point, he asked him, 'Would you shoot me?' Byrne nodded and replied 'If it was either you or me.' The sergeant simply laughed. Then, after the truck had rolled into the fire station Byrne was interrogated by enemy officers. They asked him where he had been during the rebellion. His defiant response was: 'In Jacob's Biscuit Factory, fighting for Ireland.'[22] Incredibly, young Byrne was then treated to a meal of steak and onions by the arresting sergeant in a stable, before being transported with several other prisoners to Richmond Barracks.

In Kilmainham Gaol, meanwhile, some of the British officers charged with informing the court-martialled prisoners of their verdicts and death sentences took to their task once again with an almost inhuman relish. A sergeant showed one such officer into Jack Plunkett's cell, where he read out the death sentence, followed by a prolonged pause to observe the condemned man's response. Plunkett denied the officer a reaction, and simply stood, poker-faced. This eventually frustrated the officer enough to make him venomously spit the words: 'And commuted to ten year's penal servitude.'[23] The sergeant standing next to the officer, feeling somewhat more sympathetic towards the prisoners, smiled when he heard that Plunkett's sentence had been commuted. As if to congratulate him, he shook his arm. The officer was disgusted and stormed out of the cell, calling the sergeant to follow him.

In Countess Markievicz's cell, a young officer, unnerved by the glare she gave him as he stepped inside, stuttered and fumbled the announcement of her life sentence as passed down by the court martial. When asked by the countess to 'Repeat it, this time clearly,'[24] he began again. When he had pronounced the sentence for the second time and the words 'penal servitude for life' had sunk in, she sighed and said despondently, 'I wish you had the decency to shoot me.'[25]

At 6 p.m., large detachments of Volunteer prisoners from outside Dublin began to arrive in Richmond Barracks. The first group was another contingent from Wexford, among them Captains Seán

Etchingham and Séamus Doyle. Both men had been to Dublin the previous Sunday to meet the late Commandant Pearse in Arbour Hill to verify the surrender order. They had since overseen the peaceful surrender of the Volunteer garrison that had taken over the town of Enniscorthy for the latter part of Easter Week. They were the last in the country to surrender – at 2 p.m. on Monday 1 May. The Wexford Volunteers were sent to the gymnasium as soon as they arrived. Then the selections began again.

Volunteer companies from Belfast, Dundalk and Drogheda were next to march in and were allocated immediately to barrack rooms. They were followed in turn by several hundred Galway men, who, unlike their fellow brigade comrades who had already been brought to the barracks, had been transported to the capital by train, not by sea. Night was beginning to fall.

Lieutenant O'Brien informed the officer in charge of the prisoner escort that there was no room in the barracks for any more prisoners. It was then decided to shift the bulk of them to Arbour Hill while squeezing an additional 25 men into an already overcrowded nearby barrack room. The new arrivals, horrified at the cramped and unsanitary conditions, began to exchange tales of the fighting in their own areas and counties. Liam Tannam, now surrounded by Galway men, was just one of the many prisoners from Dublin who was encouraged to learn that the fight against the empire had spread beyond the capital. Tannam was delighted to discover that he shared the same Irish surname – Ó Tainnín – as two of the men who had fought under Commandant Mellows. They told him of the pulsating skirmishes that had taken place around Clarinbridge, Oranmore and Carnmore, as well as the cat-and-mouse manoeuvres throughout east and south Galway – not to mention the naval bombardment. Tannam shared his tales of the fighting he had seen in Dublin.

As the evening darkened, Áine Ceannt, Commandant Éamonn's wife, was shown into her husband's cell in Kilmainham Gaol. She had been redirected there on foot from Richmond Barracks, where she had initially sought him out. Major Lennon was given authority to permit the visit by Viscount Powerscourt – Mervyn Wingfield – who was on the Provost Marshal's staff in the barracks.

Now, an NCO stood in the cell's darkening doorway as Ceannt and his wife looked at each other without speaking. The air in the cell was heavy and damp. The soiled post-combat condition of her husband's normally impeccable uniform struck her. It showed clear signs of battle. His Sam Browne belt was missing.

The presence of the sergeant in the doorway deprived Mr and Mrs Ceannt of an opportunity to discuss anything other than personal matters. Áine, however, did manage to suggest to her husband that the Rising had been a fiasco, only to be instantly rebuffed: 'No, it was the biggest thing since '98,'[26] (the 1798 rebellion). She then spoke of a newspaper article that claimed he had been handed a three-year sentence. Commandant Ceannt did not contradict her. In his heart he knew this would not be the case, but he did not want to take all hope away from his wife. When the time came for Mrs Ceannt to depart, she made him promise that he would send for her no matter what was to happen to him.[27] He assured her that he would.

In the neighbouring cells, other prisoners wondered in the growing darkness if the following morning would bring news of their fate. The waiting was almost unbearable. The hours of darkness dragged on as the already frigid temperature in the prison plummeted further. Prisoners, worn out from combat, demoralised from defeat, cold and hungry, shivered and paced their cells, while on the floors and landings chain-smoking guards strode up and down. The guards appeared cheerier than usual on Saturday night when news arrived that most of the prisoners' sentences were being commuted. A great many of the rank-and-file British infantrymen had by now concluded that the shabby, tattered men locked behind the rusty cell doors were fundamentally decent human beings. They were the enemy, but it gave them no pleasure to see them taken out and shot. They now felt relief, expecting that the ghastly business of execution had ceased. But they were wrong.

12

Four More Are Shot

'I am to die tomorrow at dawn'

Shortly after dawn on Sunday 7 May, Captain Arthur Dickson of the 2/7th Sherwood Foresters and a section of men under his command arrived at Kilmainham Gaol from Richmond Barracks. They had been detailed to transport Countess Markievicz to Mountjoy Prison. Several cabs had been ordered and soon pulled up outside the gaol. Markievicz was roused by the rattling of her cell door. When she was told what was happening, however, she refused to travel with enemy soldiers in a vehicle. After considering the situation for a few moments, Captain Dickson ordered his men to escort her on foot and the cab drivers were dismissed. The curfew was still in place and would be for several hours yet, but the military escort would make sure that she arrived safely at the prison, which was situated just off the North Circular Road, roughly two and a half miles away.

Markievicz walked in the middle of the road, while two files of soldiers, each six men strong, marched on the footpaths on either side, trying to keep to the slow pace of their prisoner. Markievicz was hungry and exhausted. An hour later, Dickson handed his prisoner over to the governor of Mountjoy. She was then taken away into the bowels of the prison. Captain Dickson had been struck by the fortitude and dignity displayed by the countess. He returned with his foot soldiers to Richmond Barracks, where more escort duties awaited them.

Later that morning, the infantrymen of the 2/5th Leicester Battalion were ordered to the Royal Dublin Showgrounds in Ballsbridge to await further orders. They were instructed that additional search parties would be required, but that until the precise details were ascertained, they were to rest. Many took the opportunity to bathe in the nearby River Dodder. Others attended packed church services in Ballsbridge. The suburb, like the rest of the city that morning, was warmed by sunshine.

Captain John Orchard was not as fortunate as his fellow officers. He was placed in charge of more urgent raiding parties, with almost a dozen trucks and cars involved. The mood among those conducting the raids was unforgiving. There were numerous arrests. Nevertheless, many of the addresses ransacked implicated other places of interest, as well as revealing valuable intelligence. One such address was 15 Russell Place, near Sherrard Street, the residence of Seán MacDermott. There Captain Orchard came across a bundle of envelopes, each containing a mobilisation order signed 'Seán MacDiarmada'. Each address on the envelopes was subsequently raided. More arrests were made. Impromptu interrogations took place in hallways, kitchens and parlours of both tenements and more exclusive dwellings. Some inhabitants protested their innocence; others remained silent, having expected such a visit. The net was now closing in on Seán MacDermott.

In Kilmainham Gaol that morning, the female prisoners were taken to the prison chapel to attend Mass. Seated in the gallery, they could only see the altar and the front seats[1] below them, where Éamonn Ceannt, Michael Mallin, Con Colbert and Seán Heuston knelt in prayer. Cumann na mBan members and sisters Lily and Annie Cooney leaned out of their seats to get a better look over the parapet. Several more women tried to look, including Kathleen Murphy, but their wardresses pulled them back into their seats. When the Mass ended, the male prisoners were escorted out in rows. The four prisoners in the front were the last to leave. Each of them looked up to the balcony on his way out. The women waved and smiled, trying their best to encourage them. Con Colbert fixed his gaze on Annie Cooney and nodded as he left.

James Burke had also been in the chapel. He bumped into Éamonn Ceannt after they had been escorted out. Ceannt told Burke he was glad to see him. He had not been aware that Burke had been out during Easter Week. When Burke asked his commandant if he thought they would all be executed, Ceannt replied: 'They will do in the other signatories

A mobilisation order for the Rising similar to those discovered by the raiding party at Seán MacDermott's home on Sunday 7 May. COURTESY OF KILMAINHAM GAOL ARCHIVES

and myself, but I think you will be all right.'² Both men were then sent back to their cells. No sooner had Burke's cell door been slammed shut behind him than it was opened again and an NCO ordered him to his feet. An officer stepped inside and ordered Burke to attention, before announcing that he had been sentenced to death. Burke sat down under the weight of the news. The officer barked at him, pitilessly, to stand to attention, which he did, then told him, sounding disappointed, that his sentence had been commuted to three years' penal servitude. The officer and the NCO then departed to inform other prisoners of their verdicts and sentences. A different officer broke the news of the verdicts to prisoners Ceannt, Mallin, Colbert and Heuston. There was, however, no subsequent announcement of leniency. They were to be executed at dawn the following day. At the same time, General Maxwell was dispatching the condemned men's files for promulgation. He also sent the file on Thomas Kent to Cork.

Commandant General James Connolly had recently been operated on in the hospital wing of Dublin Castle. The 47-year-old had been wounded twice during the fighting in and around the GPO – first in the arm and then the ankle. The latter injury was a dreadful one. A ricocheting bullet had smashed through his ankle and into his shin, tearing through bone and tissue as it went. Connolly had been treated by Captain Mahoney in the GPO. Mahoney, struck by the fortitude of Connolly under the circumstances, did all he could to help. Connolly had then resumed command of the garrison until he was physically unable to, his wound having become gangrenous.

Since his surrender, Connolly had been treated by military doctors, who did the best they could. After his operation, it was decided, despite his continuing weakness, that he would be fit to receive visitors in a day or so. Captain Stanley had promised Connolly's daughter Ina the previous Wednesday that he would notify her or her family as soon as her father was fit to see visitors. He kept his promise. He sent a note, addressed to Mrs Connolly, to the Dublin address where the Connolly family were staying – the residence of William O'Brien. 'If Mrs Connolly will call at Dublin Castle Hospital on Monday or Tuesday after 11 o'clock she can see her husband.'[3]

When Connolly's wife, Lillie, read the note she feared the worst. Her other daughter, Nora, pointed out to her, however, that this at least proved that he would not be executed on those days, and that time meant hope. Minutes later there was a knock at the front door. Lillie's son, Roddy, who had been released from Richmond Barracks, stood at the door with a young comrade, both filthy and exhausted. Lillie embraced both youngsters. They quickly changed out of their soiled clothes, washed and sat down to eat. They explained that they had been unexpectedly released with some other teenage Volunteers. As they ate they spoke of what they had seen and heard in Richmond Barracks. Their audience was an attentive one.

Fathers Albert and Augustine spent Sunday afternoon in Richmond Barracks attending to the spiritual needs of the prisoners. When they had finished, they made their way once again to the 59th Division's HQ on the North Circular Road. They had been led to believe that there were to be no more executions and wanted to make sure of this. They received unwelcome news. Their services would be required once again the following morning for four more executions. A car would be sent to the friary to collect them at the appropriate time. The priests returned to Church Street and did their best to rest and prepare for the inevitable call.

Fathers Albert and Augustine were not the only ones preparing for what lay ahead in Kilmainham Gaol that night. During the evening, lists of visitors were collected from the condemned men. Transport was arranged and police constables stood by, ready to act as navigators for the military.

Seán Heuston, Michael Mallin and Éamonn Ceannt requested family members to attend the gaol. Con Colbert, however, wished only to see a priest before his departure from this world. Colbert feared it would be too upsetting, both for his family and for himself. He opted, instead, to write letters to his family and to those dear to him.

Colbert had grown up in a large family in Athea in County Limerick. Short but physically formidable, resolute, physically and mentally tenacious, Colbert epitomised both the beliefs and the physical attributes of the Fianna, which he had joined in 1909 at its inaugural meeting. He was a committed Republican and a deeply religious man. A bakery clerk in civilian life, he had immersed himself in the nationalist and Republican causes. He had joined the IRB in 1912, and the Volunteers in 1913. He was a drill instructor, instilling the virtues of fitness, knowledge of history and abstinence from alcohol in those he led. During the Rising he had been deployed, with the men and women under his command, to Watkin's Brewery in Ardee Street. The position had subsequently become redundant. He had then redeployed to Jameson's Distillery in Marrowbone Lane, where he shared joint command with Captain Séamus Murphy. During a pivotal battle, Colbert's decisiveness had proved instrumental in seeing off enemy forces.

Colbert eventually changed his mind about visitors, and asked to see Kathleen Murphy, the wife of his officer comrade Séamus, having remembered seeing her along with the other women at Mass in Kilmainham earlier that morning.

That night, Gerald Doyle, lying on the bare floor of his cell, was woken by the tramp of marching feet. He listened intently to the rattling of keys and the opening and shutting of doors.[4] He rushed to his own cell door and strained to see through its spy hole. In the half-darkness outside, he could make out the silhouettes of two soldiers, with bayonets fixed, standing at attention next to the concourse staircase, their eyes fixed to Doyle's right. William Corrigan's cell adjoined Doyle's on that side. Doyle kicked furiously at the adjoining wall, fearing his comrade was about to be executed. Then, to his relief, he heard Corrigan respond with kicks of his own. He went back to the spyhole. He then saw a British major and two subalterns descending the staircase, followed by Con Colbert and Commandant Ceannt. Colbert turned suddenly to Ceannt, who nodded at him. Then they continued their descent, followed now by Michael Mallin and Seán Heuston. A six-man section and an NCO followed. The four condemned men were being moved to cells on the ground floor to wait for their relations.

Meanwhile, back in Richmond Barracks, a peculiar event was taking place. In the room now housing Count Plunkett and Commandant de Valera, another court martial was under way. This was a mock trial, presided over by Count Plunkett. Seán T. O'Kelly acted as prosecutor and Larry O'Neill spoke for the defence. De Valera was the defendant. De Valera had been charged by his peers with 'being a pretender to the throne of Muglins,'⁵ referring to the tiny island near Dalkey in Dublin.

The case was presented as pure farce, but at least raised a few laughs and cheers from the audience, until its conclusion, when the president announced a guilty verdict. A prisoner then brought a piece of black cloth for him to wear as he pronounced the death sentence. Count Plunkett stopped short, however. The atmosphere changed, a sense of foreboding quickly filling the room and dispelling all joviality. Soon afterwards, Larry O'Neill slid over to de Valera, muttered 'this is terrible' and pressed a small crucifix into de Valera's hand.⁶

On the night of Sunday 7 May, it was again raining heavily in Dublin. Éamonn Ceannt's brother Michael was sitting at home with his boots off, warming his feet by the fire, when a knock came at his front door. He answered to find a policeman who handed him a note from the commandant of Kilmainham Gaol. When he read the note his heart sank. His brother was to be executed. Michael was ushered into the waiting military motor car. His sister-in-law Áine, his sister Nell and his brother Richard were also passengers. They sat silently as the car was driven to Kilmainham.

On the way to the city from Drumcondra, Michael Mallin's brother Thomas, Michael's wife Agnes and their two youngest children, John (aged 10) and James (12), were also being driven to Kilmainham. Constable Soughley sat in the car with them. Thomas Mallin spoke quietly with Soughley, the latter confirming his brother's death sentence. Agnes still held out hope that her husband would be spared, but Thomas prepared her for the worst, hoping that when they met for the final time she would bear up and not make the sentence even harder for his brother to bear.⁷ For the rest of the journey they sat in subdued silence.

At roughly the same time, the tyres of another military vehicle sloshed through the puddles on the cobblestones of Fontenoy Street. It contained four members of Seán Heuston's family, who had just been collected from their terraced cottage there. It was a short drive to Kilmainham, but the car was stopped roughly half a dozen times at checkpoints on the way. Each time the words 'King's messenger' from the policeman sitting in the front passenger seat had the desired effect of parting the cordons of soldiers, whose bayonets glistened in the vehicle's headlights.

The first relation to arrive at the prison that night was Seán Heuston's brother Michael. He was a priest based at the Dominican Priory outside the village of Tallaght to the south-west of Dublin. Another priest accompanied Michael – Father Michael Browne, the priory's master of novices. When the clergymen entered Seán's cell, both the Volunteer captain and the priests stood silently for a few moments, until Seán spoke: 'Well, Michael, how are you? Don't cry now.'[8] Michael was losing the battle to hold back his tears. His brother, however, appeared calm and steadfast. Michael gathered himself, determined not to upset Seán's composure by losing his own. He drew a deep breath, and they began speaking. When their words turned to the Rising and the fighting at the Mendicity Institute Michael asked Seán, 'Did you kill any yourself?'[9] Seán replied, 'I had only automatic pistols and they would not carry'[10] – referring to their limited range. Seán spoke of one Volunteer, Richard Balfe, whom he presumed had been killed. Balfe had been badly wounded in a hand-grenade explosion, and in the heat of battle, had appeared dead. He was, however, recovering in hospital. They then spoke of the suspected casualty rate among the British Army in Dublin. Michael then assured Seán that the people were now siding with the Volunteers, and each execution was strengthening public feeling. When Seán asked Michael how many had already gone, referring to those already executed, he answered that there had been eight.

When they heard a cry of grief from a nearby cell, Father Browne left the cell to see if his services might be required. He approached a soldier on guard duty and asked him what had happened. The soldier answered that some of Michael Mallin's family had just arrived. Father Browne asked if he could see them. Without a permit, however, the soldier was forced to decline his request. Then the crying escalated. It was Mallin's wife. The soldier began to look very uncomfortable. Father Browne asked him the same question again. The soldier replied, 'Just walk in.'[11] The priest thanked him, then quickly stepped inside to console Mrs Mallin.

At roughly 10.45 p.m., Heuston's other relations also entered his cell. The first thing they noticed was that the young soldier standing in the cell holding a candle had tears streaming down his face. Heuston's cousin Lil began to sob loudly when she saw Seán. Michael calmed her, telling her softly, 'This won't do. You're only making it harder for him.'[12] Seán's mother, Maria, was aghast at her son's dishevelled appearance, muttering to herself, 'He's only the wreck of the fine, strong young man that went out on Easter Monday morning.'[13]

Brothers James and John Mallin sat quietly together on the ground floor in the prison's shadowy concourse. Soldiers and policemen passing through spoke with one another in hushed tones and looked sadly at the boys as they passed. Soon their uncle Thomas appeared and told them their father wished to see them. On the way to his cell, they passed several half-open cell doors, leaking flickering candlelight into the passage, and they could hear muttered prayers. When they arrived at their father's cell a soldier opened the door. Their father stood before them with a sad smile on his face. He had an old blanket draped around his shoulders. He told them: 'I am to die tomorrow at dawn.'[14] His wife broke down again at these words. James felt suddenly assailed by a bewildering array of emotions. His father had always spoken to him as if he were an adult. Now, however, he felt like a small child again – confused and frightened. The only thing he was certain of was that he would never see his father again.

As Mallin and his family said their farewells, Éamonn Ceannt's family, having had their names checked, were led to his cell by a soldier carrying a lantern. Ceannt had been sitting at a table writing his final letters by the light of a candle. When he heard the key turning in his cell door he stood, walked over to his wife, embraced her and kissed her tenderly. His brothers and sister stepped outside to allow them their final moments together. Roughly 15 minutes later their brother asked for them. He told them that Father McCarthy had visited his cell earlier and had hinted that there was hope of a reprieve.[15] Michael, however, knew his brother well, and could tell by his manner that he was merely trying to give hope to Áine. Then one of the sentries called, 'Time's up.' As the family prepared to leave, Commandant Ceannt told them that he had asked to see Father Augustine, but had heard nothing of him since. Richard asked a nearby sentry if the priest was coming. The sentry took him to Major Lennon to find out.

When Ceannt and his family had said their final farewells, Michael looked back one last time. His brother stood in the candlelight in his green Volunteer uniform, looking down at the table where his letters lay. Michael began to well up with tears. In his mind's eye, he saw the young boy he used to walk to school, not a high-ranking and resolute Irish Volunteers officer. Michael forced himself to remain composed. Then he said to his brother, almost fiercely, 'God's blessing on you.' Éamonn looked reassuringly towards him, and answered: 'May God favour you.'[16] Then the cell door creaked closed. Moments later, Richard returned from having seen Major Lennon. Lennon had assured Richard that Father Augustine would soon be there, but when told of the reprieve spoken of by Father McCarthy, had replied emphatically: 'There is no reprieve. Go back and tell your brother.'[17] It was what Commandant Ceannt had expected to hear. After his brother departed and the cell door was locked, Ceannt returned to his letters.

By now, time had also run out for Michael Mallin to say his farewells to his family. Thomas had one final question for his brother. As the rest of the family stood silently he asked him, 'Is it worth it?' Michael paused, then replied: 'It is worth it. Ireland is a grand country, but the people in it are rotters.' He added, 'The first Irishman to join the British army was a bastard.'[18] Mallin threw his arms around his brother and kissed him. Then, bidding him a final farewell, Michael asked Thomas to look after his wife and children. He embraced and kissed each of them in turn, struggling to conceal his heartbreak, particularly for his children, before saying a final goodbye.

In Seán Heuston's cell, the conversation had turned to the practical question of what would happen to his body. His mother wanted to inter him in Glasnevin Cemetery with the rest of his family. Seán explained to her that he would be buried in Arbour Hill, alongside the other executed men. He added that the others would be buried in their Volunteer uniforms. His mother's response was: 'Yes, and you have no uniform; you couldn't afford it.'[19]

The Heuston family then knelt together and prayed. When the instruction to leave followed soon afterwards Seán's mother began to cry. He looked to her, pleading, 'Don't cry now mother, don't cry,' then looked to his brother, saying, Michael, you won't let mother cry. Pray, pray hard for me.'[20] They left, accompanied by the soldier who had held the candle to light the cell. When Heuston was suddenly thrust into pitch darkness he cried through the cell's locked door, 'Won't you leave the light?'[21] The soldier assured the Heuston family that he would return with the candle as soon as he had seen them out.

In the section of the prison that housed the female inmates, Kathleen Murphy was called out of the cell she shared with fellow Cumann na mBan member Lily O'Brennan. A soldier, accompanied by a wardress, asked her if she knew 'anyone of the name Colbert.'[22] Unsure of their intentions, she replied that she would not know unless she saw the individual in question. She was taken to Major Lennon. He asked her a few questions before ordering a guard to escort her to Con Colbert's cell. Colbert was now lying on the floor, covered by a blanket.

When she stepped inside Colbert jumped up. He asked her how she was, but before she could say anything in reply he added that he was one of the lucky ones. He then said to her: 'I will be passing away at the dawning of the day.'[23]

Then he began pressing keepsakes on her, presenting her with the buttons from his uniform, and handing her a prayer book to pass on to his sister. Kathleen asked him why he had not sent for his sister. He said that he did not want to cause her any trouble. Kathleen, dismayed at this, insisted that his sister would have been able to take the news with composure and dignity. After they had spoken for a while, Colbert told her that he had never felt happier; he had never thought he would have the honour of dying for Ireland.[24] Kathleen assured him that he was setting an example of how soldiers should die. The soldier holding the candle began crying and said, 'If only we could die such deaths.'[25] Soon, Kathleen was told that the time was up. As she was leaving, Colbert asked her to pray when she heard the volleys that would soon be fired at him and his comrades. He also handed her a letter for Annie and Lily Cooney. Kathleen walked slowly to the cell door, but turned as she was leaving, and said: 'A martyr's death is a noble one.'[26] Colbert smiled at her and said goodbye.

At 1.30 a.m. on Monday 8 May, for the fourth time since the previous Wednesday morning, a military car arrived at the Capuchin Friary in Bow Street. This morning, Fathers Augustine and Albert were waiting. When they arrived at the prison about fifteen minutes later, they were told the names of those who were to die. They were initially taken to the cells of Éamonn Ceannt and Michael Mallin, then divided their time between the four condemned men. When Father Augustine entered Ceannt's cell he found the prisoner still writing letters. Ceannt said calmly to the priest, 'Father, you have to make other visits, haven't you?'[27] 'Yes, I do,' replied Augustine. Ceannt glanced at his pocket watch, and asked, 'Father, I have yet an hour, have I not?' These words cut straight to Augustine's heart. He answered as he turned away, 'Yes, Éamonn, just another hour.'[28]

The noise level rose as British Army staff cars began arriving at the prison. Soon it was a hive of activity. Outside the prison were numerous military checkpoints, their frequency increasing proportionately with proximity to the prison and nearby Royal Hospital. Major Heathcote and Captain Whitehead paced around the Stonebreakers' Yard, ensuring that everything was in order. Gerald Doyle was still awake. He began pacing in his cell. James Burke and Willie Corrigan waited apprehensively in theirs. Kathleen Murphy listened for the volleys that Con Colbert had earlier alluded to, as the dawn light began to leak through the prison bars.

Captain Dickson, along with three other young officers from the 2/7th Sherwood Foresters, had been charged with overseeing the morning's firing squads. Having mustered and briefed the requisite number of riflemen they marched towards Kilmainham. On their way, Dickson overheard one of the men say: 'Pity to dirty all these rifles; why can't we do him in with a bit of bayonet practice?'[29] There was no response.

When they arrived at the prison, Major Heathcote gathered Dickson and the other three officers around him in the Stonebreakers' Yard. In the adjoining yard, four sections, each of 12 men, with an additional NCO, were ordered to stand ready. Heathcote explained to his lower-ranking officers how the executions were to be carried out. When the major was certain that each of them understood his instructions, he told them their place in the execution sequence, detailing an officer to oversee each firing squad. The officers then went to their men. Dickson took the opportunity to go over the procedure once again with his fellow officers. Then the first squad was led in.

Father Augustine was standing in the courtyard between the prison and execution yard when, at 3.45 a.m., the signal was given to proceed.

Caught unaware, he hurried back to the prison to attend to the prisoner, only to see Éamonn Ceannt being led out, already prepared. He was blindfolded and the white card had been pinned to his chest. His bound hands gripped a crucifix that Augustine had given him earlier. Two soldiers walked on either side of him, each holding an arm.

Ceannt was led into the Stonebreakers' Yard, where the first squad waited, kneeling and standing as before. A large wooden soapbox had been placed in front of the sandbagged wall. Ceannt was placed sitting on it. An officer asked him to stretch his legs out.[30] This would steady the victim, and make it less likely that any shots would miss the pinned-on target. Ceannt stretched out one leg at a time. Tragically, however, moments later, the efforts made to help ensure accuracy would prove futile. Ceannt's death, like Tom Clarke's, would not be instantaneous.

When the officer gave his signal, rifle fire shattered the silence. Ceannt tumbled backwards off the soapbox, groaning desperately. He was still alive. The firing squad had been unable to steady their rifles. Some of their shots missed their target altogether, smashing into the sandbagged wall behind him. Those that hit him had failed to hit the white target, and instead struck his upper body haphazardly, creating multiple wounds. Captain Stanley ran forward, frantically signalling to the officer. But the officer needed no signal: he was already drawing his revolver and hurrying to the bound figure twitching and moaning on the ground. Seconds later, he ended Ceannt's agony with a bullet to the head.

From her cell, Rose McNamara, initially startled by the 12 rifle shots, heard Ceannt's moans, then a single shot, then silence.[31] In the Stonebreakers' Yard, Father Augustine ran to pick up the blood-spattered crucifix that Ceannt had held. The three men awaiting execution had also heard the dry crack of the officer's pistol shot, as well as the groans of their comrade that preceded it.

Gerald Doyle dropped to his knees and began praying. In the cell beside him he could hear Willie Corrigan also praying.

Captain Stanley had had enough. He was sick of the slaughter.[32] There and then he decided that he would no longer be part of it. He demanded to be relieved of his duty. In his place, the soldier in charge of binding and blindfolding the prisoner was handed the white targets. Ceannt's remains were wrapped in a sheet, labelled and removed.

Father Augustine hurried to Michael Mallin's cell. At the same time, Father Albert was walking with Seán Heuston towards the corridor

Captain Seán Heuston, pictured in a Fianna uniform, executed on 9 May 1916. Courtesy of Kilmainham Gaol Archives

leading to the prison yards. Shortly before 3.55 a.m., the soldier bound and blindfolded Heuston and pinned the white marker to his chest. Father Albert looked back along the corridor to see Michael Mallin and Father Augustine approaching. The seconds ticked away. Heuston bent forward and kissed the crucifix in Father Albert's hands, whispering,

'Father, sure you won't forget to anoint me?'[33] Two soldiers, one on either side, led him out. On their way through the first yard they passed Michael Mallin's waiting firing party. In the Stonebreakers' Yard the bloodstained soapbox awaited Captain Heuston. He too was placed sitting with his legs stretched out. Another officer oversaw the second 12-man firing party. As Father Albert stepped away he heard Heuston cry out, 'My Jesus, Mercy!'[34] A volley rang out. Heuston was hurled off the box with the force of the shots, but they had been true. Unlike Ceannt, Heuston was killed instantly.

Kathleen Murphy and Lily O'Brennan prayed fervently as they heard the shots, unsure which volley was dispatching whom to the hereafter. By now the entire prison was awake as the gunfire reverberated around its walls. The muttering of prayers could be heard from almost every cell. Dr Kathleen Lynn had recently arrived in Kilmainham. She and her two cellmates felt as if their hearts were being torn out with every gunshot.

Fog had descended on west Dublin as Father Augustine walked out into the misty dawn[35] with Michael Mallin at 4.05 a.m. Mallin's mind was taken up with thoughts of his pregnant wife and children. He too was placed into position on the soapbox as the new firing party stood ready, awaiting the silent signal from their officer. As soon as Mallin felt the soldiers on either side release their grip, he cried out: 'Lord Jesus, receive my spirit!'[36] He had barely finished the words when the third hail of lead that morning smashed into his chest and heart. Mallin died instantly. Cordite hung heavy in the mist as his body was wrapped and taken away to join the others in the nearby wooden shed.

Shortly before 4.15 a.m., it was Con Colbert's turn to have a target pinned to his breast. Colbert looked down as it was applied and suggested: 'Wouldn't it be better to pin it up higher – nearer the heart?'[37] The soldier looked at him and then changed its position, struggling to steady his hands. Colbert was then blindfolded. The last firing party was already in position and awaiting their final prisoner. Colbert, like the others, was hustled and shoved into the Stonebreakers' Yard. Moments later, the shots that killed him instantly resounded throughout the prison and the surrounding area. In Richmond Barracks, Seán T. O'Kelly, Count Plunkett, Larry O'Neill, and Éamon de Valera sat quietly with their comrades, wondering who was now gone, and praying for their souls.

Colbert's remains were also wrapped, labelled, and brought to the wooden shed. Meanwhile, in Arbour Hill, Father Farrington stood by,

Con Colbert, executed by firing squad 8 May 1916 at 4.15 a.m. Courtesy of Kilmainham Gaol Archives

waiting for the morning's cargo of bodies to be interred in the quicklime pit. As they were loaded into the waiting ambulance in Kilmainham, Captain Dickson addressed his subdued men: 'Right, you have done a good job of that.' When no response or reaction came, he spoke up again, saying: 'Remember we had all lost some good pals on our first days' active service.'[38] He was referring to the battle of Mount Street Bridge and Northumberland Road. Then, the squads were marched back out of Kilmainham.

13

The Endgame Approaches

'I have to make a nice corpse, you know'

Shortly before 11 a.m. on Monday 8 May, Lillie Connolly and her eight-year-old daughter Fiona arrived at Dublin Castle to see Lillie's husband, James. Both Lillie and Fiona were searched on the way in. Those overseeing the searches wanted to ensure that neither Connolly's wife nor his daughter was carrying anything that James could use to take his own life.[1] Lillie was made to promise not to speak to her husband of events since the rebellion.

James Connolly had a naturally cheerful persona. It was an attribute that had seen him through the bitterest of life's tragedies and the toughest hardships. Raised in the slums of Edinburgh, he was widely travelled, and regarded as one of the most formidable speakers of his time. His quick wit and boundless intelligence and energy captivated most who knew him. He could outshine the most eloquent of debating opponents and, almost in the same breath, tear apart the harshest verbal assaults from less well-cultivated antagonists. The men and women under his leadership adored him, knowing that each of them was treasured for their character, and not for their connections. Connolly was a founding member of the Irish Citizen Army, which he led into battle on Easter Monday, placing himself in harm's way time and again. Connolly had been a soldier in the British Army at the age of 14. He knew what made young infantrymen tick. With each passing day in Dublin Castle he had won the enemy guards over, exchanging stories with them of adventure and misadventure while empathising with the desperate dangers and hardships they had encountered in the trenches of the Great War.

When Lillie and Fiona approached his bedside, Connolly, still desperately weak, was filled with delight. After embracing them, he asked Lillie about their other children. She reassured her husband that the children were safe. Connolly breathed a deep sigh of relief. They then spoke of personal matters for a time. All too soon, the visit was over, and Connolly's wife and daughter left the castle. Lillie was in a much more positive frame of mind. She was concerned, of course, that her husband was still seriously ill, but now she firmly believed that his life would be spared.

In Kilmainham Gaol on the same morning, the air seemed weighty with malaise. Prisoners sat quietly in their cells, reflecting on their families, their aspirations, their current situation, and their growing desire for revenge. The Stonebreakers' Yard was empty, apart from service personnel who entered and left periodically as they made their rounds. Military and civilian vehicles joined the growing traffic outside the walls, as did the local trams, as normality continued to crawl back into the streets of Dublin.

Gerald Doyle was sitting in his cell when, at around noon, a British major arrived to tell him that he had been sentenced to death. Doyle sat silently, unmoved. The major asked sternly, 'Do you understand?' When Doyle answered 'Yes,' the major continued: 'The court, having considered your case, has commuted the death sentence to life imprisonment – but on further consideration – taking your age into account – the sentence is commuted to three years' penal servitude.' He then repeated, 'Do you understand'? Doyle again answered 'Yes.' He was then told, 'You are now a convict and a felon and will be transferred to one of His Majesty's prisons in England.'[2] Doyle offered no response. The major then moved on to the cells of other prisoners: Jack Shouldice and William Corrigan had their sentences reduced to five years; James Burke received three years. Neither Gerald Doyle nor his fellow inmates felt any joy in the news. They were simply worn out. However, Doyle found some consolation in the fact that he would soon join his deported comrades.

Opposite Kilmainham Gaol, in the Royal Hospital, General Maxwell and Lieutenant Wylie sat at a dining room table discussing the list of pending trials. Maxwell handed Wylie a telegram, from Prime Minister Asquith. It advised that that the trials and executions should cease, as they were having an adverse political effect in England. Maxwell asked Wylie who was next on the list to be tried. Struggling with the pronunciation of the surname, Wylie replied that it was Éamon de Valera. Maxwell asked, 'Who is he, Wylie? Is he important?' Wylie answered that he was not. He added that de Valera was a schoolmaster and unlikely to cause trouble in the future. Maxwell then asked who was next after de Valera.

'James Connolly.'

Maxwell said, almost as a reflex, 'Well, we cannot let him off.' Wylie explained that Connolly was wounded, and that perhaps they should wait until he had recovered and was fit for trial. Maxwell, however, had other plans in mind for James Connolly. He asked Wylie to procure a report from Dublin Castle's doctors. If Connolly was fit, Maxwell argued, he could be tried in hospital.

The pair then discussed the female prisoners. Wylie's impression was that most of them could now be released, but that 18 or so should remain in custody, pending further investigation. He reasoned that the latter group were 'older, better educated, and real believers in a free Ireland'.[3] Maxwell felt very reassured by this. He had been uncertain of the appropriate course of action to take with those he referred to as 'silly little schoolgirls'.

By Monday afternoon, notices of who had been executed were circulating far and wide in Dublin. Some of the names made no sense to the vast majority of the public who read them – they were unknown. People began to wonder when it would end. Horrific stories were also spreading like wildfire, such as the murderous rampage of a deranged British officer, Captain Bowen-Colthurst, in the Rathmines area. The captain had shot three people in the street, and subsequently ordered and overseen the execution without trial of three others, one of whom was the pacifist Francis Sheehy Skeffington, in Portobello Barracks. The sentiment was one of increasing disgust. It was as though Dublin's citizens were watching a stream of blood coming from beneath a closed door,[4] and there was nothing they could do about it.

In Richmond Barracks, at 2 p.m., the trials of Éamon de Valera, Thomas Ashe and Dr Richard Hayes were about to begin. Moments earlier, when de Valera was escorted out of his barrack room, the men there, fearing they would never see him again, had asked him for keepsakes. Sean T. O'Kelly was given his pen. De Valera then shook hands with the men, the last of whom was Galwayman Peter Howley. Following the handshakes de Valera said 'Be brave men, it is for a noble cause.'[5] He was then marched out to the green in front of the courthouse. Other prisoners were already gathered there. Commandant Ashe and Dr Hayes soon joined them. The sun shone. The rain of the last three days was no more.

The trials proceeded as the previous ones had. Two witnesses appeared for the prosecution in de Valera's case: Captain Hitzen and an officer cadet named Mackey. Mackey had been held prisoner in Boland's Bakery, 3rd Battalion HQ during the Rising. Mackey testified to having been detained there until his release on Sunday 30 April. He made no complaints about his treatment while he was a prisoner under de Valera. Captain Hitzen testified to having overseen the garrison's surrender, under the same man now standing before the court, and their subsequent detention in the Royal Dublin Showgrounds. Hitzen appeared to hold de Valera in high regard as a fellow officer. The discipline and general manner of his men since their capture had impressed him.

When Thomas Ashe's turn came, a number of witnesses testified to having been attacked by Ashe's battalion at Swords, Donabate and Ashbourne. Frank and James Lawless and Richard Hayes were also identified as Volunteer protagonists by the same policemen. When the trials ended, the men were marched under guard to Kilmainham Gaol to await sentencing.

At 3 p.m., in Kilmainham Gaol, Gerald Doyle was ordered out of his cell. He saw fellow prisoners to his left and right standing outside their own cell doors. He recognised three of them; Jack Shouldice, James Burke and William Corrigan. The prisoners were then ordered outside into the yard, where half a dozen policemen, backed up by a section of soldiers, formed a cordon that funnelled them towards a horse-drawn Black Maria carriage, used for transporting prisoners. A dozen prisoners were herded in. When the vehicle was secured it set off to Mountjoy Prison. Two horses pulled the carriage, a section of soldiers following on bicycles. Doyle discovered on the way that this was not the first such journey. Other Volunteers, no longer under sentence of death, had also been transported to Mountjoy, including Edward Duggan, William Cosgrave, Piaras Béaslaí, Liam Tobin and the two Plunkett brothers. Civilians stopped and stared as the carriage passed, some cheering their support.

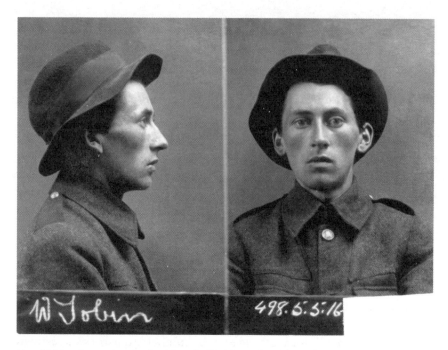

Liam Tobin, pictured soon after his arrival in Mountjoy Prison. COURTESY OF KILMAINHAM GAOL ARCHIVES

When they arrived at Mountjoy Prison roughly 45 minutes later, they were welcomed with surprising cordiality by British cavalrymen who had been detailed to garrison the prison. They were then taken into the prison reception, where a line of warders awaited them. After being searched and having their names taken, they were taken to the prison bath house. Soon they were immersed in steaming hot water. For men who had not washed in two weeks this was a most welcome experience. Gerald Doyle was delighted to wash away the stale, damp stench of what he and his comrades referred to as 'His Majesty's Hotel'. Then they were handed prison clothes. Some of the warders also gave them cigarettes, before escorting them to the prison's 'A' Wing. They were put into cells, one man to each cell. Gerald Doyle took to his new surroundings as if he had been placed unexpectedly in a luxury hotel. Compared with Kilmainham, Mountjoy was indeed luxurious. He lay down on his flat-boarded bed with its fibre mattress, crawled under the clean blankets and fell asleep.

By 6 p.m., another deportation of prisoners had been arranged. On North Wall Quay, another cattle boat awaited its latest contingent of human cargo. The men of the 2/5th Sherwood Foresters, having by now been summoned to Richmond Barracks from the Royal Hospital Kilmainham, assembled on the barracks square. Barrack rooms and corridors were once again cacophonous with the banging of doors, the tramping of feet, the murmur of hundreds of voices, and shouted commands. The prisoners were ordered to assemble outside.

Andrew McDonnell and the 11 young comrades confined with him soon found themselves on the square. Peter Howley, Frank Hardiman and a large number of their fellow Galwaymen stood nearby, as did other groups of Volunteers from various parts of the country. Once again Seán MacDermott stood on the square, this time next to Gearóid O'Sullivan and Maurice Collins. Amid the clamour of boots and the shouting of orders MacDermott told those next to him that he did not think he would make it out. Collins said they would all make it out together. MacDermott, however, saw the G-men approaching, as did Collins. The G-men pulled men out here and there as they drew closer. Finally one of them stopped and stared at MacDermott and ordered him out with a sneer. By now, the detectives had received word that a witness had been found who could link the man they so badly wanted to the mobilisation order they had found. MacDermott's trial papers were being prepared – he was going nowhere. O'Sullivan was also removed from the assembled ranks.

Rations were handed out to those deemed suitable to send on their way. They numbered approximately four hundred. Andrew McDonnell and the other teenagers, having been given their rations, were ordered to one side, away from the main body of men, whom the Sherwood Foresters surrounded. Then the British officers' instructions to the sergeants were relayed as loudly barked orders to the enlisted men to 'Forward march!' with their prisoners. Soon afterwards, the tail end of the column disappeared from McDonnell's sight. Fearing that they would be relieved of the rations they had just been handed – as had happened the previous Friday when they had similarly stood by while their older comrades were deported – they stuffed them inside their clothes. When an NCO and a section of soldiers arrived to commit the very act they had feared, McDonnell insisted that they had not received any rations. They were then led away to a room, where they soon tucked into the food.

Seán MacDermott and Gearóid O'Sullivan were taken to a room allocated to prisoners selected for court martial. There, MacDermott noticed Séamus Doyle, one of the Enniscorthy officers. MacDermott had last seen Doyle on Good Friday, when the command of the Wexford Volunteers was officially detailed. The two men began discussing the momentous events since.

Back in Kilmainham Gaol, at 7.30 p.m. cell doors once again began to creak open. Teams of guards and wardresses told the female prisoners to 'Get ready'. They were soon congregated on the concourse's ground floor, where a group of British officers, including Major Lennon, awaited them. Father McCarthy was also there. Several of the women asked where they were going now. An officer joked, 'Off to Jamaica to pick oranges.'[6] At this, his fellow officers guffawed, one of them adding, 'Hurry up, the boat is about to sail!' Then a list of names was called out. Anyone whose name was not on the list was ordered back to their cell.

Then Lieutenant Wylie stepped forward and addressed the women. He told them that they were to be released. He then insisted that they reflect on their future behaviour, warning that they were to be 'good in future, or else'.[7] Wylie then gave them a choice: since it was now evening, and the military curfew was still in place, the released women would risk arrest at army checkpoints; so, if they wanted, they could remain in the prison until the following morning. Most of them, however, had had enough of Kilmainham Gaol and decided that they would take their chances. Father McCarthy offered to escort them out. When Annie Cooney and her sister left the prison, a British NCO approached, saying he had something for them and that they should return the following morning to receive it.

As dawn broke on Tuesday 9 May, Thomas Kent was handcuffed in Cork detention barracks. He had been attended during the night by a priest, Father Sexton, who had given him a set of rosary beads to hold. When asked if he had any last requests, his response was simply that no Irishman be asked to shoot him.

He was now led, barefoot, towards the prison's execution yard, where a chair awaited him. The 12-man firing squad was under the command of a naval officer, Hereward T. Price. The barrack's medical officer asked him if he required a stimulant – rum. Kent responded: 'No, I am an abstainer'. He had also, the previous night, refused a dinner, luxurious by prison standards, offered to him when the British officers had heard from a nurse within the barracks that Kent was an educated and cultivated man. They had hitherto thought of him as being 'of peasant stock'.

At first Kent refused to sit in the chair, until Father Sexton convinced him to. A soldier then stepped forward to blindfold him. This was declined by Kent until it was made clear that he had no choice but to wear it. Within seconds of it having been applied Price gave the signal and a volley resounded throughout the barracks. Most of the barracks staff stopped momentarily when they heard the abrasive cracks, looking uneasy. They then returned to their tasks. Back in the yard a private picked up the bloodstained rosary beads. He washed the blood from them and gave them to Father Sexton.

Back in Kilmainham, at 7.00 a.m., the women who had chosen to remain overnight at Kilmainham Gaol left the prison and returned home. They felt subdued relief. Their freedom was welcome, but the recent memories of hearing the harsh volleys of gunfire at dawn doused any feelings of joy.

Soon after the women had left, Annie and Lily Cooney returned to the prison to seek out the sergeant who had spoken to them the night before. They were now also looking for information on their father, whom they discovered was also a prisoner, possibly in Kilmainham Gaol. The sergeant handed them Con Colbert's watch and the letter he had written to them. The prayer book Colbert had given to Kathleen Murphy to forward to his sister was also there. Mrs Murphy was still being detained in the prison, and the sergeant did not know how much longer she would be held. He asked the Cooney sisters if they would see to its delivery, which they later did. They did not, however, find their father in Kilmainham that morning.

General Maxwell spent the morning at his HQ. He read one of the baleful letters that had recently started to arrive, before putting it into a drawer. Within weeks, the drawer would be filled with similar letters. The general was beginning to realise that things were not proceeding as planned. As far as he was concerned, he had been called to Dublin at short notice to deal with a dangerous and volatile situation that required a vigorous and diligent response. Now, however, it appeared that his government was getting cold feet about the whole business of the trials and executions.

After some consideration, Maxwell concluded that he would need to clarify the situation to his political overseers. Lieutenant Brucknill was summoned to his office. The lieutenant had already prepared most of Maxwell's responses to the government and his services were now called on again. By late morning, Brucknill had written a dispatch to Field Marshal Lord French, asking him to inform the prime minister that the trials in Dublin were practically finished, and that the insurgents from the provinces would be next. He added that James Connolly and 'John MacDermott' were now due to be tried that day – Tuesday – and that to the best of his knowledge, these men would be the last to suffer capital punishment,[8] unless any cases of the murder of policemen or soldiers could be proved against others.

Later that day, Lord French relayed the message to Prime Minister Asquith, who replied immediately that he was satisfied with what the general had said. He also asked for a report on James Connolly's health, and his likelihood of recovery. General Maxwell had already received a report from Dublin Castle stating that Connolly's memory and understanding were entirely unimpaired and that he was fit to stand trial.[9] This was enough for Maxwell: Connolly's trial could proceed.

Seán MacDermott also received the news that his court martial was imminent that day. As soon as he heard, he persuaded one of the Richmond Barracks guards to lend him a razor. As he shaved, he turned to his comrades: 'I have to make a nice corpse, you know.'[10] When his name was eventually called by the officer standing at the barrack room door, he said his goodbyes to Captain Doyle and the others, and limped to the door. In the corridor, he met his old IRB comrade Denis McCullough, who had been arrested in Belfast. MacDermott embraced McCullough, told him his own number was up and bade him farewell. Outside on the green he met Frank Thornton, Harry Boland and Gerald Crofts, who were also waiting for their trials to commence.

Colonel Sapte was overseeing these trials. Harry Boland was the first to stand before the colonel. The only witness against him was a sergeant named Henry, whom Boland had taken prisoner in Fairview and had subsequently brought to the GPO. When the GPO could no longer be held, the sergeant had been released. He then hid out in the Coliseum Theatre for five days, unaware that the enemy had surrendered. The sergeant betrayed his bitterness at his experiences when he saw Boland waiting outside the court, gloating that the boot was on the other foot now, saying, 'He who laughs best, laughs last.'[11] Boland, undaunted, and living up to his reputation for quick-wittedness, shot back, 'Yes, chum, I am laughing! I am not whinging as you were when I took you prisoner.'[12] This prompted sniggers from both friend and foe as they entered the courtroom.

At Frank Thornton's court martial, the evidence against him centred on the fierce fighting in and around Marlborough Street towards the latter part of Easter Week. However, when he was then accused of taking part in the raid on the Magazine Fort in the Phoenix Park on Easter Monday he was shocked. He had been in many places during Easter Week, but the Phoenix Park was not one of them. Soon his trial too was over, and he joined Boland and his comrades on the green outside.

When Seán MacDermott finally faced his court martial, there were seven witnesses ready to testify against him. Detective Daniel Hoey was the first. Hoey, who came from King's County (Offaly), had known Seán MacDermott for quite some time. He knew that the lame man now standing before the court had for many years been up to his neck in revolutionary nationalism. Since MacDermott had surfaced in Richmond Barracks nine days ago, Hoey had looked forward to getting to grips with a man whose ideology he had little time for, and whose methods he despised. Hoey now testified that he knew MacDermott, by both his English and Irish names, and that MacDermott had a long-standing association with the Volunteer leadership.

Lieutenant Ruxton of the Royal Irish Regiment, who had spoken with MacDermott briefly on the morning of 30 April in Sackville Street, was next to testify. He recounted having asked the curious-looking man, whose leg seemed to be paralysed, how he had got into such an affair. He then paraphrased MacDermott's response – that he had his place within the organisation. When MacDermott's turn came to cross-examine, he asked Ruxton if he had seen him with a weapon at the time. Ruxton said he had not.

Next up was Lieutenant Dowling of the Royal Irish Rifles, who testified that MacDermott had surrendered to him on 29 April with 23 other men. MacDermott asked Lieutenant Dowling the same question – whether he had had a weapon – and Dowling confirmed that MacDermott had been unarmed.

Colonel Fraser testified that MacDermott was a prisoner in Richmond Barracks and had been since 30 April. He then produced a document marked 'D'. This was the mobilisation order that had been handed to him in the gymnasium by the NCO on that day. Detective Hoey looked on, satisfied that the pieces were finally falling into place.

Fraser was succeeded by the prosecution's trump card, a witness who had only recently surfaced. He was Edward Gannon, a clerk at Mountjoy Prison. Gannon testified that MacDermott had been held in Mountjoy between May and June 1915. He then produced what turned out to be the final piece of the prosecution's jigsaw – the prison's cash and property register. On MacDermott's release the previous year he had signed it to retrieve his property, using the Irish form of his name – Seán MacDiarmada. Gannon was then presented with document 'D' – the mobilisation order – to check if the two signatures matched. They did. MacDermott's fate was sealed.[13]

MacDermott's trial ended, and he followed the others back out to the green. He sat down next to Frank Thornton, Harry Boland and Gerald Crofts. The four men were talking about their trials when the arrival of a taxi caught their attention. To their surprise, Eoin MacNeill, the 48-year-old history professor and executive head of the Irish Volunteers, alighted from the cab under a small guard of soldiers. MacNeill had issued the countermand order calling off the Rising the day before it was originally due to begin. Many of those who had turned out to fight detested him for this decision and held him responsible for the military failure of the Rising. He had been arrested several days earlier and held elsewhere until now. When MacDermott saw him, he struggled to his feet. MacNeill walked towards MacDermott, extending his hand. MacDermott turned his back and walked away. MacNeill was then brought into a nearby building.

MacDermott, Thornton, Boland and Crofts were ordered to march to Kilmainham Gaol, escorted by two dozen British soldiers. Boland did his best to support MacDermott; Crofts did the same for Thornton, who was suffering from a leg injury sustained during the fighting. As they trundled along, the sympathetic reaction from civilians inspired them. Shouts and cheers of encouragement came from open-topped trams making their way to and from the city centre. Old men stood on street corners and saluted them.[14] As the clusters of civilians quickly grew into small crowds, the soldiers pushed and shoved people out of their way. Then, as the four prisoners finally entered the gaol, Seán MacDermott stopped and turned to the three other men. He shook their hands and said: 'I will be shot, and it will be a bad day for Ireland that I am not.'[15] Then he looked at each man. 'You must carry on from where we have left off.'[16] MacDermott's three comrades nodded in agreement; then all four of them were led away to cells.

When the courts martial in Richmond Barracks were finished, Colonel Sapte and the members of his court were driven from Richmond Barracks to Dublin Castle. They had one more man to try that day: James Connolly.

By 5 p.m., Connolly had been propped up in his bed and made as comfortable as possible. Orderlies brought in five wooden chairs and placed them around his bed. Three chairs were for the men overseeing the proceedings: Colonel Sapte, Colonel Bent, and Major Woodward; another was for the prosecutor, Lieutenant Longworth; and the fifth was for witnesses.

Connolly grimaced in pain as the first witness took his seat. It was the same Lieutenant King who had given evidence against the Pearse brothers and Tom Clarke the previous week in Richmond Barracks. King now testified to having seen Connolly dressed in a Volunteer uniform, armed, and issuing orders to break windows in the Metropole Hotel. When Connolly was allowed to cross-examine the witness, one of his questions referred to King's treatment as a prisoner. King replied, 'We were very well treated generally by the rebels.'[17]

Longworth re-examined King, asking him to recount his memory of the abandonment of the GPO on the evening of 28 April. King testified that when the prisoners, including himself, were released as a result of the evacuation, they were told to make a run for it. They were then fired on by the rebels and two of his comrades were hit. He then, however, backtracked on his claim that the rebels had fired the shots, suggesting that he could not be sure if British troops had also been firing at the same time, conceding by implication that his comrades may have been inadvertently shot by their own side.

When King was dismissed, Major de Courcy-Wheeler took his place in the witness chair. He produced as evidence a surrender order from 'P. H. Pearse'. The order had been written by Pádraig Pearse on 29 April and subsequently signed by Connolly when he was being detained and treated in Dublin Castle. The major had then personally brought the note to Commandant Mallin in the Royal College of Surgeons the same day, to confirm to him that the formal surrender of the Citizen Army had now been ordered by its commander – James Connolly. The note was handed to Colonel Sapte, who then passed it to Colonel Bent and Major Woodward.

Lieutenant Jackson appeared next. He produced one of the documents found on John MacBride as he entered the Richmond Barracks gymnasium on 30 April. The document had been signed by James Connolly. Jackson was then presented with the document Sapte had been given by Major de Courcy-Wheeler, and asked to compare the signatures. He confirmed that they were the same. Colonel Sapte then examined both, as did his officer colleagues.

Next to testify was a lieutenant from the Royal Fusiliers named Chambers. He had also been a prisoner of the rebels in the GPO. He recounted having been tied up in a telephone box in the building for three hours. He added that he had seen Connolly, dressed in a dark green uniform and wearing a military-style hat with a feather in it, issuing orders that related to firing from the Metropole Hotel.

When Connolly cross-examined Chambers he again homed in on the treatment of the prisoners in the GPO. Chambers replied, 'The rebels did their best for us whilst we were in the Post Office.'[18] When Connolly asked him if it was he himself who had ordered the men to tie him up in the telephone box, Chambers turned to Colonel Sapte and said: 'I did not hear the accused order me to be tied up in the box.'[19] However, Chambers did claim that one of the insurgents who had tied him up had spoken to Connolly just moments before.

Connolly had prepared a written statement earlier in the day, anticipating that circumstances would compel him to make one. He began: 'I do not wish to make any defence except against charges of wanton cruelty to prisoners.'[20] He went on to suggest that these were 'trifling allegations' and that there was not a shred of evidence of cruelty to or deliberate harm of unarmed prisoners. He paused, then spoke even more resolutely. Summoning all his strength, he said that he and his comrades had gone out to establish an Irish Republic and to break the bonds with the British Empire. He concluded, 'I personally thank God that I have lived to see the day when thousands of Irishmen and boys and hundreds of women and girls, were equally ready to affirm the truth and seal it with their lives if necessary.'[21] Then his court martial was over. As the officers stood, the soldiers in the room leaped to attention. The officers left, and the infantrymen were once again told to stand at ease.

Soon afterwards, Lillie and Nora Connolly arrived at Dublin Castle. They were immediately escorted to the room where the court martial had taken place. The number of armed guards with bayonets fixed greatly disconcerted Lillie. She reasoned to herself that her husband was badly wounded and confined to a bed, and did not warrant such a demonstration of force. The display did little to dispel her escalating fears for her husband of 26 years. When she spoke with him it seemed her fears were justified. When she asked him if he was in pain, he said there was no pain, but he had just been court-martialled. Nora feared that if the authorities had been prepared to court-martial her father when he was unable to sit up in his bed, they would probably not hesitate to shoot him, despite his wounds.[22]

As they talked, James asked Lillie to pass a message to Francis Sheehy Skeffington. He wanted Sheehy Skeffington, who had been a freelance writer and journalist, to get his songs published, and to give the proceeds to Lillie. Neither Lillie nor Nora said anything about the summary execution of Sheehy Skeffington that they now knew had taken place in Portobello Barracks during Easter Week. The fact that James was giving such instructions betrayed the fact that he expected to be dead soon himself. The women looked at one another, trying to conceal their own heartbreak, while trying not to add to James's by telling him of Sheehy Skeffington's death.

They then spoke in hushed tones about the Rising. Nora told James about Commandant Mellows and the Volunteers in Galway. The newspapers said that the Galway Volunteers were still fighting. James heaped praise on the women and girls who had helped in the fight. He then spoke of his son Roddy and his recent release from Richmond Barracks. Nora told of events in the north. Pádraig Pearse had sent Nora and her sister to muster the Volunteers' Northern Division. She spoke now of the great sense of frustration she had felt when both she and her sister had subsequently walked back to Dublin from Dundalk, only to arrive after the fighting had finished. She added, as if ashamed, 'I did nothing.' Her father reached over and held her, saying, 'I think, my little woman, you did as much as any of us.'[23]

Connolly then turned to his wife. His face seemed to light up when he spoke of one of his stretcher-bearers during the evacuation of the GPO. He was just a youngster, but whenever a bullet came anywhere close to hitting the stretcher he had manoeuvred his body to cover him. When Connolly had asked the youngster his age he had replied, 'I am just fourteen, Sir.' Connolly then looked distant as he then spoke to Lillie and Nora for the last time that evening, saying, 'We cannot fail now. Those young lads will never forget.'[24]

As evening began to draw in, an NCO told Lillie and Nora that their time was up. Soon they left the castle, walking as briskly as they could, aware that the curfew was shortly to come into force in the city. For James Connolly's family, Tuesday was a long night.

14

The Final Executions and an Unexpected Visitor to Richmond Barracks

'Jaysus, lads, we're in the Gresham'

As Lillie and Nora Connolly were making their way home from Dublin Castle, a meeting was taking place in the majestic King's Inns buildings – the law school situated between Henrietta Place and Broadstone. A DMP sergeant named Fox had been summoned there by Laurence Darcy, the institution's butler.

The reason for the meeting was that a young cellar-boy named George Fitzgerald, who worked at O'Rourke's public house at 177 North King Street, had earlier contacted Darcy, whom he knew from Darcy's regular visits to O'Rourke's. Fitzgerald understood that, as a butler, Darcy was a man of significant influence.

Fitzgerald had been washing bottles in the pub's cellar when he noticed a heavy, pungent smell. He had investigated further, pulling beer barrels out of his way as he sought the source of the growing stench, until he noticed that his boots were wet with what looked like blood. It was coming from under his feet. Terrified, he had sought out Darcy and told him of his disturbing discovery. Darcy assumed that Fitzgerald was afraid to go to the police himself, and that this was why the boy had contacted him. When Sergeant Fox heard this he immediately had the information relayed to Dr Matthew Russell of the Public Health Department.[1] An investigation was scheduled for the following morning.

Just before midnight on Tuesday, General Maxwell telegraphed London to inform his superiors that James Connolly had that day been deemed medically fit for trial, and had subsequently been tried and found guilty. He added that both Connolly and Seán MacDermott would be executed at dawn on the morning of 11 May.

On the morning of Wednesday 10 May, Dr Russell arrived at O'Rourke's pub. Michael Moynihan, the borough surveyor, accompanied him, as did the cellar-boy, Fitzgerald. When they descended into the cellar Fitzgerald pointed to the area where he had made his grim discovery. On discovering an area of freshly dug clay, Moynihan and Russell marked out the area before alerting a colleague of Dr Russell's named Travers. Soon afterwards, Travers arrived, followed by several of the department's sanitary staff. The marked area was then excavated.

The first discovery was a man's cap. As they dug further they began to expose a man's decomposing body. When these remains were removed, another corpse was discovered underneath. They immediately sent for the police.

James Healy and Patrick Bealen had both been missing since Saturday 29 April. Healy had been attempting to get to work, despite the frenetic battle still raging that day, when he had gone missing. Bealen, the pub's foreman, had been taken away by soldiers on the same day.

Soon after the arrival of the police, a crowd gathered outside the pub. Among them was James Healy's wife. When she heard that bodies were being removed from the cellar she was overwhelmed by dread. She rushed to the building's entrance, only to be refused access. When she persisted, the police ordered her to return home. Within minutes of her arrival home, Mr Moynihan turned up, holding a small piece of paper that had been taken from the pocket of one of the corpses. When she saw the handwriting, she knew for sure that her husband was dead. A short time later, Catherine Bealen identified the body of her own husband, Patrick.

These suspicious deaths added to the growing unease in London over unlawful killings by British Army men in Ireland. Indeed; on the same morning, Dublin was again taking centre stage in London's corridors of power. In the Horse Guards building, Major Sir Francis Fletcher Vane had an audience with Lord Kitchener. Vane had been stationed in Portobello Barracks during the Rising. When he was confronted with what appeared to be a cover-up in Irish Command relating to the shootings there on 26 April he had considered taking matters to Kitchener himself. The final straw was when the intelligence officer based in Dublin, Major Ivor Price, had spoken to him of the shootings, saying, 'Some of us think it was a good thing Sheehy Skeffington was put out of the way.'[2] Vane now sought out the man in charge – the Secretary of State for War.

Following his meeting with Vane, Kitchener relayed the information without delay to his Prime Minister, who in turn demanded a full explanation. Kitchener then telegraphed General Maxwell in Dublin, requesting a full account of events. Maxwell's response read: 'Skeffington was shot on morning 26th April, without the knowledge of the military authorities. The matter is now under investigation.'[3]

That afternoon, when the Prime Minister took his seat in the House of Commons, William O'Brien MP, of the Irish Parliamentary Party (IPP), spoke of the executions in Dublin. Coincidentally, O'Brien, a namesake of the ITGWU leader currently held at Richmond Barracks, had been imprisoned in Kilmainham Gaol himself in 1881, along with Charles Stewart Parnell. O'Brien asked the Speaker, 'Does the number of executions published include the case of Mr Sheehy Skeffington and two others who were murdered, without any form of trial, by a subordinate officer?'[4] Harold Tennant, the Under Secretary of State for War, replied that he did not know for certain at that point if they were included.

As arguments began to rage across the floor of the House, IPP Deputy Leader John Dillon, who had also served time in Kilmainham in 1881, asked if any further secret trials and executions had been carried out since the four executions of the previous Monday. Asquith replied: 'The trials by court-martial of those who took an active part in the rising in Dublin are practically finished, and, beyond two sentences which have already been confirmed, we have the best reasons for hoping and believing that there may be no further necessity to proceed with the extreme penalty.'[5]

Dillon asked the House if any of the prisoners had been shot without trial. Then he sought an explanation of the shooting of Mr Sheehy Skeffington. This was followed by another question from IPP member Tim Healy regarding the other two men – Thomas Dickson and Patrick McIntyre – who had been shot along with Sheehy Skeffington. He asked if the Prime Minister had enquired if these men had been shot without trial. Asquith referred to the telegram sent by General Maxwell to Kitchener stating that the matter was under investigation. He added that the officer at the centre of the enquiry had been under arrest since 6 May. Asquith had avoided answering John Dillon's question about whether there had been further executions since 8 May. Dillon, unsatisfied with this, called for an adjournment of the House until the following day. The House agreed.

At 4.35 p.m. on Wednesday, Prime Minister Asquith, having by now returned to Downing Street, sent a telegram to General Maxwell: 'No more executions until further orders.'[6] All evening, a series of telegrams flowed between the two men. That same evening, however, both James Connolly and Seán MacDermott received official word that they had been sentenced to death. Sentence was to be carried out at dawn the following day – 11 May.

At 8 p.m., Father Patrick Browne from St Patrick's Seminary, Maynooth, arrived at Kilmainham Gaol asking to speak with the commanding officer. When he met Major Lennon, he asked if he could see Seán MacDermott, explaining that he was a good friend. Lennon allowed the priest half an hour on his own with MacDermott. With his execution fast approaching, MacDermott paced restlessly around his cell, chain smoking. Father Browne sat on a small stool and listened as MacDermott spoke of personal matters. At one point, he came to the subject of Eoin MacNeill. He suggested the rebellion would have been formidable had it not been for his countermand order. They continued speaking – for far longer than the 30 minutes allocated by Major Lennon.

At 10.45 p.m., General Maxwell, now back at the Royal Hospital Kilmainham, was feeling uneasy about the executions scheduled for the following dawn. The frequency of the telegrams bouncing back and forth all evening suggested the government was feeling ambiguous. Seeking clarification, he now sent a message asking if he should commute the sentences. An hour later the response arrived: 'Do not commute the sentences ... But suspend execution until further orders.'[7] A flurry of telephone calls followed. One was the instruction to stand down the night's firing parties. Another went to Major Lennon. When Lennon received it, he sent notification to the nearby DMP station. MacDermott had provided a list of those he wished to see before his death. This was now no longer necessary, considering the change in circumstances. Any police escorts could now stand down. He then went to MacDermott's cell, where he was surprised to see Father Browne still sitting there, almost four hours after having been admitted. Lennon gave

MacDermott the news. MacDermott turned to the priest, saying, 'It is only postponed, but you never know! Life is sweet.'[8]

Major Lennon and Father Browne then left MacDermott fashioning a pillow by wrapping his coat around his boots. Lennon asked Father Browne to join him in his office. He warned him about going home during the curfew, advising him to stop immediately if challenged by soldiers. He asked him if he would have a drink with him. Then, when the priest accepted, Lennon confided that he did not think there would be any more executions.[9] Browne noticed a look of relief on Lennon's face as he spoke.

General Maxwell had a restless night. Shortly after sunrise on Thursday 11 May, he summoned Lieutenant Brucknill. Over breakfast, they drew up a memo that Maxwell called 'A Short History of Rebels'. In the memo, he placed the executed into three categories: A – those who had signed the proclamation, including James Connolly and Seán MacDermott; B – those in command of rebels who had shot soldiers, police and civilians; and C – those found guilty of murder. He placed Thomas Kent in the third category. The memo was telegraphed to London.

At 8 a.m. the same morning, after tea and dog biscuits were served to the remaining prisoners in Kilmainham Gaol, two Black Marias stood by outside, ready to transport another contingent of prisoners to Mountjoy. Those leaving 'His Majesty's Hotel' this morning included Harry Boland, Thomas Ashe, Frank Thornton and Éamon de Valera. In Richmond Barracks, meanwhile, charge sheets were handed to those who were to be court-martialled that day. The process was relentless.

At 2 p.m., Father Aloysius visited James Connolly in Dublin Castle. He found Connolly suffering terribly with his ankle, which had been operated on recently. He was feverish from infection and had barely slept since his wife and daughter left the previous evening. Realising that Connolly needed to rest, Aloysius decided to return the following day in the hope that he would be more amenable to a visit. He then left, but just after he walked beneath the Castle Gate a sudden feeling of trepidation overcame him. He went back to the castle, seeking Captain Stanley's reassurance that nothing was in danger of happening to Connolly that night.[10] After searching for what seemed like hours he eventually located Stanley, who was happy to reassure the priest. It seemed that a huge weight had been lifted from his shoulders when he said, 'No, nothing; have you seen the papers? Asquith promised there will be no more executions pending a debate which is on tonight.'[11] Aloysius, tremendously relieved, thanked Captain Stanley and left, feeling similarly unburdened.

At the same time, the political and military grapevines in London were buzzing with rumours coming thick and fast from Dublin. Both Prime Minister Asquith and Lord Kitchener knew that most of them, such as the story about a massacre of 50 men at Dublin's Royal Barracks, could simply be ignored. However, the previous day's revelation of bodies being dug up in a pub cellar in North King Street was most disconcerting. Another victim of Captain Bowen-Colthurst's murderous rampage in Rathmines had become known. The captain had shot James Coade, an unarmed teenager, with his revolver at close range on the street. The drip feed of such revelations was causing growing consternation in London. Asquith wanted to put an end to it. He decided that the best course of action was to get the last executions out of the way once and for all, and draw a line under them. He was satisfied with Maxwell's earlier memo categorising those sentenced to death, and now wanted to have done with it. Shortly before 3 p.m., Kitchener sent Maxwell a telegram: 'Unless you hear to the contrary from Mr Asquith you may carry out the extreme sentence of death on MacDermott and Connolly.'[12] Asquith, meanwhile, made his way to the House of Commons.

That evening, the atmosphere in the House was highly charged. The IPP MP Alfred (Alfie) Byrne asked the Home Secretary, Herbert Samuel, if any inquiries were now pending into the deaths of Mr Sheehy Skeffington and four other men who had died in suspicious circumstances in North King Street – in this case number 27. Samuel referred him to the Prime Minister's statement of the previous day – an inquiry would be held.

John Dillon now took the floor. He made a long and impassioned speech in which he declared that the rebels in Dublin had, no doubt, been wrong in their actions; nonetheless, they had committed no acts of savagery. He recounted speaking with General Maxwell about the conduct of the Dublin Fusiliers. Maxwell had spoken highly of their loyalty and their steadfastness during the recent fighting. He then mentioned the sentiment among Dublin's populace at the time of the insurrection, and the support that a great many had shown for the British Army.

Dillon then launched an attack, stating emphatically that the government's actions were turning the tide of public opinion against the same soldiers. The aforementioned loyal civilians were now being driven to sympathise with the rebels and their leaders, a sentiment rapidly spreading through the entire country of Ireland. He went on to detail precisely what he himself had heard of the shooting of Sheehy Skeffington and the other two victims of Bowen-Colthurst. He painted an ugly picture of a madman at the helm of a platoon of unquestioning infantrymen, running amok on the streets of Dublin, who, at least thus far, appeared unaccountable for their actions.

Dillon's tone became even more vehement when he spoke of the executions in Kilmainham Gaol. He insisted that the government could not understand the damage they were doing. He conceded the point that if a man committed murder he must, of course expect a trial – and justice – but that the men being shot by military firing squads were insurgents. He went on to say: 'It is insurgents who have fought a clean fight, a brave fight, however misguided, and it would be a damned good thing for you if your soldiers were able to put up as good a fight as did these men in Dublin – three thousand men against twenty thousand with machine-guns and artillery.'[13]

Then Dillon came to Thomas Kent's case, driving home the point that his rapidly orchestrated court martial and subsequent execution were as unjust and counterproductive as the cases of the other 12 men executed so far in Kilmainham.

Asquith referred to Maxwell's 'Short History of Rebels' memo to rebuff Dillon's protests. He explained the general's methodology in drawing up the memo, and insisted that each of the 13 men executed so far fell into one of the three categories in the memo: those who had signed the Proclamation of the Provisional Government, of whom five had so far been executed; those in command of rebels, of whom seven had been executed; and, finally, those guilty of murder – for which Thomas Kent had been tried and sentenced. He spoke of the two other men recently sentenced to death. He had received confirmation from General Maxwell that both had signed the proclamation, and that one of them – James Connolly – was the most active of all the rebels. He then stated: 'I do not see my way, and the Government do not see their way, to interfere with the decision of Sir John Maxwell that in these two cases the extreme penalty must be paid.'[14]

The Prime Minister then spoke of General Maxwell's actions since his arrival in Dublin on Friday 28 April. He praised the general for displaying discretion, humanity and depth of mind, and repeated that he had no intention of interfering with the general's actions. Finally, he said, 'I have come to the conclusion that it is my duty, without delay, to go to Ireland, which I propose to do in the course of a few hours, not with any intention of superseding the executive authority there, I need hardly say, but for the purpose of consulting at first hand with the civil and military authorities.'[15]

In Bow Street in Dublin, at 9 p.m. Captain Stanley, having been driven by motor car from Dublin Castle, knocked at the Capuchin Friary's doors. When a priest answered the door, Stanley asked for Father Aloysius. When they spoke moments later, Stanley told him in a subdued tone that his services would be required at 2 a.m. the following morning. He added, 'I am not at liberty to say more.' He did not need to.

At midnight, a British Army motor ambulance arrived at the house where the Connolly family were still staying. The officer knocked at the door and said he was looking for Lillie Connolly. He told her that James Connolly was very weak and wished to see his wife and eldest child.[16] As they got into the motor ambulance Lillie apprehensively asked the officer if they were going to shoot her husband. The officer, however, told her he could say nothing more.

When the ambulance reached Dublin Castle Lillie and Nora climbed the same staircase as on their previous visit, which this time was lined with soldiers; some were dozing, while others, in full equipment, stood at attention. Lillie and Nora's hearts were palpitating at the news they feared they were to hear. As they entered the room, James looked over at them, saying, 'Well, Lillie, I suppose you know what this means?'[17] Lillie broke down, protesting, 'Not that, James, not that!' Her husband replied, 'Yes, it is. They woke me at 11 p.m. to tell me I was to die.' Her heart sank as she exclaimed, 'Your beautiful life, James!' Connolly consoled his wife. 'Hasn't it been a full life and isn't this a good end?'[18] He then looked at Nora, told her not to cry and, gently patting her hand, whispered to her to put her hand under the bedclothes. When she did he slipped the written statement he had read to his court martial into her hand for her to smuggle out of the castle.

Connolly tried to cheer his wife and daughter with some of the more humorous stories from the fighting in the GPO. One of these concerned a Dubliner who was unwilling to accept the fact that he could not purchase stamps, even though the building was now the headquarters of a revolution. The man had protested, 'What is Dublin coming to when you cannot buy a stamp at a post office?' The family spoke of shared memories and laid out, as best they could, plans for the family's future without him.

The officer who had escorted them in the ambulance then came and told them that their time was up. Lillie, overcome with grief, could not drag herself away from her husband's bed. Connolly tried to pull himself up from a lying position to embrace her, but was too weak. A nurse named Sullivan stepped forward and gently escorted Lillie from the room. Lillie asked the nurse to get a lock of her husband's hair for her. Nurse Sullivan later fulfilled her request. Nora made it as far as the door, but then turned and ran back to her father, embraced him and kissed him. Connolly's final words to her were, 'Nora, I am very proud of you.'[19] They kissed again and she left.

On the far side of the River Liffey, at roughly 1 a.m., a motor car arrived at the Capuchin Friary on Bow Street. Father Aloysius was standing ready. Father Sebastian accompanied him to Dublin Castle.

Back in Kilmainham Gaol, Seán MacDermott's visitors had arrived. MacDermott had been given final confirmation of his execution several hours earlier and had sent for Min (an old sweetheart) and Phyllis Ryan; his landlady, Elizabeth Dunne; and his accountant, Seán Reynolds, whom MacDermott had summoned to take his last will and testament.

When the formality of dictating his will was out of the way the five sat and talked. MacDermott told them that he held no hard feelings towards those who had not turned out for the Rising, and that he now felt no ill will for Eoin MacNeill. He handed around keepsakes to his visitors. MacDermott dropped the occasional hint to the others to leave himself and Min Ryan alone in the cell to say their final goodbyes, but they seemed to fall on deaf ears. MacDermott chain-smoked again as he recounted some of the funnier aspects of the rebellion. To those standing outside the cell there seemed to be many such stories, and the volume of laughter belied the gravity of the occasion. But at 3 a.m., when Father McCarthy entered the cell, the laughter stopped. The priest's arrival reminded everyone why they were there. When the soldier standing guard saw the priest he took it as his cue to call out, 'Time's up.' MacDermott bade his final farewells. Min Ryan went to him before she left, looked into his eyes and whispered: 'We never thought it would end like this, that this would be the end.'[20] MacDermott smiled and simply answered 'Yes'.

Back in Dublin Castle, James Connolly, following his confession and Holy Communion administered by Father Aloysius, was given a light meal while Captain Stanley and Father Aloysius waited outside next to a horse-drawn ambulance. When Connolly had finished his meal he was transferred from his bed to a stretcher, then carried out of the room by a group of soldiers. He was still wearing his pyjamas. A nurse named Lucinda MacDermott clasped his hand and held it as they were led slowly down the staircase, which was lined with silent soldiers and weeping nurses. Connolly was taken to the waiting ambulance. The sky was slowly brightening. When he had been secured in the back of the ambulance a military doctor, Dr Tobin, injected him with a dose of morphine, enough to dull the pain but not enough to render him unconscious. Father Aloysius, Father Sebastian and Dr Tobin climbed into the ambulance, followed by a four-man infantry section, who formed a guard. Father Aloysius asked Connolly if he would pray for the soldiers who were about to shoot him. Connolly replied, 'I'll pray for all brave men who do their duty according to their lights.'[21]

In Kilmainham Gaol, Major Heathcote was overseeing the imminent execution of Seán MacDermott. Moments before 3.45 a.m., Heathcote, standing in the yard adjoining the prison and the Stonebreakers' Yard, gave the order to proceed. MacDermott, by now blindfolded and with a target pinned to his chest, was grabbed by a soldier on either side and hurried out through the first yard, his damaged leg dragging on the ground every couple of steps, forcing the two soldiers to slow down as they took him through the archway that led to the Stonebreakers' Yard. He was placed in front of the firing squad, once again comprising 12 riflemen, six standing and six kneeling. The sandbagged wall had been built up again.

On the officer's silent signal – a raised arm – each infantryman pulled the stock of his rifle firmly into his shoulder and lined up his rifle-sights on the white card ten yards in front of him. In his peripheral vision he was aware of the officer raising his arm, higher again – the signal to present. When the signal was given, his index finger rested on the trigger, giving it the lightest of squeezes. He held his breath, enabling him to focus his aim on the small white card fluttering ever so lightly in the dawn breeze. Then the officer's arm dropped. His finger squeezed harder on the trigger. He heard the deafening crack of the rifles next to him, as well as his own as it recoiled violently into his shoulder, but his body, poised to absorb the force of the four-kilogram weapon, quickly recovered. His eyes were drawn instantly to where he had aimed his shot to see if it was true, but now the white marker was gone, replaced by a wall of bloodstained sandbags. His duty was done. Eleven bullets had struck MacDermott's chest. He had been killed instantly.

Soon after Seán MacDermott's bloody remains were wrapped in a sheet to be labelled and transported, Constable Soughley, who had been on duty that night, left the gaol. Soughley, the police constables sharing his shift and the prison staff were all greatly relieved that the grim work was finished.[22] Military staff cars carrying officers also sped away from the prison. However, just as Constable Soughley and his colleagues stepped into the police station next to the gaol they noticed the staff cars returning. A section of soldiers trotted at the double into the gaol. The policemen also ran back. It was then they noticed the arrival of the horse-drawn ambulance carrying James Connolly, his entourage and his guards.

As the ambulance came to a halt inside the prison yard, Captain Stanley jumped down and issued a blindfold to one of the soldiers sitting in the back. The soldier tied it around Connolly's eyes. Father Aloysius and Father Sebastian alighted, as did Dr Tobin. Tobin briefed Major Heathcote on the condition of the prisoner to be executed. Back in the ambulance, Captain Stanley checked on the man whose care he had overseen for over 12 days. He bade Connolly farewell, and returned to his seat in the front of the ambulance, wanting nothing more to do with the proceedings.

Connolly's stretcher was carefully unloaded from the ambulance and placed next to a chair. One of the soldiers told Connolly that they were about to lift him from the stretcher in such a way that he could stand on his uninjured leg.

Major Heathcote could now see for himself the dreadful condition the prisoner was in. He summoned two members of the firing squad to one side, and instructed them to aim for the head to ensure that Connolly had a quick death. It was abundantly clear to everyone present that this man had suffered enough. The rest of the squad were to train their rifles on the white card marker pinned to Connolly's chest.

When Connolly was placed on the chair his hands groped around and he asked groggily, 'What is it?' A soldier replied: 'It is a chair for you to sit on, Mr Connolly.'[23] The morphine was having the desired effect. The soldiers stretched out Connolly's leg. His head rolled back. His hands gripped the rungs of the chair behind his back as he braced himself. The firing party lifted their rifles as the officer raised his arm. His arm dropped and a volley rang out. Its coarse echoes shattered the stillness, then dissipated. Once again, the air hung heavy with cordite. Spent cartridges were ejected from rifle chambers, still smoking as they fell to the ground. Connolly had died instantly, shot through the heart and head. His broken and bloodied remains were anointed and wrapped, ready for removal, along with MacDermott's. The area was again silent, save for the dawn chorus of birds and the footsteps of soldiers in the prison yards. It was 4.15 a.m. on Friday 12 May. Dr Tobin spoke up suddenly, breaking the silence. He looked to Connolly's wrapped remains and said aloud: 'He was one of the bravest men I have ever known.'[24] Both bodies were transported to Arbour Hill, where Father Farrington once again oversaw their interment. Fourteen bodies now filled the quicklime pit.

Later that morning, most of the women still held in Kilmainham Gaol were released, among them Kathleen Murphy. Seven others – Helena Moloney, Brigid Foley, Marie Perolz, Ellen Ryan, Winifred Carney, Countess Plunkett (mother of the late Joseph Plunkett) and Dr Kathleen Lynn – were transported to Mountjoy Prison. All of them were glad to see the back of the miserable gaol and the gut-wrenching dawn volleys. Mountjoy was a far more welcoming facility by comparison. The wardresses there saw them as something of a novelty compared to the ordinary inmates and did their best for them when they arrived.

In Richmond Barracks, following the customary morning latrine run, Liam Tannam was lining up in front of the barracks cookhouse for breakfast. Tannam could not help but notice that something was different about the barracks this morning. The guards seemed less menacing and the general atmosphere not as tense as on previous days. But further courts martial were scheduled and business as usual appeared to be the order of the day. Tannam could not quite put his finger on it. Then he saw his comrades leaving the cookhouse just as he was about to enter himself. He had to look twice at their plates to confirm that he was not hallucinating from the hunger that had plagued him for as long as he

James Connolly, who was executed on the morning of 12 May 1916. NATIONAL LIBRARY OF IRELAND

could remember. The men's plates were loaded with eggs and ham. When he went inside and reached the top of the line he was offered eggs and ham, as well as bread and butter, cheese, jam and porridge. He breathed in the aroma. A broad Dublin accent behind him shouted boisterously, 'Jaysus, lads, we're in the Gresham,' referring to the hotel in Sackville Street, at which the rest of the queuing men, including Tannam, fell into fits of laughter. He took everything that was on offer. As he made his way back to his barrack room he saw soldiers lining the route, begging for food from the prisoners. Friendly faces among the soldiers were handed tins of jam or hunks of cheese, accompanied by friendly jibes. Those who had been less cordial to their prisoners were passed without a glance. It appeared that the tide was beginning to turn.

As the morning progressed, word began to spread in the barracks of who had been executed that dawn. Reactions were sombre. Word also spread of an important visitor – Prime Minister Asquith. The Prime Minister was presently visiting General Maxwell; then he would call at Richmond Barracks. Every subaltern and NCO in the barracks was under strict orders to have their men ready to present on parade. However, when Asquith eventually arrived, he wanted – to the incredulity of the military officers and men – to see the rebels first, not those who had helped to subdue them. This sent a powerful signal to the prisoners – that they had not fought in vain.[25] Asquith's presence signified that they had succeeded in making their mark; the rebellion had been felt. The British Empire was fighting for its life in a Great War, yet the Prime Minister charged with overseeing that empire, by visiting the barracks with the primary intention of inspecting the Volunteers for himself, betrayed the significance of their cause. As soon as Asquith and his attendants and guards left the barracks, Volunteers' caps flew into the air amid cheers of 'Victory!' The soldiers in the barracks seemed in shock. Many of the Volunteers began to turn on the guards, taunting those who had robbed and humiliated them. Afterwards, Asquith spoke very highly of the impression made upon him by the Volunteers.

In Mountjoy Prison the atmosphere was more subdued. Countess Markievicz received two visitors that day: her younger sister, Eva Gore-Booth; and Eva's lover, the suffragette Esther Roper. Both women had been warned not to mention James Connolly's execution to the prisoner. They were shown into a room and told to stand at a barred window. Across a small corridor there was a large grille, at which Markievicz appeared slowly, almost ghost-like. Her first question was whether Connolly had been shot.[26] Eva and Esther's deafening silence was all Markievicz needed. Tears began streaming down her face. She said despondently, 'You needn't tell me, I know,' before asking in frustration, 'Why didn't they let me die with my friends?'[27]

Later that day, in the exercise yard of Mountjoy Prison, Frank Thornton was walking the circle behind Éamon de Valera. Suddenly, to the astonishment of both men, Prime Minister Asquith stepped into the yard. They had to look twice to be sure it was actually him. As his entourage looked on, Asquith approached de Valera, extending his hand. De Valera ignored him, and simply walked on. Asquith then tried to shake the hands of several more prisoners, only to receive the same response. He and his entourage quickly left. As soon as they had left the Volunteers looked in wonder at one another. It struck them that they might have lost the first battle in Ireland's war for independence, but the war itself was far from over.

Back in Richmond Barracks, Andrew McDonnell and his teenage comrades, now including Vinny Byrne, were lined up on the parade ground. When a sergeant shouted 'Right turn! Quick march!' they feared they were about to be deported. Then the gate was opened and they were marched out. When the gate closed behind them and they realised that there was no escort of soldiers it dawned on them that, astonishingly, they were free to go. One of them cried out, almost in disbelief, 'Oh God, lads, we are out.'[28]

Later that afternoon, Gerald Doyle and 30 fellow prisoners in Mountjoy were unexpectedly handed back their Volunteer uniforms, or, where appropriate, their civilian clothing. When Doyle asked a warder what was happening, he replied that they were 'off to England'. Soon they were loaded once again into Black Marias, which then set off down the North Circular Road towards the port. Just after they had entered Seville Place, Doyle, looking through the grille at the back of his vehicle, saw a friend of his, Harry Tuite, looking on as the vehicles passed by. Tuite was a member of Geraldines Gaelic Football Club, as was Doyle himself. Doyle shouted out: 'Up the Geraldines!' at the top of his voice. It took Tuite a few moments to realise who had called out. Minutes later, when Doyle was walking up the gangplank to a waiting ship he heard a shout: 'Good luck Ger! Up the Geraldines!' It was Tuite. Doyle laughed and waved at his friend. Then he and his comrades disappeared into the bowels of the ship.

Doyle's was not the last of the deportations from Dublin. For weeks afterwards, Volunteers and suspected Volunteers, as well as those who had yet to be court-martialled, would follow. Meanwhile, in Dublin, the aftermath of the executions had left a bitter taste in people's mouths. This, together with the continuing revelations of murders and cover-ups relating to episodes such as those in Rathmines and North King Street, and the continuing deportations and internments without trial of those completely innocent of involvement in Easter Week, set the scene for a backlash that General Maxwell simply did not see coming.

15

Internment

'I could wipe my nose with the skin of my belly'

Most of the Volunteers and Citizen Army who were deported after the Rising, as well as hundreds of civilians who had played no part, were for a time scattered throughout England's prisons before being marshalled together in Frongoch Internment Camp, three miles to the west of the village of Bala, in north Wales. Séamus Grace, having endured a sea crossing to Holyhead so rough he had expected the boat to capsize, was initially sent in his stinking uniform to Wakefield Prison in Yorkshire. He was held there alongside many other no less dishevelled prisoners, including Joe O'Connor, Séamus Daly and Michael Staines.

All the prisoners in Wakefield were kept in solitary confinement for the first few weeks. They were only released from their cells for an hour, or slightly longer, each day. Hunger was a constant companion, as was cold. When rumours filtered into the prison regarding the continuing executions in Kilmainham, messages were tapped in Morse code on cell walls to communicate the news. Those without fellow Volunteers in adjoining cells heard the same messages shouted by their comrades from cell windows. Communications and conditions eventually improved. Prisoners could now exercise together, a luxury that was soon augmented by visits from groups of Irishwomen from the nearby city of Leeds offering support in the form of food and clothing.

Grace, O'Connor, Daly and Staines were sent to Frongoch by train with their fellow inmates in June 1916. Frongoch was originally a German prisoner-of-war (POW) camp that held 1,800 prisoners. All but three of the Germans had been removed by the time the first contingent of Republican prisoners arrived. One of those who was left was dying of consumption. His only vocabulary was a selection of swear words taught to him by the prison guards.

Frongoch was selected as an internment camp because of its location, close to the ports of Holyhead and Liverpool. Additionally, the authorities believed that the local population would be hostile towards the internees. This was later discovered to be untrue. Many of them were native Welsh speakers, and sympathised to a degree with the Irish nationalist cause.

The camp was divided into two sections – the north and south camps. By the time the prisoners had arrived, the north camp (known as Camp 2) was in the final stages of construction; it would eventually contain 27 wooden huts, each of which would hold 25 men. The south camp (Camp 1) was positioned on the site of an old granite-walled distillery that had been appropriated by the British government in 1914 and converted into a POW camp. Its three-storey storehouse was converted into dormitories. The two German POWs whose grasp of English was better than their dying comrade's were quick to point out to the Volunteers that the south camp was better than the north camp. The south camp was uncomfortably warm and stuffy during the summer months; however, the north camp was unbearably cold in winter. The Irish prisoners nicknamed them Purgatory and Siberia respectively. The first Republican internees entered Frongoch on 9 June.

The camp's commandant, Colonel Frederick A. Heygate Lambert,[1] who spoke with a lisp, did his best to antagonise the prisoners at every opportunity. He got off to a bad start with his charges just after they arrived, earning the nickname 'Buckshot' when he threatened to shoot the prisoners with buckshot cartridges from the guards' shotguns should they try to escape. He did little to improve his standing among the prisoners as time passed. He delegated the day-to-day running of the camp to his adjutant, Lieutenant Burns.

Soon after arriving in Frongoch, O'Connor, Grace and Daly, and many others, were summoned to the Sankey Commission in London. This was a commission of inquiry into the Easter Rising under the supervision of Lord Sankey, a Labour politician and High Court judge. The purpose of the commission, which sat in Wandsworth and Wormwood Scrubs prisons, was to filter out those whom the authorities considered to be the least dangerous. They were, after all, being held without trial, and the authorities were keen to avoid the embarrassment of being seen to be bypassing the rule of law by detaining so many in such a fashion. Lord Sankey appeared to be under the impression that the rebel prisoners had been fundamentally misled by their leaders. All the rebel prisoners in Frongoch were compelled to attend the commission at some point, travelling to London in groups of 30 or so.

When Séamus Daly was travelling from Frongoch to London by train to attend the commission, both his and his comrades' rations were accidentally left behind in the camp. In an act of kindness similar to that displayed by Captain Hitzen and his officer colleagues in the Royal Dublin Showgrounds on 30 April, the British officer in charge of the prisoners' escort ordered his men to share their rations with them, then used his own money to buy them tea. Later, while they were on their way to Wandsworth in south-west London, Daly was even more surprised by the uplifting sight of dozens of tricolour flags being flown from the front and back gardens of houses in the Irish districts they passed through.

When Séamus Grace stood before Lord Sankey he was perturbed at what the British appeared to know about his involvement in the Battle of Mount Street Bridge. He had been advised by Terence MacSwiney, a Volunteer commander from the Cork Brigade, to say nothing to the inquiry. The advice was heeded. Séamus Daly's experience of the inquiry was significantly more cordial than Grace's. He was allowed to explain the reasons why he had fought in the Rising before being asked if he would like to see his family again. The question betrayed Lord Sankey's opinion that Daly did not pose any further threat, and he was released from Frongoch with the first of the Republican prisoners in August 1916. Joe O'Connor was also released at the same time. Séamus Grace and Michael Staines enjoyed no such fortune, however. Both were detained in Frongoch, where Staines was made commandant of the prisoners on 30 June.

Other deported prisoners were sent initially to Knutsford Prison in Cheshire, near Manchester, before being transferred to Frongoch. Knutsford had been converted into a prison for British soldiers the previous year and many of the guards there were prisoners themselves. They did not really know what to make of their Republican captives when they first arrived. They were neither prisoners of war in the official sense, nor criminals in the ordinary sense – other than having committed the crime of taking up arms for a cause. Nevertheless, they felt little affection for them. The 99-year-old prison, known locally as 'Knutsford Hotel', was bleak. It was always bitterly cold, whatever the weather, apart from the uppermost floor, which became unbearably hot during summer.

Frank Robbins was among the first detachment sent to Knutsford on 1 May. When he first landed in Holyhead he was subjected to a venomous barrage of abuse by onlookers, who shouted at him and his comrades, accusing them of being traitors and murderers. Once they were on board the train to Knutsford, however, the abuse stopped. To Robbins' surprise, for the rest of his journey he found the soldiers guarding them much kinder than those in Dublin. It would be his last agreeable surprise for quite some time.

When Robbins eventually arrived at the prison he slept in his cell for two days, completely worn out. The Volunteers who accompanied him there included Arthur Shields, Seán O'Duffy and Joe Good. A dreadful regime awaited. Good was kept in solitary confinement for two months and subjected to repeated abuse from a particularly vicious sergeant. Others who followed them to Knutsford, two days later, on 3 May, included Richard Mulcahy, Joseph Lawless, Thomas Pugh, Robert Holland and William J. Brennan-Whitmore. On the train from Holyhead to Knutsford some of the British soldiers on board were as good-natured as those who had travelled with Frank Robbins. They shared cigarettes with the Volunteers. The Volunteers themselves were in a sorry physical state, and their clothing reeked from the filthy conditions on the cattle-boat. When Voluntary Aid Detachment (VAD) women – who provided field nursing to British soldiers – saw their pitiful condition they handed them food, only to react angrily when they later discovered who they really were.

The solitary confinement that awaited each prisoner in Knutsford was a cruel experience. They were plagued with hunger; Robert Holland complained to a comrade through a cell window, 'I could wipe my nose with the skin of my belly.'[2] What meagre food they did receive was of the poorest quality. After each meal Holland would lick his thumb and use it to collect the crumbs that fell to the floor of his cell. To alleviate the terrible boredom, he counted the bricks in the cell walls, frequently hoping to get it wrong and have to repeat the same futile exercise. He improvised a calendar to count the days by scratching vertical lines into the wall, seven at a time, crossing off each day and week with a horizontal line. He stuck a nail he had found into his cell floor to act as a sundial, calibrating it to the daily arrival of what passed for dinner, which was brought to the cells at noon. At times, he counted the flies climbing his cell walls, occasionally bidding the insects 'good morning' when he rose from his wooden plank bed.

Other Volunteers occupied themselves with such mundane activities as flipping buttons and then trying to find them on the floor with their eyes closed, fearing they would lose their minds otherwise – and some did. Thomas Pugh had his bible and all reading materials removed on arrival in the prison and was forced to use his boots as a pillow.

Over the next couple of weeks, word of the leaders' executions in Dublin filtered in from the gloating guards. Frank Robbins learned of Commandant Mallin's execution and Countess Markievicz's life sentence by messages in Morse code tapped on his cell wall – the same means of communication as that employed in Wakefield.

When Liam Tannam arrived in Knutsford on 6 June, he too was placed in solitary confinement. Luckily, he still had some provisions left over from Dublin. The following day he met some of his comrades in the exercise yard and was struck by their shabby beards. Captain Brennan-Whitmore looked like a down-and-out. His trousers, having been ripped to shreds from the fighting in Dublin, were now also badly discoloured from being disinfected in the prison. As Tannam walked in circles around the yard he began eating an orange. He was horrified at the sight of Volunteers behind him scrambling to devour his discarded peels. The following day he shared his remaining supplies among the starving men.

Nights were a horrendous, and frequently sleepless, ordeal for prisoners struggling to maintain their sanity in Knutsford. On some nights, the incessant yelling of British soldiers under punishment in the lower section of the prison reinforced the brutal atmosphere. Robert Holland wished at times that he had been killed during the fighting, and thanked providence that their executed leaders had been spared the torture of prison.

Despite the appalling conditions, however, the Volunteer prisoners maintained their discipline. When offered a respite from their misery through prison work to assist in the war effort, or even release from the prison itself on the condition that they would serve in the British Army, they refused to aid their enemy in any way. When it was suggested that their recent impressive performances as combatants would see them quickly ascend through the military ranks, they took some cheer from the commendation, but stood their ground.

Complaints about the poor food and the beatings were supressed by the prison governor when several politicians, eager to observe the Volunteers for themselves, visited the prison. One such politician was the prominent IPP member Alfie Byrne. He was almost run out of the prison by angry Volunteers, who mistrusted his motives. Many prisoners felt that the IPP had usurped the Volunteer movement in 1914 for its own ends, and had since condemned the rebellion. Among the prison staff in general there was little sympathy for the prisoners' complaints – as far as they were concerned they were lucky not to be fighting against the Germans in muddy Flanders.

The conditions in Knutsford began to improve. Prisoners received visits from women who travelled from Manchester and Liverpool with food and other items considered mundane in everyday life but lavish by prison standards. The visits were organised by a priest, Father Fogarty, who visited to attend to the prisoners' spiritual needs. Some of the female visitors asked for the men's autographs. Captain Brennan-Whitmore, having by now enjoyed a change of clothing, donated the buttons from his tunic to the women as souvenirs. The grateful Volunteers adored these women. Thomas Pugh's wife lived in Manchester, where she worked as a schoolteacher, and she too was permitted to visit. Letters and parcels were soon allowed in, as were newspapers, which carried reports of the Great War that suggested the British were having a tough time. The Volunteers showed as much support as they could for the Germans as a means of antagonising the guards who had boasted to them of their leaders' executions. They cheered throughout the prison when they heard in early June that Lord Kitchener had been killed. Kitchener's ship had been struck by a German mine near the Orkney Islands and had sunk, killing Kitchener and several hundred seamen.

The Knutsford prisoners were transferred to Frongoch on 17 June. Liam Tannam was sent to the north camp, where he was a hut leader, before being transferred to the south camp, where he was joined by Frank Robbins, among others. Arthur Shields and Seán O'Duffy also ended up in Frongoch, as did Richard Mulcahy, Joe Good and Joseph Lawless.

Volunteer prisoners in Frongoch Camp. NATIONAL LIBRARY OF IRELAND

Generally, there was a sense of novelty among the prisoners when they first arrived in Frongoch, despite the hardships, particularly considering the far worse conditions they had just left. The hilly countryside and the bracing air were a tonic for many. Route marches were organised by the Volunteer officers and the prison guards. Some of the guards, such as the camp's rough-and-ready sergeant major, Newstead, whom the prisoners nicknamed 'Jack-knives',[3] shared a mutual respect with the prisoners. They were, after all, fellow soldiers – albeit on opposing sides. Others treated them with contempt – and the sentiment was reciprocated. In the main, however, the guards, taken from British Home Service battalions, were impressed by the discipline and demeanour of the Volunteers, particularly their penchant for sports such as athletics and football. Games were contested with a fighting spirit that made some of the onlooking guards think they were glad not to have faced these men in combat. The Volunteers named their small Gaelic football pitch Croke Park, after the pitch in Dublin. Concerts, games and debates were held in the camp's damp, draughty, rat-infested dormitories, as well as classes in Irish, bookkeeping and shorthand. Later, these 'classes' evolved into lectures on military tactics, and, perhaps more importantly, how they could be applied most effectively in Irish terrain.

Joe Good, Thomas Pugh and Frank Robbins were soon summoned to the Sankey Commission from Frongoch, as were Joseph Lawless and Captain Brennan-Whitmore. Frank Robbins was kept in Wandsworth while waiting his turn at the commission. Many of his fellow inmates there were English conscientious objectors, who often wondered when the war would end, and who were treated brutally by the guards, who considered them mere cowards. Thomas Pugh was also in Wandsworth at the time of the Sankey Commission. He was incarcerated near a group of Australian military prisoners with whom he struck up a boisterous rapport.

Frank Robbins' experience of the commission was as cordial as Séamus Daly's. Lord Sankey seemed to take a liking to him. When Robbins described his trade as a driller, Sankey asked him jokingly if that was because he 'drilled holes in soldiers'.[4] Robbins, to much laughter from the commission's other attendees, informed him that a driller was a dockyard trade. When asked if he had killed anyone during the Rising he replied, 'I could not say – not being at the other end', referring to his rifle. The response elicited even more laughter.

Joseph Lawless was also held at Wandsworth pending his appearance at the Sankey Commission. At one point he was escorted through London's streets with other Volunteers on a double-decker bus. There was a sense of excitement among them as they saw the vast city. A curious novelty that struck the prisoners was that women seemed to be working everywhere in the city, as the war had by now taken so many of the men.

Thomas Pugh was taken aback by the amiable disposition of the enemy soldiers. On a train heading through London that was packed with both civilians and guards, a particularly boorish Londoner approached him and told him venomously that once he himself got off the train he hoped it crashed and killed the lot of them, meaning Pugh and his comrades. The guards told the man to back off, shouting at him: 'Go away you big fat so and so – these men fought at least.'[5] Similarly, on the train that took him back to Frongoch from London, troops from the London-Scottish Regiment were equally kind, even taking the Volunteers' letters to post for them.

On arrival back at Frongoch, however, he found that not all the Volunteers had had such pleasant experiences at the Sankey Commission. Brennan-Whitmore noticed that many of their senior officers had not returned and had been sent instead to Reading Gaol. The authorities appeared to want the men leaderless. Joe Good, who had been detained at Wormwood Scrubs, near Hammersmith, while in London, returned without five comrades who had provided their names and addresses in advance to the commission. Henceforth no more names would be provided. This tactic of withholding names eventually led to prolonged conflict between the camp authorities and the prisoners. In late autumn things really came to a head. 'Colonel Buckshot' was determined to get the prisoners to reveal their names so that those with English addresses, who would consequently be eligible for conscription into the British Army, could be handed over. This dilemma rode hot on the heels of another dispute – which became known as the 'Ash-pit strike'[6] – when Volunteers were punished for refusing to empty the refuse from the guards' quarters and huts.

'Colonel Buckshot' made numerous attempts to overcome the solidarity of the prisoners during both disputes. He ultimately failed, but not before men had gone on hunger strike, had been incarcerated in punishment blocks and refused privileges, including mail. Paddy Daly maintained a hunger strike for two weeks while in isolation. He was subsequently court-martialled and dispatched to Wilton Gaol in Liverpool where, ironically, he spent two months enjoying better food than at Frongoch, while tending to the prison garden under the direction of the governor, who accepted him as a political prisoner. The governor came to respect Daly, and expressed regret when he was sent back to Frongoch.

The conscription stand-off was not without its tragic side effects. One of the camp doctors, Dr Peters, was instructed by 'Buckshot' to defy his Hippocratic oath and withhold medical treatment from prisoners who refused to identify themselves. This provoked such a crisis of conscience in the doctor that he drowned himself in the nearby river. Both sides in the dispute blamed the other, and mourned the doctor equally.

Eventually, the energetic young men interned in the camp, being more or less left to their own devices, organised themselves along similar military lines to those who had ultimately led them there. This was done under the very noses of those whose aim was to oversee the dissolution of such structures. It also led to the ascent to prominence of men such as Michael Collins, who arrived in Frongoch in July 1916 from Stafford military prison. Collins had been incarcerated in Stafford alongside Frank Henderson, as well as many Volunteers from Galway

Republican prisoners in Stafford Prison 1916. Michael Collins is fifth from the right.
COURTESY OF THE MILITARY ARCHIVES

and elsewhere. The conditions there had been far less severe than in Knutsford.

Once in Frongoch, Collins organised a lot of mischief, creating as much distraction and irritation for his captors as he possibly could. On one occasion, the entire complement of prisoners insisted on a full medical examination at the same time. After much furore their demand was finally agreed to. The camp doctors, somewhat to their astonishment, determined that there was not a single case of venereal disease among the 1,800 prisoners who had been examined, one after the other. A comrade joked afterwards that consequently their prisoner-of-war status no longer applied, i.e. they could not be recognised as an authentic military force until at least some of them had symptoms of VD. A prison doctor in Knutsford had similarly been struck by the absence of venereal disease among the Irish prisoners, in contrast to the British Army, of which he estimated 15 per cent of its rank and file were suffering from the condition at any one time.

As the months passed in Frongoch, many of the camp inmates became increasingly aware that Michael Collins was at his best making war in some shape or form. Collins had worked in the Post Office Bank in London from the age of 15, and his job had fine-tuned his knack for record keeping and number crunching for a decade by the time he returned to Ireland in January 1916 to prepare for his part in the rebellion. He had an almost superhuman memory and a penchant for skulduggery and one-upmanship. The latter talents led many to dislike and dismiss him. His irrepressible confidence grated on some, who saw him as nothing more than an overbearing oaf and egotist, but it also helped him win people over. He did just that with some camp guards and sympathetic local civilians who served the camp, arranging for supplies and small luxuries to be smuggled in, as well as messages and letters to be smuggled out – beyond the reach of the camp's censor. Richard Mulcahy, somewhat less charismatic than Collins but no less formidable, was another whose talents for meticulous organisation and leadership became evident in Frongoch. His frequent lectures on combat tactics regularly alluded to the type of pitiless conflict they could expect to have to fight in the future to free their country from British rule.

Frank Robbins was released at the same time as Séamus Daly, in August 1916, as were Arthur Shields, Charles Saurin, Seán O'Duffy and hundreds of others. Séamus Daly disembarked at Kingstown port one August morning accompanied by Saurin and Shields. This was when they discovered at first hand the positive change in sentiment from Dublin's civilians towards them since their deportations four months earlier. When they boarded a tram to Dublin city to view its ruins they recognised a conductor who had been hostile to them before the Rising, when they had often travelled by tram in their Volunteer uniforms – he now shook their hands. From the city centre, they made their way to Dollymount Strand to enjoy the seaside on their way home. When they arrived at Dollymount they were greeted and cheered by onlookers with shouts of: 'The boys are coming home!'[7] As soon as Daly was settled back at home in Clontarf he began to attend 'dancing classes' – Volunteer meetings. He soon got the Clontarf branch of the Gaelic League up and running again in the town hall. When the general amnesty came in December his Battalion company (F) had already been re-formed. During November 1916, Vice Commandant Cathal Brugha, who had been very badly wounded during the Rising but had since largely

The young Michael Collins in Volunteer uniform. Collins became more prominent as a leader and organiser during his incarceration in Frongoch camp. NATIONAL LIBRARY OF IRELAND

recovered, organised a meeting attended by 50 prominent Volunteer members from across the country. These men had either avoided arrest or had returned from internment. During the meeting, a committee was set up whose purpose was to gather all the fragments of the Volunteer movement and to reunite it. Following the meeting, reorganisation and recruitment began in earnest, including Seamus Daly's 2nd Battalion. The Volunteers then set about taking up the fight once again.

Frank Robbins took a train from Kingstown to Westland Row, where he was struck by the crowds of well-wishing civilians. Word had quickly spread in Dublin of the prisoner releases. The policemen trying to maintain order among them were swept aside by the crowd who surged forward to cheer Robbins and the other Volunteers who alighted from the train with him. He eventually returned to his home in North Strand, where, after a time, he tried to pick up the threads of the Citizen Army in Dublin, but with little success. He ended up making his way to New York, eventually working alongside Liam Mellows in procuring arms for the movement. Arthur Shields, meanwhile, returned to work as an actor in the Abbey Theatre.

In September, following the release of so many comrades in August, the remaining men in Frongoch's north camp were transferred across to the south camp, where they stepped up their campaign of passive resistance. Conditions improved: it was not quite as crowded and stuffy and there was a little more food to go around. Thomas Pugh was one Volunteer among many who, in spite of this, found it very difficult during roll calls to have to listen to the names of prisoners to be released, and not hear his own name. Séamus Grace found it even more frustrating when he and others frequently had to march into the nearby village alongside those being released, knowing he would not be travelling home with them. He and several others considered taking over the village just to put it up to their captors.

In spite of this, Pugh, Grace and the rest of the camp inmates, unbeknownst to them, had only a few months left to wait in Frongoch – but they were cold months. A vicious wind swept constantly from the barren hills, freezing everything in its path. By late 1916 a bitterly cold winter had north Wales firmly in its grip, but even so, it was not enough to chill the spirits of the Volunteers. On one particularly glacial day they built a snowman, complete with Volunteer hat and Sam Browne belt, and with its right hand raised in salute.

Returning prisoners greeted by crowds on Westland Row. NATIONAL LIBRARY OF IRELAND

Christmas 1916 saw all of Frongoch's internees released under a general amnesty. Hundreds of Volunteers, including Joe Good, Thomas Pugh, Séamus Grace, Liam Tannam, Richard Mulcahy, Joseph Lawless, William J. Brennan-Whitmore, Michael Collins, Seán McLoughlin, Patrick and Garry Holohan, found themselves on their way to Dublin again via Holyhead. They still, however, refused to give any names to 'Colonel Buckshot' before they left the camp, despite the colonel's insistence that no one would be given tickets for the trip without first doing so. Their unity held fast, however. 'Buckshot' was forced to relent, and each man returning home had passed out from the Frongoch 'academy' with flying colours.

When the ship ferrying Joe Good and numerous other men arrived in Dublin's docks on Sunday 24 December, the quayside was deserted. However, he noticed a huge change in the demeanour of Dubliners in the city towards himself and his fellow Volunteers. When the festive season was over, Good quickly took up the baton once again as a member of D Company, 2nd Battalion under its commander, Dick McKee.

Thomas Pugh found himself on board a first-class train carriage from Frongoch to Holyhead. The carriage was heated, a fact the passengers greatly appreciated; a brutally cold wind had driven ice and snow into their faces as they waited, shivering, on the station's platform. Once on board, Pugh eagerly went to open a bottle of whiskey he had brought from the camp to celebrate with his comrades. Their exuberance was quickly dampened, however, when they realised that the camp guards, as a parting gesture, had drunk the whiskey themselves and refilled the bottle with water.

When Pugh arrived in Dublin the reception put on for him and hundreds of his fellow travellers was a spectacle he would never forget. The entire length of Westland Row, as well as the surrounding streets, was thronged with supporters. Their cheers were tremendously uplifting. Pugh also immersed himself immediately in the resurrected movement, eventually becoming secretary of his local IRB circle.

Garry Holohan was similarly welcomed back on Dublin's streets following his release from internment. His first port of call following the euphoric reception was to his cottage near Summerhill in Dublin city centre. His good friend and comrade from the fighting of Easter Week, Éamon Martin, who had been badly wounded during the Rising, had been staying at his home. Holohan was shocked to see that Martin was skeletally thin. Martin stayed with the Holohan brothers until New Year's Eve, when he set sail from Kingstown, and ultimately to the USA for recuperation. Paddy Daly, who had led both men during their daring assault on the Magazine Fort, returned home to his family in Clontarf, and soon began to help reorganise his Volunteer company.

Séamus Grace had a different mission in mind when he arrived back in Dublin during Christmas 1916. Having witnessed the enthusiastic welcome given to the Volunteers, he set about acquiring three rifles, and travelled, accompanied by fellow 3rd Battalion Volunteers – Micheál and Seán Cullen – to the graveside of his good friend Lieutenant Michael Malone, who had died fighting alongside him the previous April. Malone's grave, in Glasnevin Cemetery, had been opened for the purpose of identifying his body. He had initially been buried in the garden of 25 Northumberland Road before being re-interred in Glasnevin. Malone's sister Áine had identified her dead brother by his teeth. It was

Séamus Grace (*seated at centre*) and his comrades from the Battle of Mount Street Bridge, pictured in the garden of the deceased Lieutenant Michael Malone's house on Grantham Street, near Dublin's South Circular Road, on the battle's first anniversary. The Walsh brothers, who escaped captivity, are to the left and right of picture. NATIONAL LIBRARY OF IRELAND

almost eight months to the day since her brother had been killed and there had been significant decomposition of his body. However, Grace immediately recognised Malone's bloodstained Volunteer tunic. Three volleys of shots then echoed out in the still and freezing air, fired over Malone's grave in salute by Grace and his two companions.

Grace was reunited with his comrades from the Battle of Mount Street Bridge soon after his return. Four of them – Thomas and James Walsh, James Doyle and Willie Ronan – had made a daring escape from Clanwilliam House during the battle. Ronan, like Grace himself, was captured soon afterwards, but Doyle and both Walsh brothers managed to evade the authorities for months, before coming out of hiding voluntarily in December 1916, awarding themselves a similar 'amnesty' to the rest of their comrades returning from Frongoch. They came together on the first anniversary of the battle – 26 April 1917 – and posed together for photographs in their Volunteer uniforms to mark the occasion in the garden of the late Michael Malone's house in Grantham Street. They, too, were reorganised into their battalion companies. Vice-Commandant O'Connor saw to it that the 3rd Battalion's recruiting net was cast far and wide throughout Dublin's southside, as the Volunteer movement steadily regained traction.

16

Triumphant Return to Dublin

'Good old Ireland – That's the stuff to give them'

Unlike their comrades who had been deported without charge, and ultimately marshalled together in Frongoch, the Volunteers and Citizen Army members who had been court-martialled following the Rising, and since rotated through Mountjoy Prison, found themselves sent to different prisons in England to serve sentences ranging from three years to life.

Frank Thornton was sent to Dartmoor Prison in Devon, accompanied by Harry Boland, Con O'Donovan, Éamon de Valera and Austin Stack – the Commandant of the Volunteers' Kerry Brigade. Commandant de Valera, now the Rising's most senior commander, and Thomas Ashe, the second most senior, demanded POW status. However, the prison's governor, Major E. Reade, did his utmost to treat the prisoners as ordinary convicts. Commandant Ashe had arrived by train, accompanied by Frank and James Lawless, Seán Etchingham, and several others from Wexford. They were escorted by infantrymen of the Sherwood Foresters, who seemed to enjoy the company of the men they were guarding. They appeared particularly impressed with the charismatic persona of Commandant Ashe. Not only did Ashe stand out due to his powerful physique, he also treated his fellow passengers to a multitude of jokes, songs and anecdotes, lifting the spirits of friend and foe alike.

The POW issue became something of an open sore in Dartmoor as the prisoners spent day after day in solitary confinement and enforced silence. They found some consolation in the fact that the guards displayed a good deal more respect for the Republican prisoners than the ordinary inmates who shared their spartan surroundings. Séamus Doyle, who had arrived with Seán Etchingham, was incarcerated in an old part of the prison that had been built to house prisoners from the Napoleonic Wars. The comfort of its inmates had not been high on the architects' agenda. They passed their time making mailbags, longing for home. The authorities' refusal to allow them to receive letters was a particular source of anguish. The prisoners were not allowed to write home until September 1916.

Frank Thornton found the food intolerable and was particularly affected by the cold West Country winds that swept through the prison. To add to his woes, Dartmoor's drinking water contained so much iron that flakes of it would float on the surface of his tea. Over time, this began to cause some painful tooth-decay issues for prisoners. Any complaints about the conditions, however, merely resulted in bread-and-water punishments. Harry Boland was regularly punished; he appeared wholly unable to observe the rule of silence. His gregarious charm, however, endeared him to everyone in the prison, including the chief warder, who took a liking to his irrepressible light-heartedness.

Eoin MacNeill was also a prisoner within the bleak walls of the 107-year-old prison. Commandant de Valera witnessed MacNeill suffering the indignity of a strip-search – performed on all inmates on arrival. Ever the opportunist, de Valera used the occasion to throw down a gauntlet to the prison authorities. Soon after MacNeill was searched he was escorted by guards down a staircase. At the bottom of the staircase 20 prisoners were lined up for exercise. De Valera shouted "Shun [Attention] – eyes left!' When most of the prisoners came smartly to attention de Valera was pushed back into his cell by guards and threatened with flogging. De Valera's fellow inmates understood his meaning, however. He was displaying to the authorities that they were a disciplined military force, saluting their overall commander, and not simply criminals. More important, de Valera was showing who was in charge – himself. De Valera quickly gained a reputation as a firebrand with Major Reade.

As the time passed, Séamus Doyle regularly chatted with Professor MacNeill when the periods of enforced silence had finally passed, some weeks after their arrival. MacNeill confessed during one of these

Captains Séamus Doyle (*top right*) and Seán Etchingham (*centre left*) of the Wexford Volunteers. Both were deported following their courts martial at Richmond Barracks.

exchanges that he was beginning to think that Pádraig Pearse and the other leaders of the Military Council had been right in striking their blow against the Crown when they did, particularly when word began to filter in about the changing attitudes of Dubliners towards the Rising.

In August news came to Dartmoor of Roger Casement's execution in Pentonville Prison, and was greeted with great sadness. Casement, a former knight, had attempted to land in Ireland from a German submarine just before the Rising, having sought aid earlier from Imperial Germany to support it. He was subsequently arrested, tried for treason, and executed.

Following his period of detention in Mountjoy Gaol, Gerald Doyle was sent via Holyhead with others, including Liam Tobin, to Portland Prison on the south coast of England. While they were awaiting a train in Holyhead, they were welcomed by the VAD women, and this time treated to boxes of cigarettes. When the women discovered, to their horror, that they were Irish Volunteer prisoners they reacted angrily, shouting and spitting at them. At another stop on what became a two-day journey, crowds of angry women spat at their train windows. When the train was waiting at Portsmouth station the Volunteers were taken aback to see numerous other trains passing, loaded with huge howitzers. It then struck Doyle just how powerful the empire was that they had taken on with so little. A comrade reassured him, saying that in spite of their defeat in Dublin, what they had done during Easter Week would resound throughout the world. Doyle then thought again of what Tom Clarke had said to him in the cell at Kilmainham about the Rising being merely the beginning. When the train began moving again, a British soldier who had been in Dublin spoke of the fighting there. He said that he initially thought he had arrived in France when his ship had pulled into Kingstown to unload him and his comrades. He added that the fighting in Dublin was 'bloody hot while it lasted.'[1] The soldier then asked Doyle for his rosary beads. He was soon to be sent off to Flanders, and felt he had a far greater need of them.

Portland Prison was located on the eastern side of the Isle of Portland, just to the south of Weymouth in Dorset, and less than a mile from a huge Royal Navy base. Once Doyle, Tobin and the others got to the prison, they, like their comrades in Dartmoor, were put to work making mailbags while being kept in solitary confinement. The only time they could communicate with fellow prisoners was at Mass, and it was here that news filtered in about Roger Casement's trial at the Old Bailey. Word also came in of the increasing number of German Zeppelin raids on London. They prayed for Casement on the morning of his execution.

September provided some relief from the crushing daily monotony for Doyle and his comrades. The entire prison suddenly began to vibrate as if an earthquake had struck. A German U-boat had surfaced in the English Channel within range of the huge naval guns that protected the adjacent base. When the submarine's raised periscope disturbed a flock of seagulls, causing them to take flight from the water's surface, the base's spotters were quick to react, and sent several salvos of high-explosive shells out to sea, each shot making the prison walls reverberate. Some days later Portland saw the feared Zeppelins launch an air raid on the naval base. Most of the prison's inmates were taken to the basements as a precaution. Except for the Irish prisoners – they were left behind in their dank cells.

The following month, word was brought to the Irish prisoners by their chaplain of the release of the first batch of prisoners at Frongoch. Conditions in Portland began to improve at the same time. As the weeks passed, bundles of letters started to arrive from the released Volunteers, filling the prisoners in on what was happening both in Frongoch and at home.

By 13 November, the British authorities had decided to bring all the convicted Republican prisoners together under one roof. They chose Lewes Prison in Sussex. Prison restrictions were to be relaxed. The prisoners were, in effect, to be led to believe that they were receiving political status, which they were not.

Frank Thornton and the other Republican prisoners from Dartmoor were transported in chain gangs to Lewes on 13 December 1916. When asked to give their word that they would not attempt to escape en route, they had refused. After leaving Dartmoor they were viciously attacked at the railway station by civilians. To their surprise, the soldiers guarding them came to their rescue, driving the attackers back with rifle butts and elbows, and shouting to the men among them that at least the prisoners they were guarding had fought for their country, unlike the 'conscription dodgers' now attacking them. The prisoners were then herded into specially assigned railway carriages. When they finally arrived at Lewes they sang rebel songs as they were led into the prison. The prisoners from Portland were also transferred to Lewes at around the same time. Their journey was less dramatic.

The conditions in Lewes were less severe than in Dartmoor and Portland. The prisoners were even treated to Christmas dinner, which they ate with spoons and forks. Gerald Crofts and Seán Etchingham kept them entertained over the festive season – the former with songs and the latter with a barrage of jokes. Thomas Ashe devoted his more creative energies to poetry, writing a poem entitled 'Let Me Carry Your Cross for Ireland, Lord'. Éamon de Valera spent his time in the prison setting up a clandestine communications system with the Volunteers who had returned to Ireland. One of the first communiqués was taken back to Dublin by Gerald Crofts, following his release due to ill-health. Volunteer Captain Simon Donnelly, who had helped oversee an avalanche of supporting fire to his 3rd Battalion comrades during the Battle of Mount Street Bridge during the Rising, and was now back in Dublin from Frongoch, regularly received timed and dated dispatches from his wily commandant.

Following the Roscommon by-election the following February, the mood in Lewes Prison greatly improved. Count Plunkett, as well as being the father of Joseph – whose death at the hands of a firing squad had radicalised him – had two other sons serving in English prisons, George and Jack. His wife's arrest and deportation had further copper-fastened his determination to strike back. He did this by contesting the Roscommon election, which he won, marking the Sinn Féin party's first parliamentary victory. This was a clear sign of the changing political tide in Ireland. Letters soon began to arrive in Lewes Prison stating that 'Caitlín Ní Úallacháin' was well and her health was improving. This was a coded message indicating that the situation in Ireland was getting better from the nationalist perspective. The prison governor, Major R. A. Marriot,[2] having read so many letters with Ms Ní Úallacháin's name while censoring the mail, joked during an address to the prisoners that he would like to meet with this mysterious lady on a trip he was planning to Dublin.

The governor's residence was close to the prison, and at the time was badly in need of renovation. A pragmatic man, the governor knew that a significant proportion of the Volunteers were tradesmen, so he decided on a solution he felt would be favourable both to his own budgetary limitations and to the prisoners themselves. He would ask them to carry out the necessary work, a great deal of which involved painting. The prisoners obliged, glad to have some distraction from the daily

Volunteer Joseph
McGuinness in uniform.
NATIONAL LIBRARY
OF IRELAND

routine. Frank Thornton, whose family ran a decorating business, was among them, as was Gerald Doyle. When the job was completed several weeks later the governor was so delighted with the quality of their workmanship, particularly the painting, that he promised to use his contacts in the Board of Works to secure a job for any man among them, should he request it, on his release. Unfortunately for the governor – or perhaps fortunately – he had no idea of the significance of the colours chosen by the prisoners to paint the house, both inside and out. They painted the walls, doors and windowsills in various shades of green, white and orange – the colours of the Irish tricolour.

Joseph McGuinness, also a prisoner in Lewes since December, had stood as a Sinn Féin candidate in the hotly contested Longford South by-election in May 1917, despite being incarcerated. McGuinness, with the full support of the prisoners in Lewes, had initially refused the nomination, feeling that it would compromise the traditional Republican attitude of contempt for a foreign parliament.[3] Ultimately, however, his nomination stood. Michael Collins, back in Ireland since the previous December, used his boundless energy and his Frongoch-honed penchant for mischief to help push the much-used slogan, 'Put him [McGuinness] in to get him out.' The strategy paid off. McGuinness won the election, after a recount, and by only 38 votes; but this was a huge propaganda victory for the Republicans. The Volunteers now had their own MP in the prison. When news of the hard-fought victory arrived via smuggled newspapers, there was celebration among the prisoners. They used the victory as a means of antagonising the guards. McGuinness was carried shoulder-high while singing broke out throughout the prison – even among the German POWs held there, who shouted 'Good Old Ireland'[4] with characteristic gusto. The Volunteer prisoners returned the compliment by loudly singing a German song they had recently learned, 'The Watch on the Rhine.'[5]

The joviality was, however, short-lived. Commandant de Valera was quick to seize the initiative resulting from both the propaganda victory and the fact that the recently formed, but increasingly vociferous, anti-partition group, the Irish Nation League, had recently called for the Irish prisoners to be treated as POWs. Once de Valera received word from the outside showing support, he ordered the Volunteer prisoners, on 28 May, to refuse to carry out any work whatsoever within the prison owing to their continued lack of full official recognition as political prisoners. The prisoners were then confined to their cells as punishment. The issue quickly escalated into a near riot. As a countermeasure, de Valera was sent to Maidstone Prison in Kent, where he was joined by Séamus Doyle and several others. In Maidstone, de Valera continued the policy of non-compliance, despite numerous confrontations with the prison governor. The Republican prisoners were quick to earn the respect of the guards in Maidstone by refusing to flinch in the face of punishment. Meanwhile, the rest of the Lewes prisoners were broken up into separate groups and dispersed.

Liam Tobin was sent, as punishment for his part in the Lewes disturbances, to Broadmoor Prison on the Isle of Wight. Gerald Doyle was soon on his way back to Portland, accompanied now by Frank Thornton and Peadar Clancy, among others. On the way their train stopped at Southampton and their paths crossed with a trainload of infantrymen from the Royal Dublin Fusiliers, who began shouting abuse at them and calling them 'Casement's Bastards'.[6] At Portland, Doyle and the others continued to refuse to work. They insisted that, come what may, they would stand their ground demanding full political status. The answer from the prison authorities came in the form of bread-and-water punishments, and no light was permitted in the cells of those refusing to co-operate. The standard 'three-day rule', the maximum period of time a prisoner was supposed to endure solitary confinement with no light, was discarded, and the men would be confined for spells of ten days. The only time the prisoners would be allowed to leave their cells was for a once-daily visit to the latrines and to empty out their slop buckets. There was also a weekly visit to the prison barber. No braces or shoelaces were permitted to the prisoners enduring such punishments, as the authorities feared suicide attempts by hanging.

Mercifully for the prisoners, these terrible conditions were short-lived. In June the prison chaplain brought the Volunteer prisoners news of the general amnesty that now applied to all Republican captives in English prisons. In Portland they were overjoyed. The prisoners were now to be marshalled together at Pentonville Prison, transported there by warders, before being sent home to Ireland as free men. The chief warder at Portland implored them to behave themselves and leave peacefully when the time came. They did no such thing. Instead, when Thornton, Clancy, Doyle and the rest of the half-starved Volunteers assembled in the yard they started singing rebel songs, finishing with their anthem, 'The Soldiers' Song'. The rest of Portland's prisoners were inspired by what they heard. Scores of them began banging on their cell doors and shouting, 'Good old Ireland – That's the stuff to give them.'[7] The men's morale was raised again when they left the prison and came across a detachment of Australian soldiers who loudly hailed them as heroes. Frank Thornton marched proudly alongside the others to the nearby train station, where they winked at girls on the platform.

They arrived at Waterloo station in London several hours later, next to a Red Cross train unloading wounded British and German soldiers, some of whom were in a very bad way. Gerald Doyle noticed an Irish girl, who had come to Waterloo to assist the released Volunteers, see, to her surprise, her brother, a British soldier, lying wounded on one of the stretchers. This soldier later became an Irish Republican Army (IRA) volunteer in London. As it transpired, the German wounded had arrived at Waterloo that day just in time to almost get killed by their own side, as the station and the surrounding area were bombed by Zeppelins. When the bombing stopped, Londoners who had found out who the Volunteers were started picking up rubble from the recent explosions and throwing it at them. This resulted in an almost full-scale riot as Thornton and the others gave as good as they got, hurling back whatever masonry they could lay their hands on. There were several injuries before order was restored and, eventually, they were on the move once again to Pentonville, five miles away, near Holloway in north London. Liam Tobin and his fellow former inmates from Broadmoor also arrived in London to a reception of rocks and missiles thrown by angry civilians that smashed some of the train windows. They, too, were transferred to Pentonville. De Valera and the prisoner contingent from Maidstone arrived shortly afterwards.

The Volunteers' sojourn in Pentonville was brief but unpleasant. The prison was infested with lice, fleas and an assortment of other unpleasant bugs. Nevertheless, they knew they were on their way home and their morale remained buoyant.

When, on 17 June 1917, the Republican prisoners eventually left Pentonville, they were dressed in civilian clothes provided by the authorities. On the way out they passed Roger Casement's grave. The letters 'RC 1916' were inscribed into concrete on the wall close to it. Then, less than a mile from Pentonville, at Euston train station, when they were boarding the train to Holyhead, crowds of well-wishers handed them gifts of food and cigarettes for their journey to Ireland. They were overjoyed at this gesture from so many of their exiled countrymen and women.

When they arrived in Holyhead late that evening, Commandant Ashe formed the men into fours to board the ship to take them across the Irish Sea, while de Valera insisted to the crew that his men be allowed to travel first class. This was initially refused, but when they simply pushed past the ticket collectors and took the seats, the ship's captain decided that a fight was best avoided, and he relented. This added to the men's jubilation. When the ship pulled away from dock many of them rushed to the decks. They had been confined for over a year in dark, claustrophobic prison cells, and the fresh sea air soothed lungs that now ached from the copious amounts of tobacco smoked on the train from

The last of the Republican prisoners return home in June 1917 – seen here receiving a jubilant welcome outside Westland Row Station. National Library of Ireland

London. Also on the decks were groups of soldiers returning to Ireland on leave. Some of them shouted insults at Séamus Doyle and Frank Thornton, protesting that they themselves were 'as Irish as any of them'. When, shortly after daybreak the following morning, the Wicklow Mountains appeared in the distance, their lingering jibes were drowned out by the boisterous singing of Harry Boland, who treated them to a celebratory rendition of 'Dawn on the Hills of Ireland'.[8] Some of the still half-drunk British soldiers taking the early morning air on deck ended up singing songs with the Volunteers, and by the time the ship had pulled into Kingstown a few of them had even learned off by heart the words of 'The Soldier's Song'.

When they disembarked at Kingstown they were greeted as heroes by a crowd of about the same size, ironically, as the one that had gathered the previous year to welcome the British Army to subdue their insurrection. When they got to Westland Row in Dublin, however, a crowd they could never have imagined filled the streets. The prisoners had smuggled their 'felon's caps' out of prison with them. They now wore them with pride. The former prisoners were pulled at by huge numbers wanting to congratulate them. When de Valera and Thomas Ashe arrived the crowd seemed to go completely mad.

The first person to greet Frank Thornton was Michael Collins. The two Volunteer captains eventually ended up in Fleming's Hotel on Gardiner Place, where a feast awaited them. De Valera and Ashe followed, as did large numbers of civilians, one of whom – 14-year-old Charlie Dalton – waited for several hours to hear what he hoped would be a speech from de Valera. Dalton was disappointed – there was no speech. His first impression of de Valera was not a good one. Gerald Doyle made his way to Sackville Street, transfixed by the ruins, but elated at the sight of the tricolour flag flying once again from the roof of the shell of what had once been the GPO. Dublin was a changed city.

17

Hunger Strikes and a Movement Reborn

'Nothing additional remains to be said'

It was not just the male prisoners who were deported following the Easter Rising. After their brief incarcerations in Mountjoy Prison the seven women transferred there on 12 May were also dispatched across the Irish Sea. Dr Kathleen Lynn was one of them. When her family successfully intervened in her case, she ended up working with another doctor in the picturesque town of Bath in Somerset. She returned to Dublin in December 1916, but was forbidden to practise her profession. Dr Lynn and others began organising food parcels to be sent to Frongoch for Christmas. When the prisoners were released, however, they decided instead to gorge themselves on the parcels in Liberty Hall. The occasion provided a respite from a very hungry period for most of Dublin's Republicans. Food was scarce in Dublin during the cold winter of 1916–17. In spring 1917 Dr Lynn became involved in organising the first annual commemoration of the Rising, and marched with hundreds of others from Liberty Hall to the GPO on its anniversary, where the tricolour was once again raised on its roof – presumably the one that still fluttered in the breeze when Gerald Doyle observed the same building two months later on his own return to the city.

Following her detention in Mountjoy, Countess Markievicz wound up in Aylesbury Prison. It was a cold, filthy, utterly depressing institution built in 1847 in the Buckinghamshire countryside, and could not have been further removed from the trappings of wealth and status Markievicz had turned her back on when she immersed herself in the Republican movement. Markievicz was the only woman among those incarcerated in Aylesbury to have been convicted following the Rising and was treated as a common criminal. The others – Winifred Carney, Helena Moloney, Marie Perolz, Ellen Ryan and Brigid Foley – being internees as opposed to convicts, were kept segregated from the other prisoners until their eventual release in December 1916. Markievicz, on the other hand, shared her incarceration with murderers, thieves and prostitutes in appalling conditions that drove many to take their own lives. There were numerous suicides by hanging; and some women even swallowed needles, considering such a painful departure from the world as a release – a testament to the dismal conditions they faced in Aylesbury. One woman set her own cell on fire when she was locked in it to spare herself the further torment of solitary confinement.

Markievicz returned to Ireland in June 1917. She had lost a lot of weight – the food in Aylesbury Prison was, in the main, barely palatable. On her return she immediately re-immersed herself in the Republican movement, eventually becoming the first female MP elected to parliament in Westminster, standing as a Sinn Féin candidate.

Winifred Carney, when she was released from Aylesbury, returned to her native city of Belfast. In autumn 1917 she was elected president of Cumann na mBan Belfast.

Most of the other women who had been detained following the Rising waited patiently for news of their male Volunteer counterparts. When they began to return to Ireland between autumn 1916 and summer 1917 the 'silly little schoolgirls', as General Maxwell had described them, quickly returned to their tasks as Cumann na mBan members, and waited until the time was right to strike again. When General Maxwell expressed his relief to Lieutenant Wylie when he released these women from Kilmainham Gaol, he thought he had seen the back of them. He had no idea that he had just set free the very backbone of the Republican cause.

Summer 1917 was not without its tragedies for the women pursuing the nationalist cause. On 9 July, Thomas MacDonagh's 31-year-old widow, Muriel, was drowned in the sea while swimming close to Shenick Island off Skerries, in north County Dublin. This left their two children,

Dr Kathleen Lynn, Irish Citizen Army, who was deported following her imprisonment in Dublin. She returned to Dublin in December 1916 and once again immersed herself in the movement. COURTESY OF THE ROYAL COLLEGE OF PHYSICIANS OF IRELAND

Donagh and Barbara, orphaned. Muriel had been holidaying with several other prominent Republican widows, including Grace Plunkett, Lillie Connolly, Áine Ceannt and Agnes Mallin.

The British military command in Ireland was rejigged as the dust settled following the Rising. General Maxwell remained in Ireland until the autumn of 1916. He became greatly disillusioned when he saw how far public opinion had swayed towards radical nationalism since the 14 executions in Kilmainham Gaol. He expressed his exasperation in frequent letters to his wife. His ability to score own goals in terms of propaganda was not confined to his actions during May 1916, however. Scathing comments he later made about what he felt was the Catholic Church's misguided sympathy for the Republican revolutionaries further fuelled the fires of nationalist dissent in Ireland. He was eventually reassigned to Northern Command in the north-east of England, and was appalled at being moved to what he considered a backwater. General Blackader, on the other hand, was ordered to the Western Front in late June 1916. Brigadier Colonel Maconchy was promoted to the temporary rank of Brigadier General on 6 June 1916. He was also posted to the Western Front, with the Sherwood Foresters Regiment, in February 1917. After the war, he took up poultry farming.

Thomas Ashe, Michael Collins and Diarmuid Lynch were quick to reorganise the IRB on their return to Ireland. Ashe, a long-standing member, was elected its president, a position that had been vacant since the shooting of Pádraig Pearse the previous year. Ashe immediately employed his tireless energy travelling far and wide throughout the country, making speeches and campaigning for Sinn Féin. His incarceration had done nothing to dampen his charisma and physical presence. He was well over six foot tall, with a distinctive waxed moustache and a wild head of hair. He didn't walk – he strode. His reputation as the only commandant whose forces had comprehensively beaten the enemy in the field of battle the previous year added to his allure as a leader. This, allied with his oratorical skills, gave him a growing countrywide audience.

Éamon de Valera, who was now held in similarly lofty esteem to Thomas Ashe – owing principally to his position as commandant of the last Dublin Brigade battalion to surrender following Easter Week – spent a brief period at home with his family following his release from prison. He then turned his energies to politics, contesting a seat for Sinn Féin in the East Clare by-election in July 1917, which he won by a significant margin. De Valera and Ashe were the only two of the original commandants who had fought in 1916 who were still alive and in Ireland. Liam Mellows, the other, had escaped to the United States in autumn 1916. Considering that the seven signatories to the Proclamation of the Irish Republic had all been executed in Kilmainham, and that another seven of the Volunteer movement's more prominent figures were also lying in the same unmarked mass grave in Arbour Hill, there was a void to be filled in telling the Irish people that the movement, far from having been put to death with its leaders after Easter 1916, was now resurrected. De Valera and Ashe quickly filled that void.

Michael Collins had been typically busy since his release from Frongoch in December, not just during the Longford by-election that had seen Joe McGuinness elected MP. Kathleen Clarke, aware of Collins' inexhaustible energy and his aptitude for meticulous bookkeeping, had appointed him Secretary of the National Aid and Volunteer Dependants' Fund during the early months of 1917. Kathleen had set up the fund, along with Áine Ceannt and 27-year-old Sorcha MacMahon (who had stepped in when Kathleen suffered a miscarriage). Frank Thornton worked alongside Collins in his new role, as the two men strove to help reorganise the Volunteers. Money quickly flowed into the fund. Both Joe Lawless and Garry Holohan also became involved. Holohan became somewhat disenchanted with Collins, accusing him of spending too much time drinking in the Stag's Head pub close to Dame Street. Seán McLoughin was put in touch with Collins, also through the fund. McLoughlin was elected to the role of Commandant-General of the Fianna in early 1917, a rank suited to the leadership abilities he had shown in the cauldron of fire that was Moore Street during the climax of the Rising's fighting. McLoughlin was dispatched to Belfast in his new role, but following a warrant being issued there for his arrest he was sent back to the south, eventually ending up in Tipperary.

The political upheaval throughout Ireland in 1917 was not without a backlash from the authorities. Any signs of dissent were monitored and, where possible, subdued. Patrick Holohan was imprisoned for six months in 1917 for singing anti-establishment songs. Thomas Ashe was arrested after making a seditious speech on 15 July 1917 in Ballinalee, County Longford, having been in the county with Michael Collins. He was sent under armed guard initially to the Curragh camp in Kildare, and from there to Mountjoy Prison. He was sentenced to two years' hard labour. In prison he and six other Republican prisoners, including fellow Kerryman Austin Stack, and Seán Treacy – one of Éamon de Valera's bodyguards – demanded prisoner-of-war status, just as the Volunteers had done in England, insisting on wearing their own clothes and on being able to associate with other prisoners. They also refused to carry out any prison work. When POW status was denied they went on hunger strike on 20 September.

The hunger strike rapidly escalated as more prisoners joined in. When, as a result of their protest, they were prevented from using the exercise yard, they began continuously ringing the bells in their cells. The bells were soon removed. Not to be outmanoeuvred, they then began kicking continuously on their cell doors. This prompted the chief warder, as an act of retaliation, to enter Ashe's cell with two other warders and remove his bedding, stove and table. They then returned and took his slippers, and even his bible, before forcibly removing his boots. Ashe and his fellow prisoners were appalled. This level of retribution for the prisoners' POW protest was unprecedented – in England they had refused to work and obstructed the regime at every available opportunity, but had never been treated with this level of contempt.

Ashe was left in a bare cell to sit and lie on a cold floor for over two days. He maintained his hunger strike, refusing to be branded a criminal. Word of the hunger strike quickly spread through the country. Joe Good witnessed huge crowds gathering outside Mountjoy Prison to pray for Ashe and his comrades. At one point, when Michael Collins arrived there with Cathal Brugha, the crowd, spurred on by the presence of Brugha, a man whose exploits during the Rising were now the stuff of legend, nearly erupted into a riot.

The authorities, however, aware of the huge level of support for the hunger strikers, were desperate not to have any more Republican martyrs on their hands. The memories of May the previous year and the public reactions to the executions in Kilmainham were still raw. The decision was therefore made to force-feed the prisoners. This process was brutal in the extreme, particularly in Ashe's case because he was already weak from the inhumane conditions in his cell. After he was restrained, his wrists and arms were strapped to a tall wooden chair while his head was held back. His mouth was then prised open with a wooden spoon while a feeding tube that had already been used on several other prisoners, and rinsed with cold water each time, was forced down his throat. This would cause Ashe to vomit violently every time it was removed. On the third day of the force-feeding, 23 September, Dr Lowe, an assistant to the prison doctor Mr Dowdall, whose only experience of 'artificial feeding', as he called it, was having force-fed five of the other prisoners, forced a tube down Ashe's throat that pierced his lung. The mixture of milk and beaten eggs that was subsequently forced into the feeding tube filled the damaged lung, in effect drowning him. He was rushed to the adjacent Mater Hospital where, two days later, on 25 September, he died of lung and heart failure.

Ashe's brutal death was seen as a national tragedy. He had captured the hearts of the Irish public and was hugely respected, not only for his profession as a schoolmaster and his prowess as a commander, but also

Thomas Ashe, whose brutal treatment and gruesome death from force-feeding while on hunger strike in September 1917, and his subsequent funeral, marked a turning point for the Volunteer movement. COURTESY OF KILMAINHAM GAOL ARCHIVES

for his oratory and his poetry. The poem he had written in Lewes prison, 'Let Me Carry Your Cross for Ireland, Lord', was widely publicised, as was the maxim he regularly alluded to: 'It is not those who can inflict the most, but those who can suffer the most, who will prevail.' Frank Thornton was at a concert in Kells in County Meath the night Ashe died. When the news came of his death the concert was stopped and speeches were made in tribute to him.

Ashe had been a founding member of the Volunteers. His body was dressed in a Volunteer uniform and sent to St Mary's Pro-Cathedral on Marlborough Street. From there it was taken by horse-drawn hearse to City Hall, escorted by several dozen Volunteers, including Captain Simon Donnelly, who marched with his revolver at the ready. Thousands looked on as it passed. Ashe's body lay in state in the majestic building for two days with a round-the-clock guard of honour comprised of Volunteers and younger Fianna scouts, under the very noses of the authorities next door in Dublin Castle, not to mention the British military in the hall itself, who chose discretion over valour and made themselves scarce. City Hall's ornate statues still bore the bloodstains of the vicious close-quarter fighting witnessed there during the Rising, and the soldiers did not wish to risk history repeating itself. Instead of gunpowder hanging in the air, however, the hall now smelled of flowers from the huge number of wreaths that were brought inside. Thousands paraded past the coffin to pay their respects. Ashe was the first dead Volunteer leader whom the public at large, not just the Volunteers themselves, had been given an opportunity to mourn properly, having been denied the previous year by the clandestine interment of the executed leaders in the quicklime pit in Arbour Hill. Ashe's death became the conduit of a mass outpouring of public sympathy, as well as an opportunity for the Volunteers to honour a fallen leader suitably, and at the same time to signal to the Irish people that they had not gone away.

On 30 September, the day of Ashe's funeral, over 30,000 people from throughout the country turned out in their best, thronging the streets between City Hall and Glasnevin Cemetery, three miles to the north. Movie cameras recorded the event, initially filming outside City Hall, where droves of youngsters ran about, intrigued by the novelty of the cameras. G-men mingled with the crowd, notebooks at the ready. Military personnel looked on from the upstairs windows of Dublin Castle.

Inside the hall, six Volunteers were detailed as pall-bearers. On hearing the command, in Irish, 'Up!',[1] they raised Ashe's coffin, now draped in a tricolour, to their shoulders, and, preceded by clergymen, carried it out of the Castle Street doors and down the steps to the same hearse that had transported the remains two days earlier. The glass-sided hearse, drawn by four raven-black horses, was covered in a kaleidoscope of floral wreaths. A short time later, after a momentary silence among the gathered crowd as the coffin was loaded, a loud command in Irish – 'Face front!'[2] – echoed around Castle Street's imposing façades, and the Volunteers flanking the hearse joined the scores of those both in front and behind in a slow march through Dublin's cobble-stoned streets. As the cortège passed, mourners lining the streets removed their hats and stood silently. Six-to-12-man Volunteer sections had been detailed to various points and junctions along the route to ensure there was minimal interference by potential troublemakers or the authorities. This was the first occasion since the Rising that fully uniformed Volunteers had paraded in public. They intended to make an impact. The authorities opted to avoid a confrontation.

The procession grew as it made its way through the streets, bolstered by the thousands who followed it once it had passed them. Well over an hour later, as the hearse approached Glasnevin Cemetery, a British Army lorry driver, having lost his patience with the lengthy proceedings, attempted to barge his way through. One Volunteer, Joe Leonard, who was positioned close to Joe Good, grabbed his revolver and pointed it at him, quickly putting an end to the interruption. The assembled Volunteers from the Dublin Brigade waiting in the cemetery stood to attention and saluted the hearse as it entered. Joe Lawless, standing among them, saw Volunteers manning the gates to ensure that no policemen came in.

Shortly afterwards, as the cemetery filled with Volunteers and mourners, the coffin was removed from the hearse and carried shoulder-high by the same pall-bearers to the graveside, where its flag was removed and folded. A piper played in the background. A priest addressed the gathered crowd for a time before anointing the coffin in its grave. A firing party, formed from Ashe's 5th Battalion, quickly assembled at attention in two ranks under the direction of the recently appointed commandant of the Dublin Brigade, Richard Mulcahy. It consisted of Joseph Lawless and 11 other Volunteers. Dick McKee had made sure there were enough

Richard Mulcahy, who commanded the firing party over Thomas Ashe's grave on 30 September 1917 and went on to become the Commander-in-Chief of the Irish Republican Army during the War of Independence. NATIONAL LIBRARY OF IRELAND

rifles and ammunition for the occasion. A cameraman stood to the firing party's left with the camera rolling.

There was a moment of silence after the priest said his final words over the grave. Then three commands from Mulcahy heralded the first volley of shots. The entire cemetery echoed to the sharp, piercing cracks of a dozen rifles. Outside the cemetery gates, policemen, alerted by the shots, jostled fiercely with the dense crowds who closed ranks to deny them entry as another two volleys rang out in rapid succession. Michael Collins then took his place at the head of the grave as those within the

Volunteers fire volleys over Thomas Ashe's grave in Glasnevin Cemetery. NATIONAL
LIBRARY OF IRELAND

cemetery closed in to hear him. Collins was visibly emotional. He had
developed a tremendous liking and respect for Ashe in the few months
since the latter's return from England and had been devastated when he
heard of his horrific death. Collins now addressed those gathered – also
filmed by the cameraman – standing with his back to a huge Celtic cross.
He seemed barely able to contain his emotions as he spoke, the words
wrenched from his chest: 'Nothing additional remains to be said! That
volley which we have just heard is the only speech which it is proper to
make above the grave of a dead Fenian!'[3] He was standing in the same
spot where Séamus Grace and his comrades had fired volleys over
Michael Malone's grave the previous Christmas. Malone's grave was to
Collins' immediate left. Ashe's was roughly six feet to his front.

Richard Mulcahy saw to it that the firing party was quickly dispersed
within the grounds of the graveyard. By the time the policemen managed

to get through the wrought-iron gates and cover the hundred yards or so to the graveside, all that was left of the firing party was the acrid smell of gunpowder lingering in the air. Dick McKee had arranged for civilian clothes to be made available to the firing party to change into before they made their escape.

Soon afterwards, the Volunteers and the crowds made their way back towards the city. They expected trouble as a result of the shots fired in Glasnevin, but most of them had pre-arranged to proceed along Whitworth Road and to dissolve into the surrounding terraces of red-brick houses that lined its north-eastern side. In the end, there was no trouble.

* * *

Thomas Ashe's death and funeral seemed to resurrect the sentiments of the previous year following the summary executions and callous burials of the Rising's leaders. It once again highlighted to a great many people the apparent brutality of Ireland's rulers. A huge portion of the Irish people who had been reasonably content with the general order of life, despite recent difficulties, now baulked at what they perceived as further evidence of the authorities' disregard for them.

The funeral itself represented the first large-scale marshalling of the Irish Volunteers Dublin Brigade under arms since Easter 1916. Having resurfaced as a cohesive force under the direction of officers recently 'graduated' from Frongoch and the various English prisons, the way forward now was to continue to reorganise and prepare for the next phase.

Michael Collins's short but powerful graveside speech that day turned out to be a similar harbinger of turbulent times as that made by Pádraig Pearse, also in Glasnevin and mere yards away, two years earlier at the funeral of Jeremiah O'Donovan Rossa – a similarly well-orchestrated occasion. Collins' words echoed the same uncompromising sentiment, and suggested that the fight for Irish independence from Britain was far from over. He would soon be proved right. The funerals of both Ashe and O'Donovan Rossa were also dress rehearsals of sorts, requiring levels of co-ordination between battalions and units that confirmed to the officers and men of the Volunteers that discipline was sound, and that plans could be made to take the fight once again to the enemy when the time was ripe and enough arms were available.

Events confirmed Collins's prophetic graveside oration when the War of Independence began in earnest in 1919. This conflict would be a wholly different affair from that of 1916. It would be prolonged and unforgiving. Instead of set-piece battles between battalions marshalled under their officers, it would feature the type of guerrilla warfare that had been effective during Easter Week at Swords, Donabate, Garristown and Ashbourne, carried out notably by the battalion under the overall command of Thomas Ashe, and led in the field during the Ashbourne engagement by Richard Mulcahy. Mulcahy himself would go on to become Commander-in-Chief of the IRA during the War of Independence. This war would be characterised by flying columns, assassinations, hunger strikes, torture, and vicious acts of revenge and murder by the despised Black and Tans and Auxiliaries,[4] underpinned by an intelligence war under the direction of Michael Collins, during which, for the first time in military history, the British intelligence services would meet their match. It gave many of those who had played comparatively minor parts in the Easter Rising the opportunity to take on far more prominent roles, as well as introducing men who, for whatever reason, had been denied a chance to strike at Britain in 1916, and who intended to make up for what they considered a lost opportunity. Since the 'Tan War', as it was often called, came after the end of the Great War, the ranks of Volunteers were also bolstered by ex-British Army personnel, primarily from Irish regiments, some of whom were highly trained NCOs and officers, and most of whom were combat veterans. The war was unrelenting and ruthlessly contested. Within a few years, many of those who stood to attention at Thomas Ashe's funeral would themselves be interred in adjacent plots, including the speechmaker himself; in his case – as in numerous others – put there by his own countrymen in the subsequent civil war.

Ultimately, it was the aftermath of the Easter Rising, the courts martial and executions, the deportations, internments and imprisonments, and the marshalling of Volunteers together in Frongoch and elsewhere that became the forge that tempered the Republican and nationalist movement for what was to follow. Thomas Ashe's death and funeral was just one – albeit a hugely significant one – of many catalysts during the period from 1916 to 1919 that propelled the movement once again to war. Ashe's inquest, the judgment of which was unambiguously scathing of his brutal and inhuman treatment, served only to deepen the resentment felt towards the British authorities, and helped ensure that, as winter 1917 approached, Ireland's fight was far from over. The fight would be a predominantly political one in 1918, and would eventually result in a landslide victory for Sinn Féin in December of that year. Earlier, during April 1918, the threatened introduction of conscription (with the Military Service Bill) suggested that the British had learned nothing from their litany of public relations disasters since the Rising. They managed, yet again, to ratchet up support for their adversaries, this time by attempting to introduce legislation that would force conscription into the British Army, in order to bolster manpower on the haemorrhaging Western Front. This was followed by the arrests of Sinn Féin leaders in May 1918, when they were incorrectly suspected of plotting with Germany. This action merely served to displace the more moderate members from positions of influence, and facilitate the further ascent of radicals like Michael Collins. Widespread arrests and round-ups among the populace continued, frequently for the most ridiculous of misdemeanours, such as speaking Irish at Gaelic League events, serving once again to alienate legions of young men and women, whom they then frequently incarcerated alongside seasoned Republicans, who could now instruct them in how to exact revenge.

Opposite the strategic blunders of the authorities, preparations in both the command structure and the rank and file of the Volunteers accelerated. The ground was prepared throughout 1918 for an altogether different and far more lethal contest to the comparatively chivalrous Rising, with an increase in the number of raids on RIC barracks and other establishments throughout the country to obtain weapons and ammunition, as well as a return to the tried-and-tested methods of bribing soldiers to smuggle guns and ammunition from their barracks.

In many ways, therefore, Thomas Clarke's assertion to Gerald Doyle in Kilmainham on 2 May 1916 – the night before Clarke stood in front of his wavering firing party – was proved by subsequent events to be accurate: the Rising and executions were indeed only the beginning of this particular episode in Ireland's centuries-old fight with her neighbour. The many comments in the same vein made by the other executed men were no less prophetic, particularly Seán MacDermott's suggestion that their cause would be lost if there were no executions. The condemned men's widely reported stoicism as they met their fate served, as time went on, to bolster further the spirits of thousands who took up the fight, or re-immersed themselves in it. Indeed, it is arguable that it both galvanised the determination of the Republican movement to such an extent that it helped it to see off a host of tenacious, robust and brutal enemies; and also, ironically, through the same symbolic power, contributed to the sentiment that subsequently fuelled the Civil War. Many saw a compromise of any kind with the enemy, or with those who would treat with it, as a betrayal of the gallantry and sacrifice of those they now held in such high, and in many ways holy, regard. The history of warfare is laced with such unforeseen paradoxes.

It is beyond doubt, however, that very few of those Republicans who returned from prisons and camps in England and Wales in 1916 and 1917, or those who remained in Ireland, would have predicted that within a few short years they would be taking up arms against their comrades. For now, their sights were focused squarely on the task at hand – the war against the British Empire, the conflict that Richard Mulcahy had, in his many lectures in Frongoch, suggested would be contested ruthlessly and without pity. There would be far fewer examples of the camaraderie displayed to each other by soldiers on opposing sides during the Easter Rising. Richmond Barracks and Kilmainham Gaol saw numerous examples of such fellowship between men who faced the same risks, discomforts and terrors, despite serving different masters in different uniforms. Similarly, Volunteers imprisoned in England following the Rising were, considering the circumstances, looked on with both respect and admiration by a great many of their adversaries. This sentiment would not last when the fight took the form of ambush, assassination and reprisal.

Neither Richmond Barracks nor Kilmainham Gaol – as a functioning prison – was destined to survive the foundation of the Irish Free State, whose genesis owed so much to both establishments. Following the War of Independence, and the establishment of the Irish Free State in 1922, the barracks was handed over by the Royal Irish Regiment to the recently founded National Army of the Free State, and renamed Keogh Barracks. Soon after, it was taken over by Dublin Corporation and used for civilian purposes, including housing and schools.

Kilmainham Gaol housed political prisoners during both the War of Independence and the Civil War. In 1924 it permanently ceased to operate as a prison. Following decades of neglect, it was eventually restored during the 1960s, and today serves as a poignant reminder to hundreds of thousands of visitors of the sacrifices and hardships endured by so many of our ancestors. In its ability to transcend time, it has few equals.

Richmond Barracks has also seen significant restoration in more recent years. Events in its gymnasium sealed the fates of both the selection victims and, ironically, in the course of time, some of the selectors themselves. Today, it is difficult not to be moved by the haunting history that resonates from its walls.

The Royal Hospital Kilmainham today justifies its position as the oldest classical building in Ireland. Its elegant floors continue to overlook much of the western axis of a city steeped in history. Its clock tower and medieval entrance gates remain both historical and geographical landmarks. Following the establishment of the Free State it was considered as a potential home for the Irish Parliament – Oireachtas Éireann. When this did not come to pass it served as the headquarters for the Irish Civic Guards – An Garda Síochána – from 1930 to 1950. Today it houses the Irish Museum of Modern Art (IMMA).

Arbour Hill graveyard still retains the remains of the 14 men referred to by Con Colbert in a letter written before he was executed as 'those of us who must die'.[5] Today, the plot is, both aesthetically and symbolically, far removed from the simple mound of disturbed earth left there originally from their hasty interment in 1916. The same piece of ground is now meticulously maintained and surrounded by modest horizontal stone memorials to the executed, which are themselves set within a simple but picturesque mosaic of hexagonal flagstones. The plot today serves as a setting for annual state commemorations, as well as a host of other official and unofficial ceremonies. It is also a place of reflection for the individuals and small groups who visit daily. Adjacent is a crescent-shaped, ornate limestone wall. Set within the wall, a gold-coloured cross overlooks the final resting place of those who so indomitably faced the reluctant firing squads of the Sherwood Foresters. Carved into the wall, in both English and Irish, is the proclamation that underpinned the struggle they spearheaded, and the subsequent campaign embarked upon by their male and female comrades, and their successors, in 1919 – and beyond.

Epilogue

'The position of citizen soldiers'

VERBATIM WITNESS STATEMENT

Bureau of Military, 1913-1921
Statement by Witness
Document Number W.S. 336
Witness: Garry Holohan
Identity: Senior Officer, Fianna Eireann, 1914-1921

Some time in 1917 Cathal Brugha and Count Plunkett were holding a meeting in Beresford place when the police interfered and one of the police inspectors was killed by a blow from a Fianna officer named Eamon Murray, who had taken part in the Rising (he was in the Magazine fort attack). Murray ran towards Abbey Street, followed by a policeman, and he would have been arrested and hanged only he happened to have a revolver in his possession. He turned round to shoot the policeman, who got such a fright that he ran away. It was a very near thing with Murray, as the first bullet jammed in the revolver, and had the policeman realised that there was something wrong with the revolver he would have got Murray. Murray went on the run and was sheltered by the Countess Markievicz and her friends until he was smuggled out to America. He came home after the Truce, and fought with us during the Civil War. He later joined the Civic Guards, but lost his reason and is now a patient in Grangegorman Hospital.

The reason I relate this incident is to have a record of the first men to kill a British officer after 1916. It is stated in Desmond Ryan's book that Soloheadbeg was the first event of the kind. Eamon was in charge of the Fianna Sluagh at 41 Parnell Square at the time. He should not have been at the meeting and he should not have been carrying arms.

There was a tremendous difference for me in the Movement before 1916 and after. Before 1916 I had five comrades on the Volunteer Executive, as well as a number of friends, with the result that I was in the centre of all activity. As the only men who were considered reliable before 1916 were the members of the I.R.B. we were in the centre of every action and held the key positions in every movement. This was completely altered after 1916. Every man who took part in the Rising was considered tried and true, as well as the other members of his family, so the new organisation grew to enormous dimensions and the ranks were swelled with the usual crafty place-hunters and jobseekers, who were quick to realise that this would eventually mean a new party.

A number of Civil Servants were dismissed for their part in the Rising. They were employed, where possible, by the new Sinn Féin organisation, as clerks and organisers.

The movement changed from a small party of idealists, who were ready to do and die in face of all adversity, to a huge political movement embracing all classes and types.

The fighting men of limited education, like myself, devoted most of our energy to the re-organisation of military organisations, while the men of education took over control of the political machinery. In other words, men of my type were to accept the position of citizen soldiers.

When the Fianna was under way we held our first Convention in Pearse's home in St Enda's, in 1917. The splendid house was in a dilapidated condition, as it had been torn to bits by the military. Even the ceilings were damaged. I was Officer in charge of Dublin, and was appointed Quartermaster General, two posts I held until the Truce. The job of Quartermaster General took a good deal of time and energy, as orders came pouring in from all parts of the country for uniforms and leather equipment. It is hard to believe that it was still possible for me to buy ex-Army leather equipment in large quantities at Lawlors' store in Fownes' Street, and post it to all parts of the country. Alfie White was my assistant, and I can say he was energetic. This supplying of equipment continued until about 1918.

The Fianna organised a big ceilidhe in the Banba Hall, Parnell square, early in 1917. We also organised the Manchester Martyrs concert in November, 1917, at which we got de Valera to give an address. We re-occupied the ball at Skipper's Alley, and carried on with our classes and drilling as usual.

In the meantime the Great War was still going on in France and the Volunteers were constantly buying arms and ammunition from the soldiers. These guns were passed out through the railings of the different barracks in the most daring way. I raided a pawn-shop on Elliss's Quay with a party of boys at about 10.30 p.m. about November, 1917. We arranged with one of the shop assistants, who lived on the premises, to slip down and open the hall door at the appointed time. We then climbed into the lock-up shop through a fanlight over the door leading from the shop into the hall, and got away with twenty guns and revolvers. We made our way by the back streets to Mrs O'Donoghue's in Fontenoy Street. Mrs O'Donoghue was the mother of Father Tom O'Donoghue, who fought in 1916 and is now on the English mission. She lived opposite Mrs Heuston. We left the guns there until any excitement that might take place would die down.

The Fianna also marched to Bodenstown churchyard in June, where the Wolfe Tone procession was held as usual. There is just one incident that comes to mind which took place after 1916. As if to add insult to injury, the British authorities erected a large scroll or banner of bunting across the top of the columns of the G.P.O. on which was painted an appeal for recruits for His Britannic Majesty's Navy. This was too much for us, so we organised a party of the Fianna. There were about twenty of us, including Liam Langley, Hugo MacNeill and Theo Fitzgerald. We met with bicycles at George's Pocket. We had a supply of twine with lead, weights attached, and several sods of turf soaked in paraffin oil. We cycled into O'Connell Street at about half-past eleven, held up the policeman on duty at the point of a revolver, threw the lead weights over the banner, hauled up the burning sods of turf and the whole thing was in ashes in a few minutes. It was never replaced.

Endnotes

INTRODUCTION

1. W. G. Hall, *The Green Triangle: Being the History of the 2/5th Battalion The Sherwood Foresters (Notts & Derby Regiment) in the Great European War, 1914–1918* (Letchworth, 1920), pp. 27–8.
2. The Irish Volunteers was formed in November 1913, as was the Irish Citizen Army. Cumann na mBan (women's association) was founded in April 1914, and Na Fianna Éireann (boy scouts) in August 1909.

PROLOGUE

1. Alfred Brucknill, *WS 1019*, p. 2.
2. Seán Enright, *Easter Rising 1916: The Trials* (Kildare, 2014), p. 18.

CHAPTER 1: THE FIRST PRISONERS – RICHMOND BARRACKS AND KILMAINHAM GAOL

1. Seán McLoughlin, *WS 290*, p. 33.
2. Desmond Ryan, *WS 724*, p. 24.
3. Eamon Morkan, *WS 411*, p. 11.
4. Liam Tobin, *WS 1753*, p. 7.
5. Morkan, *op. cit.*, p. 26.
6. Frank Henderson, *WS 249*, p. 62.
7. Séamus Ua Caomhanaigh, *WS 889*, p. 62.
8. The IRB was a secret organisation dedicated to an independent Ireland.
9. Brian Feeney, *Seán MacDiarmada (16 Lives* series) (Dublin, 2014), p. 277.
10. Oscar Traynor, *WS 340*, p. 24.
11. *Ibid.*, p. 24.
12. Head of Military Police, in this case for Richmond Barracks.
13. Charles Saurin, *WS 288*, p. 47.
14. Diarmuid Lynch, *WS 004*, p. 10.

Chapter 2: The Prisoner Selections Begin in Richmond Barracks

1. 2nd Lieutenant Samuel Jackson. He was a Dubliner who served with the 3rd Battalion, Royal Irish Regiment. Before the war, he was a schoolteacher. He was killed in action in France in March 1918 while serving with the 2nd Battalion, Royal Irish Regiment.
2. Seán Kennedy, *WS 842*, p. 18.
3. Charles Saurin, *WS 288*, p. 48.
4. Seán McLoughlin, *WS 290*, p. 34.
5. Patrick Rankin, *WS 163*, p. 14.
6. Patrick Kelly, *WS 781*, p. 24.
7. *Ibid.*, p. 25.
8. Seán O'Duffy, *WS 618*, p. 3.
9. *Ibid.*, p. 3.
10. Joseph Good, *WS 388*, p. 20.

Chapter 3: Round-ups, More Selections and Civilian Backlash

1. Maryann Gialanella Valiulis, *Portrait of a Revolutionary: General Richard Mulcahy and the Founding of the Irish Free State* (Dublin, 1992), p. 16.
2. *Ibid.*, p. 16. Richard Mulcahy spoke the words in Irish – '*Beannacht Dé agat*'.
3. *Ibid.*, p. 16.
4. *Ibid.*, p. 16.
5. Bernard McAlister, *WS 147*, p. 9.
6. Frank Robbins, *WS 585*, p. 82.
7. Various, *Dublin's Fighting Story* (Cork, 2009), p. 155.
8. Robbins, *op. cit.*, p. 84.
9. *Ibid.*, p. 84.
10. John McDonagh, *WS 532*, p. 14.
11. Joseph Lawless, *WS 1043*, p. 131.
12. Seán McLoughlin, *WS 290*, p. 34.
13. Patrick Rankin, *WS 163*, p. 15.
14. Seán O'Duffy, *WS 618*, p. 4.
15. Charles Saurin, *WS 288*, p. 52.
16. Mortimer O'Connell, *WS 804*, p. 28.
17. Seán MacEntee, *WS 1052*, p. 121.
18. Robbins, *op. cit.*, p. 85.
19. The SS *Libau,* under the cover name SS *Aud,* attempted to transport an estimated 20,000 rifles, mostly of the Russian Mosin-Nagant model, which had been captured on Germany's Eastern Front. She also carried ammunition, machine guns and explosives. Intercepted off the coast of Kerry, she was escorted by HMS *Bluebell* towards Cobh Harbour. With the harbour in sight, the *Aud*'s captain, Karl Spindler, scuttled the ship, sending it and its cargo to the bottom of the sea.
20. Rose McNamara, *WS 482*, p. 8.

CHAPTER 4: THE DEPORTATIONS BEGIN

1. Michael O'Reilly, *WS 886*, p. 11.
2. This was the order sent out on Saturday 22 April 1916, declaring no Volunteer parades for the following day. It appeared in the newspapers on Sunday 23 April. The rebellion was postponed by one day by its leaders due to the confusion the order caused. It was the principal reason for the diminished numbers who reported for duty on Monday 24 April 1916.
3. Joseph Good, *WS 388*, p. 21.
4. Seán Prendergast, *WS 755*, p. 152.
5. *Ibid.*, p. 152.
6. Lyn Ebenezer, *Fron-Goch Camp 1916 and the Birth of the IRA* (Llanrwst, 2006), p. 84. The *Slieve Bloom* was a twin-screw steamer built in 1908.
7. Charles Saurin, *WS 288*, p. 54.
8. Michael O'Flanagan, *WS 800*, p. 39.
9. Séamus Grace, *WS 310*, p. 13.
10. William Christian, *WS 646*, p. 11.
11. Joseph Lawless, *WS 1043*, p. 133.
12. *Ibid.*, p. 135.
13. Peadar O'Mara, *WS 377*, p. 19.
14. *Ibid.*, p. 20.
15. Seán Byrne, *WS 422*, p. 18.
16. *Ibid.*, p. 19.
17. Frank Robbins, *WS 585*, p. 91.
18. Peadar McMahon, *WS 1730*, p. 3.
19. Michael Molloy, *WS 715*, p. 5.
20. Joseph Gleeson, *WS 367*, p. 10.
21. Helen Litton, *Tom Clarke* (*16 Lives* series) (Dublin, 2014), p. 198.
22. Piaras F. Mac Lochlainn, *Last Words* (Dublin, 1990), p. 42.
23. Brian Barton, *The Secret Court Martial Records of the Easter Rising* (Gloucestershire, 2010), p. 155.
24. Thomas Doyle, *WS 186*, p. 14.
25. Henry Murray, *WS 300*, p. 22.
26. Robert Holland, *WS 280*, p. 46.
27. *Ibid.*, p. 46.

CHAPTER 5: THE MILITARY PREPARE TO MAKE THEIR NEXT MOVE

1. Annie O'Brien, Lily Curran, *WS 805*, p. 12.
2. Gerald Doyle, *WS 1511*, p. 18.
3. Padraig O Ceallaigh, *WS 376*, p. 5.
4. Michael Lynch, *WS 511*, p. 9.
5. Robert Holland, *WS 280*, p. 47.
6. Jack Plunkett, *WS 865*, p. 3.
7. Brian Barton, *The Secret Court Martial Records of the Easter Rising* (Gloucestershire, 2010), p. 34.

8. W. J. Brennan-Whitmore, *Dublin Burning: The Easter Rising from Behind the Barricades* (Dublin, 1996), p. 121.
9. John McDonagh, *WS 532*, p. 15.
10. Joseph Lawless, *WS 1043*, p. 140.
11. Barton, *op. cit.*, p. 120.
12. Trial Records, Pádraig Pearse, *PRO W/O 71/345*, p. 11.
13. Liam Cosgrave, *WS 268*, p. 13.
14. *Ibid.*, p. 29.

CHAPTER 6: THE FIRST COURTS MARTIAL AND THE SECOND DEPORTATIONS

1. Seán Murphy, *WS 204*, p. 10.
2. The 178th Brigade of the 59th (2nd North Midlands) Division comprised the 2/5, 2/6, 2/7 and 2/8 Battalions of the Sherwood Forester Regiment.
3. E. U. Bradbridge, *59th Division 1915–1918* (Chesterfield, 1928), p. 43.
4. Piaras F. Mac Lochlainn, *Last Words* (Dublin, 1990), p. 27.
5. W. J. Brennan-Whitmore, *Dublin Burning: The Easter Rising from Behind the Barricades* (Dublin, 1996), p. 124.
6. Mick O'Farrell, *1916: What the People Saw* (Cork, 2013) p. 60.
7. James Burke, *WS 1758*, p. 7.
8. Gerald Doyle, *WS 1511*, p. 19.
9. William Christian, *WS 646*, p. 11.
10. Doyle, *op. cit.*, p. 21.
11. *Ibid.*, p. 21.
12. Murphy, *op. cit.*, p. 10.
13. Séamus Daly, *WS 360*, p. 57.
14. Robert Holland, *WS 280*, p. 49.
15. Bradbridge, *op. cit.*, p. 89.
16. Maryann Gialanella Valiulis, *Portrait of a Revolutionary: General Richard Mulcahy and the Founding of the Irish Free State* (Dublin, 1992), pp. 18–19.
17. Thomas Pugh, *WS 397*, p. 10.
18. Daly, *op. cit.*, p. 58.
19. John McDonagh, *WS 532*, p. 16.
20. Charles Weston, *WS 149*, p. 15.

CHAPTER 7: THE FIRST EXECUTIONS IN KILMAINHAM GAOL

1. Seán Enright, *Easter Rising 1916: The Trials* (Kildare, 2014), p. 31.
2. *Ibid.*, p. 62.
3. Rev. Fr Aloysius, *WS 200*, p. 14.
4. Kathleen Clarke, *Revolutionary Woman* (Dublin, 1991), pp. 133–4.
5. *Ibid.*, p. 134.
6. *Ibid.*, p. 134.
7. *Ibid.*, p. 135.
8. Shane Kenna, *Thomas MacDonagh* (*16 Lives* series) (Dublin, 2014), p. 255.

9. Rev. Fr Aloysius, *op. cit.*, p. 14.
10. Right Rev. Monsignor M. Curran, *WS 687*, p. 72.
11. Michael T. Sloughley, *WS 189*, p. 2.
12. *Ibid.*, p. 4.
13. *Ibid.*, p. 2.
14. Gerald Doyle, *WS 1511*, p. 22.

CHAPTER 8: COURTS MARTIAL IN RICHMOND BARRACKS GATHER STEAM

1. Kathleen Clarke, *Revolutionary Woman* (Dublin, 1991), p. 144.
2. Tim Pat Coogan, *1916: The Easter Rising* (London, 2001), p. 162.
3. Liam Tannam, *WS 242*, p. 45.
4. Michael T. Sloughley, *WS 189*, p. 2.
5. Major-General Maxwell's instructions were to hold the trials under DORA, not military or martial law.
6. Brian Barton, *The Secret Court Martial Records of the Easter Rising* (Gloucestershire, 2010), p. 88.
7. Charles Townshend, *Easter 1916: The Irish Rebellion* (UK, 2015).
8. Nora Connolly, *The Unbroken Tradition* (New York, 1918), p. 174.
9. Trial Records, Edward Daly, *PRO W/O 71/344*, p. 13.
10. Trial of Joseph Plunkett, *PRO W/O 71/349*, p. 5.
11. Liam Tobin, *WS 1753*, p. 9.
12. *Ibid.*, p. 10.
13. Trial Records, Éamonn Ceannt, *PRO W/O 71/348*, pp. 21–2.
14. Barton, *op. cit.*, p. 223.
15. Townshend, *op. cit.*, p. 279.

CHAPTER 9: AN UNEXPECTED WEDDING AND FOUR MORE FIRING SQUADS

1. Liam Tobin, *WS 1753*, p. 11.
2. Michael Staines, *WS 284*, p. 20.
3. Diarmuid Lynch, *WS 004*, p. 11.
4. Liam Cosgrave, *WS 268*, p. 17.
5. Honor Ó Brolcháin, *Joseph Plunkett* (*16 Lives* series) (Dublin, 2012), p. 404.
6. Albert Desborough, *WS 1604*, p. 12.
7. *Ibid.*, p. 12.
8. Rev. Fr Augustine, *WS 920*, p. 20.
9. David Johnson, *Executed at Dawn: British Firing Squads on the Western Front 1914–1918* (Gloucestershire, 2015), p. 47.
10. Piaras F. Mac Lochlainn, *Last Words* (Dublin, 1990), p. 95.
11. Michael T. Sloughley, *WS 189*, p. 3.
12. Tobin, *op. cit.*, p. 12.
13. Kathleen Clarke, *Revolutionary Woman* (Dublin, 1991), p. 148.
14. Eily O'Hanrahan O'Reilly, *WS 270*, p. 10.
15. Mac Lochlainn, *op. cit.*, p. 79.

16. Helen Litton, *Tom Clarke* (*16 Lives* series) (Dublin, 2014), p. 176.
17. Mac Lochlainn, *op. cit.*, p. 70. She is referring to Theobald Wolfe Tone, leader of the 1798 Rebellion, and Robert Emmett, leader of the Rebellion of 1803.
18. *Ibid.*, p. 71.
19. Clarke, *op. cit.*, p. 150.
20. Mac Lochlainn, *op. cit.*, p. 71.
21. O'Hanrahan O'Reilly, *op. cit.*, p. 11.
22. *Ibid.*, p. 11.
23. *Ibid.*, p. 11.
24. *Ibid.*, p. 12.
25. Francis P. Jones, *History of the Sinn Fein Movement and the Irish Rebellion of 1916* (New York, 1920), p. 418.
26. O'Hanrahan O'Reilly, *op. cit.*, p. 13.
27. Mac Lochlainn, *op. cit.*, p. 85.
28. Honor Ó Brolcháin, *Joseph Plunkett* (*16 Lives* series) (Dublin, 2012), p. 406.
29. Jones, *op. cit.*, p. 418.
30. Mac Lochlainn, *op. cit.*, p. 79.
31. *Ibid.*, p. 79.
32. Rev. Fr Augustine, *op. cit.*, p. 20.
33. *Ibid.*, p. 20.
34. *Ibid.*, p. 21.
35. Mac Lochlainn, *op. cit.*, p. 96.
36. Neil Richardson, *According to their Lights: Stories of Irishmen in the British Army, Easter 1916* (Cork, 2015), p. 189.

CHAPTER 10: COURTS MARTIAL CONTINUE AND ANOTHER VOLLEY AT DAWN IN KILMAINHAM

1. Gerald Doyle, *WS 1511*, p. 23.
2. *Ibid.*, p. 23.
3. Trial Records, Seán Heuston, *PRO W/O 71/351*, p. 12.
4. *Ibid.*, p. 13.
5. Trial Records, Cornelius Colbert, *PRO W/O 71/352*, p. 3.
6. Jack Plunkett, *WS 865*, p. 3.
7. *Ibid.*, p. 3.
8. Seán Enright, *Easter Rising 1916: The Trials* (Kildare, 2014), p. 99.
9. *Ibid.*, p. 101.
10. Liam Cosgrave, *WS 268*, p. 17.
11. Trial Records, Éamonn Ceannt, *PRO W/O 71/348*, p. 24.
12. *Ibid.*, p. 26.
13. Enright, *op. cit.*, p. 186.
14. http://www.findlaters.com/chapter9.html
15. Brian Barton, *The Secret Court Martial Records of the Easter Rising* (Gloucestershire, 2010), p. 216.
16. Trial Records, John MacBride, *PRO W/O 71/350,* pp. 9-10.
17. *Ibid.*, p. 10.

18. *Ibid.*, p. 12.
19. Maire O Brolchain, *WS 321*, p. 13.
20. *Ibid.*, p. 13.
21. Trial Records, Cornelius Colbert, *op. cit.*, p. 4.
22. *Ibid.*, p. 4.
23. Piaras F. Mac Lochlainn, *Last Words* (Dublin, 1990), p. 100.
24. Barton, *op. cit.*, p. 217.
25. Rev. Fr Augustine, *WS 920*, p. 23.
26. Cosgrave, *op. cit.*, p. 18.
27. Rev. Fr Augustine, *op. cit.*, p. 24.
28. Mac Lochlainn, *op. cit.*, p. 104
29. Barton, *op. cit.*, p. 219.
30. Rev. Fr Augustine, *op. cit.*, p. 24.

CHAPTER 11: CHANGING SENTIMENT IN DUBLIN AND FURTHER DEPORTATIONS

1. William O'Brien, *WS 1766*, p. 18.
2. *Ibid.*, p. 18. MacNeill would later in the day issue the countermand order.
3. Peter Howley, *WS 1379*, p. 15.
4. Gerald Doyle, *WS 1511*, p. 25.
5. Seán Enright, *Easter Rising 1916: The Trials* (Kildare, 2014), pp. 176–7.
6. *Ibid.*, p. 177.
7. Doyle, *op. cit.*, p. 27.
8. *Ibid.*, p. 28.
9. Trial Records, Michael Mallin, *PRO W/O 71/353*, p. 4.
10. *Ibid.*, p. 5.
11. http://www.findlaters.com/chapter9.html
12. It has often been suggested that Michael Mallin could have inadvertently put Countess Markievicz in front of a firing squad by making this statement to the court. But there are a number of factors worthy of consideration. (1) word had been spread among those waiting for trial from the very first day that they were to contest the charges. (2) Mallin would have known that Markievicz had already been tried, and could reasonably have assumed that she had already been sentenced; prisoners were usually told their sentence by the following day. (3) When we look at other trial records or witness statements, it becomes evident that when a Volunteer was asked the name of their commanding officer, they would give the name if the officer had already been tried. It appears that Mallin took the only option available to him, which was to give the impression he was not in command, believing that Markievicz, having received her sentence, could not be tried again.
13. Trial Records, Michael Mallin, *op. cit.*, p. 7.
14. *Ibid.*, p. 8.
15. Doyle, *op. cit.*, p. 29.
16. *Ibid.*, p. 29.
17. Andrew McDonnell, *WS 1768*, p. 20

18. Molly Reynolds, *WS 195*, p. 9.
19. *Ibid.*, p. 9.
20. W. G. Hall, *The Green Triangle: Being the History of the 2/5th Battalion Sherwood Foresters (Notts & Derby Regiment) in the Great European War, 1914–1918* (Letchworth, 1920) p. 24.
21. Vincent Byrne, *WS 423*, p. 5.
22. *Ibid.*, p. 5.
23. Plunkett, *op. cit.*, p. 4.
24. Diana Norman, *Terrible Beauty: A Life of Constance Markievicz* (Dublin, 1987), p. 156.
25. *Ibid.*, p. 156.
26. Áine Ceannt, *WS 264*, p. 35.
27. *Ibid.*, p. 35.

Chapter 12: The Authorities Reflect

1. Annie O'Brien, Lily Curran, *WS 805*, p. 12.
2. James Burke, *WS 1758*, p. 8.
3. Nora Connolly, *The Unbroken Tradition* (New York, 1918), p. 176.
4. Gerald Doyle, *WS 1511*, p. 31.
5. Earl of Longford and Thomas P. O'Neill, *Eamon de Valera* (London, 1970), p. 48.
6. *Ibid.*, p. 48.
7. Thomas Mallin, *WS 382*, p. 5.
8. Brian Barton, *The Secret Court Martial Records of the Easter Rising* (Gloucestershire, 2010), p. 253.
9. John Gibney, *Seán Heuston (16 Lives series)* (Dublin, 2013), p. 152.
10. *Ibid.*, p. 152.
11. Piaras F. Mac Lochlainn, *Last Words* (Dublin, 1990), p. 127.
12. Barton, *op. cit.*, p. 255.
13. Gibney, *op. cit.*, p. 160.
14. Mac Lochlainn, *op. cit.*, p. 126. Translated by the authors from the Irish – *Tá mé le bás a fháil le breacadh an lae.*
15. Mary Gallagher, *Éamonn Ceannt (16 Lives series)* (Dublin, 2014), p. 319.
16. *Ibid.*, p 320. He spoke the words in Irish: '*Beannacht Dé leat*'; and the reply from Ceannt was '*Go soirbhidh Dia duit*'.
17. Áine Ceannt, *WS 264*, p. 37.
18. Mallin, *op. cit.*, p. 6.
19. Gibney, *op. cit.*, p. 162.
20. *Ibid.*, p.164.
21. Mac Lochlainn, *op. cit.*, p. 112.
22. *Ibid.*, p. 151.
23. *Ibid.*, p. 151.
24. *Ibid.*, p. 151.
25. John O'Callaghan, *Con Colbert (16 Lives series)* (Dublin, 2015), p. 212.
26. Mac Lochlainn, *op. cit.*, p. 112.

27. *Ibid.*, p. 142.
28. *Ibid.*, p. 142.
29. Mick O'Farrell, *50 Things You Didn't Know About 1916* (Cork, 2009), p. 125.
30. Mac Lochlainn, *op. cit.*, p. 142.
31. Rose McNamara, *WS 482*, p. 10.
32. E. Gerrard, *WS 348*, p. 7.
33. Mac Lochlainn, *op. cit.*, p. 115.
34. Capuchin Franciscan Order, *The Capuchin Annual 1966: 1916 Rising Commemorative Pages* (Dublin, 2016), p.158.
35. A. A. Dickson, *True World War I Stories: Sixty Personal Narratives of the War* (London, 1997), p. 185.
36. Francis P. Jones, *History of the Sinn Fein Movement and the Irish Rebellion of 1916* (New York, 1920), p. 421.
37. Capuchin Franciscan Order, *op. cit.*, p. 156.
38. O'Farrell, *op. cit.*, p. 126.

CHAPTER 13: THE ENDGAME APPROACHES

1. Nora Connolly, *The Unbroken Tradition* (New York, 1918), p. 178.
2. Gerald Doyle, *WS 1511*, p. 33.
3. Charles Townshend, *Easter 1916: The Irish Rebellion* (UK, 2015), p. 285.
4. Pamela Hickson, *Seventy Years Young: Memories of Elizabeth, Countess of Fingall* (Dublin, 1991), p. 375.
5. Peter Howley, *WS 1379*, p. 15.
6. Annie O'Brien, Lily Curran, *WS 805, op. cit.*, p. 15.
7. Rose McNamara, *WS 482*, p. 10.
8. Brian Barton, *The Secret Court Martial Records of the Easter Rising* (Gloucestershire, 2010), p. 89.
9. Trial Records, James Connolly, *PRO W/O 71/354*, p. 15.
10. Piaras F. Mac Lochlainn, *Last Words* (Dublin, 1990), p. 167.
11. David Fitzpatrick, *Harry Boland's Irish Revolution* (Cork, 2003), p. 45.
12. *Ibid.*, p. 45.
13. The trial records for Seán MacDiarmada are incomplete. The last two witnesses' testimonies are missing from the file records. It is also unknown whether Seán MacDiarmada made a statement in his own defence.
14. Frank Thornton, *WS 510*, p. 25.
15. *Ibid.*, p. 25.
16. *Ibid.*, p. 25.
17. Trial Records, James Connolly, *op. cit.*, p. 11. Additionally, Lieutenant King states that Connolly was dressed in the uniform of the Irish Volunteers. James Connolly would have worn the bottle-green uniform of the Irish Citizen Army, not the light green of the Irish Volunteers.
18. *Ibid.*, p. 13.
19. *Ibid.*, p. 13.
20. *Ibid.*, p. 8.
21. *Ibid.*, p. 9.

22. Nora Connolly, *op. cit.*, pp. 179–80.
23. *Ibid.*, p. 182.
24. *Ibid.*, p. 183.

CHAPTER 14: THE FINAL EXECUTIONS AND AN UNEXPECTED VISITOR TO RICHMOND BARRACKS

1. John J. Reynolds, *A Fragment of 1916 History* (Dublin, 1919), p. 21.
2. Max Caulfield, *The Easter Rebellion* (Dublin, 1995), p. 291.
3. Hansard, HC Debates, 10 May 1916, Vol. 82, Col. 634.
4. *Ibid.*, Vol. 82, Col. 628.
5. *Ibid.*, Vol. 82, Col. 631.
6. Seán Enright, *Easter Rising 1916: The Trials* (Kildare, 2014), p. 38.
7. *Ibid.*, p. 39.
8. Rt Rev. Mgr Patrick Browne, *WS 729*, p. 7.
9. *Ibid.*, p. 5.
10. Rev. Fr Aloysius, *WS 200*, p. 16.
11. *Ibid.*, p. 16.
12. Enright, *op. cit.*, p. 231.
13. Hansard, HC Debates, 11 May 1916, Vol. 82, Col. 951.
14. Nora Connolly, *The Unbroken Tradition* (New York, 1918), p. 178–80.
15. *Ibid.*, Vol. 82, Col. 959.
16. Trial Records, James Connolly, *PRO W/O 71/354*, p. 183.
17. *Ibid.*, p. 184.
18. *Ibid.*, p. 184.
19. *Ibid.*, p. 186.
20. Brian Feeney, *Seán MacDiarmada* (*16 Lives* series) (Dublin, 2014), p. 302.
21. Piaras F. Mac Lochlainn, *Last Words* (Dublin, 1990), p. 193.
22. Michael T. Sloughley, *WS 189*, p. 4.
23. William O'Brien, *WS 1766*, p. 26.
24. Anne Marreco, *The Rebel Countess: The Life and Times of Constance Markievicz* (London, 2000), p. 215.
25. W. Alison Phillips, *The Revolution in Ireland 1906–1923* (London, 1926), p. 107.
26. Diana Norman, *Terrible Beauty: A Life of Constance Markievicz* (Dublin, 1987), p. 157.
27. *Ibid.*, p. 157.
28. Vincent Byrne, *WS 423*, p. 7.

CHAPTER 15: INTERNMENT

1. Lyn Ebenezer, *Fron-Goch Camp 1916 and the Birth of the IRA* (Llanrwst, 2006), p. 117.
2. Robert Holland, *WS 371*, p. 7.
3. W. J. Brennan-Whitmore, *With the Irish in Frongoch* (Cork, 2013) pp. 29–30.
4. Frank Robbins, *WS 585*, p. 109.
5. Thomas Pugh, *WS 397*, p. 14.

6. Joseph Lawless, *WS 1043*, *op. cit.*, p. 194.
7. Séamus Daly, *WS 360*, p. 65.

CHAPTER 16: TRIUMPHANT RETURN TO DUBLIN

1. Gerald Doyle, *WS 1511*, p. 39.
2. David Fitzpatrick, *Harry Boland's Irish Revolution* (Cork, 2004), p. 52.
3. Robert Kee, *The Green Flag*: Vol. 3, *Ourselves Alone* (London, 1989), p. 24.
4. Frank Thornton, *WS 510*, p. 33.
5. *Ibid.*, p. 33.
6. Doyle, *op. cit.*, p. 81.
7. Thornton, *op. cit.*, p. 38.
8. *Ibid.*, p. 41.

CHAPTER 17: HUNGER STRIKES AND A MOVEMENT REBORN

1. '*Suas!*'
2. '*Ar aghaidh!*'
3. Tim Pat Coogan, *Michael Collins* (London, 1991).
4. The Black and Tans were temporary constables recruited to the RIC during the Irish War of Independence. The name derives from their uniform, which was a mixture of British Army and green RIC issue. The Auxiliaries were members of the Auxiliary Division of the RIC (ADRIC), the RIC's counter-insurgency unit. Its ranks were filled with former British Army officers.
5. Annie O'Brien, *WS 805*, p. 15.

Sources

BUREAU OF MILITARY HISTORY, 1913–1921

WITNESS STATEMENTS

Aloysius, Rev. Fr. *WS 200*

Archer, Liam. *WS 819*

Augustine, Rev. Fr. *WS 920*

Balfe, Richard. *WS 251*

Banks, Henry T. *WS 1637*

Barrett, James. *WS 343*

Barton, Dulcibella, *WS 936*

Bean Uí Chonaill, Eilís. *WS 568*

Boland, Kathleen. *WS 586*

Boylan, Peter. *WS 269*

Boylan, Seán. *WS 212*

Bracken, Peadar. *WS 361*

Brady, Christopher. *WS 705*

Brennan, Robert. *WS 125*

Broderick, John. *WS 344*

Broderick, Seán. *WS 1677*

Browne, Rt Rev. Mgr Patrick. *WS 729*

Broy, Eamon. *WS 1280*

Bulfin, Eamonn. *WS 497*

Burke, James J. *WS 1758*

Byrne, Christopher. *WS 167*

Byrne, Gerald. *WS 143*

Byrne, Seán. *WS 422*

Byrne, Seán. *WS 579*

Byrne, Thomas. *WS 564*

Byrne, Vincent. *WS 423*

Caldwell, Patrick. *WS 638*

Callanan, Patrick. *WS 347*

Callender, Ignatius. *WS 923*

Ceannt, Áine. *WS 264*

Christian, William. *WS 646*

Clifford, Peter. *WS 231*

Cody, Seán. *WS 1035*

Coghlan, Francis. *WS 1760*

Colbert, Elizabeth M. *WS 856*

Colley, Harry. *WS 1687*

Collins, Maurice. *WS 550*

Connaughton, Patrick. *WS 1137*

Connolly O'Brien, Mrs Nora. *WS 286*

Connolly, Matthew. *WS 1746*

Corrigan, William. *WS 250*

Cosgrave, Liam T. *WS 268*

Costello, John. *WS 1330*

Coughlan, James. *WS 304*

Courtney, Thomas. *WS 447*

Cremen, Michael. *WS 563*

Crenigan, James. *WS 148*

Curran, Lily. *WS 805*

Curran, Rt Rev. Mgr M. *WS 687*

Daly, Madge. *WS 209*

Daly, Séamus. *WS 360*

Daly, William. *WS 291*

De Brún, Seosamh. *WS 312*

De Búrca, Feargus. *WS 694*

McCrave, Thomas. *WS 695*

McCrea, Patrick. *WS 413*

McCullough, Denis. *WS 915*

McDonagh, John. *WS 532*

McDonnell, Andrew. *WS 1768*

McDonnell, Michael. *WS 225*

McDonough, Joseph. *WS 1082*

McGarry, Seán. *WS 368*

McGuill, James. *WS 353*

McHugh, Patrick. *WS 677*

McInerney, Thomas. *WS 1150*

McLoughlin, Seán. *WS 290*

McMahon, Peadar. *WS 1730*

McNamara, Rose. *WS 482*

Molloy, Brian. *WS 345*

Molloy, Michael. *WS 716*

Molony, Helena. *WS 391*

Morkan, Eamon. *WS 411*

Morrissey, Gilbert. *WS 874*

Mullen, Patrick. *WS 621*

Murphy, Fintan. *WS 370*

Murphy, Gregory. *WS 150*

Murphy, Seán. *WS 204*

Murphy, Very Rev. Canon Patrick. *WS 1216*

Murphy, William. *WS 352*

Murray, Henry. *WS 300*

Murray, Séamus. *WS 308*

Napoli-McKenna, Cathleen. *WS 643*

Newell, Martin. *WS 1562*

Newell, Michael. *WS 342*

Newell, Thomas. *WS 572*

Nicholls, Harry. *WS 296*

Nohilly, Thomas. *WS 1437*

Nolan, George. *WS 596*

O'Brien, Annie. *WS 805*

O'Brien, Laurence. *WS 252*

O'Brien, Liam. *WS 323*

O'Brolchain, Maire. *WS 321*

Ó Buachalla, Domhnall. *WS 194*

O'Byrne, Joseph. *WS 160*

O'Callaghan, Margaret. *WS 747*

O'Carroll, Liam. *WS 314*

O'Carroll, Liam. *WS 594*

Ó Ceallaigh, Pádraig. *WS 376*

O'Connell, Mortimer. *WS 804*

O'Connor, James. *WS 142*

O'Connor, Joseph. *WS 157*

O'Daly, Patrick. *WS 220*

O'Dea, Michael. *WS 1152*

O'Donoghue, Father Thomas. *WS 1666*

O'Donovan, Cornelius. *WS 1750*

Ó Droighneáin, Michael. *WS 374*

O'Duffy, Seán. *WS 313*

O'Flanagan, George. *WS 131*

O'Flanagan, Michael. *WS 800*

Ó Flaithbheartaigh, Liam. *WS 248*

O'Grady, Charles. *WS 282*

O'Hannigan, Donal. *WS 161*

O'Keeffe, Seán. *WS 188*

O'Kelly, Fergus. *WS 351*

Oman, William. *WS 421*

O'Mara, Peadar. *WS 377*

Ó Monacháin, Ailbhe. *WS 298*

O'Neill, Edward. *WS 203*

O'Neill, Seán. *WS 1219*

O'Reilly (O'Hanrahan), Eily. *WS 270*

O'Reilly, John J. *WS 1031*

O'Reilly, Michael. *WS 866*

O'Rourke, Joseph. *WS 1244*

O'Shea, James. *WS 733*

O'Shea, Seán. *WS 129*

O'Sullivan, Séamus. *WS 393*

Peppard, Thomas. *WS 1399*

Plunkett, Grace. *WS 257*

Plunkett, Jack. *WS 488*

Plunkett, Jack. *WS 865*

Pounch, Séamus. *WS 267*

Prendergast, Seán. *WS 755*

Price, Eamon. *WS 995*

Price, Leslie. *WS 1754*

Price, Seán. *WS 769*

Pugh, Thomas. *WS 397*

Rankin, Patrick. *WS 163*

Redmond, Laurence. *WS 1010*

Reynolds, Joseph. *WS 191*

Reynolds, Molly. *WS 195*

Ridgeway, Dr. J. C. *WS 1431*

Robbins, Frank. *WS 585*

Robinson, Séamus. *WS 156*

Robinson, Séamus. *WS 1721*

Ronan, Patrick. *WS 299*

Ryan, Desmond. *WS 724*
Ryan, Min. *WS 399*
Saurin, Charles. WS 288
Scollan, John. *WS 318*
Shelley, Charles. *WS 870*
Shouldice, John. *WS 162*
Slater, Thomas. *WS 263*
Slattery, James. *WS 445*
Smart, Thomas. *WS 255*
Smyth, Patrick. *WS 305*
Soughley, Michael T. *WS 189*
Stafford, Jack. *WS 818*
Staines, Michael. *WS 284*
Stapleton, James. *WS 822*
Styles, John J. *WS 175*
Tannam, Liam. *WS 242*
Thornton, Frank. *WS 510*

Tobin, Liam. *WS 1753*
Traynor, Oscar. *WS 340*
Tuite, Daniel. *WS 337*
Twamley, John. *WS 629*
Ua Caomhánaigh, Séamus. *WS 889*
Ua h-Uallacháin, Gearóid. *WS 328*
Walker, Michael. *WS 139*
Walpole, R. H. *WS 218*
Walsh, James. *WS 198*
Walsh, Laurence J. *WS 1748*
Walsh, Thomas. *WS 198*
Ward, Patrick. *WS 1140*
Weston, Charles. *WS 149*
Whelan, William. *WS 369*
White, Alfred. *WS 1207*
Wyse-Power, Charles. *WS 420*
Young, Thomas. *WS 531*

NATIONAL ARCHIVES: PUBLIC RECORDS OFFICE, KEW

TRIAL RECORDS

Ceannt, E. *PRO W/O 71/348*
Clarke, Thomas. *PRO W/O 71/347*
Colbert, Con. *PRO W/O 71/352*
Connolly, James. *PRO W/O 71/354*
Crenigan, J. *PRO W/O 71/351*
Daly, Edward. *PRO W/O 71/344*
Dougherty, John. *PRO W/O 71/358*
Heuston, J. J. *PRO W/O 71/351*
Kelly, P. *PRO W/O 71/351*
Kent, Thomas. *PRO W/O 71/356*
MacBride, John. *PRO W/O 71/350*

MacDonagh, Thomas. *PRO W/O 71/346*
Mallin, Michael. *PRO W/O 71/353*
MacDermott, John. *PRO W/O 71/355*
McGarry, John. *PRO W/O 71/358*
O'Dea, W. *PRO W/O 71/351*
O'Hanrahan, Michael. *PRO W/O 71/357*
Pearse, P. H. *PRO W/O 71/345*
Pearse, William. *PRO W/O 71/358*
Plunkett, Joseph. *PRO W/O 71/349*
Walsh, J. J. *PRO W/O 71/358*

SELECTED READING

Books
Andrews, C. S., *Dublin Made Me* (Dublin, Lilliput Press, 2001)
Arthur, Sir George, *Life of Lord Kitchener* Vols. 1–3 (London, MacMillan and Co. Limited, 1920)
Augusteijn, Joost, *The Irish Revolution 1913–1923* (Hampshire, Palgrave, 2002)

Babington, Anthony, *For the Sake of Example: Capital Courts Martial 1914–18 – The Truth* (London, Leo Cooper, 1999)

Ballard, Brigadier-General C. R., *Kitchener* (London, Newnes, 1936)

Barker, Ernest, *Ireland in the Last Fifty Years 1866–1918* (Oxford, Clarendon Press, 1919)

Barton, Brian, *The Secret Court Martial Records of the Easter Rising* (Gloucestershire, History Press, 2010)

Béaslaí, Piaras, *Michael Collins and the Making of a New Ireland* Vol. 1 (Dublin, Phoenix Publishing Co., 1922)

Blake, J. Y. F., *A West Pointer with the Boers* (Boston, Angel Guardian Press, 1903)

Boyle, John F., *Irish Rebellion of 1916: A Brief History of the Revolt and its Suppression* (London, Constable and Co., 1916)

Bradbridge, E. U., *59th Division 1915–1918* (Chesterfield, Wilfred Edmunds, 1928)

Brennan-Whitmore, W. J., *Dublin Burning: The Easter Rising from Behind the Barricades* (Dublin, Gill & Macmillan, 1996)

— *With the Irish in Frongoch* (Cork, Mercier Press, 2013)

Byrne, Ciaran, *The Harp and Crown: The History of the 5th (Royal Irish) Lancers 1902–1922* (self-published, 2008)

Cathasaigh, P. O., *The Story of the Irish Citizen Army* (Honolulu, University Press of the Pacific, 2003)

Caulfield, Max, *The Easter Rebellion* (Dublin, Gill & Macmillan, 1995)

Clarke, Kathleen, *Kathleen Clarke – Revolutionary Woman* (Dublin, O'Brien Press, 1991)

Clarke, Thomas James, *Glimpses of an Irish Felon's Prison Life* (Dublin, Maunsel & Roberts, 1922)

Collins, Lorcan, *James Connolly* (*16 Lives* series) (Dublin, O'Brien Press, 2012)

— *1916: The Rising Handbook* (Dublin, O'Brien Press, 2016)

Connell, Joseph E. A., Jr, *Dublin Rising 1916* (Dublin, Wordwell, Dublin, 2015)

— *Who's Who in the Dublin Rising 1916* (Dublin, Wordwell, 2015)

Connolly, Nora, *The Unbroken Tradition* (New York, Boni & Liveright, 1918)

Coogan, Tim Pat, *Michael Collins, A Biography* (London, Arrow Books, 1991)

— *De Valera: Long Fellow, Long Shadow* (London, Arrow Books, 1995)

— *1916: The Easter Rising* (London, Phoenix, 2005)

Corns, Cathryn, and Hughes-Wilson, John, *Blindfold and Alone: British Military Executions in the Great War* (London, Cassell Military Paperbacks, 2005)

Cottrell, Peter, *The Anglo-Irish War: The Troubles of 1913–1922* (Oxford, Osprey Publishing, 2006)

Crozier, Brigadier General F. P., *A Brass Hat in No Man's Land* (New York, Johnathan Cope & Harrison Smith, 1930)

Dalton, Charles, *With the Dublin Brigade: Espionage and Assassination with Michael Collins' Intelligence Unit* (Cork, Mercier Press, 2014)

Dangerfield, George, *The Damnable Question: A History of Anglo-Irish Relations* (New York, Barnes & Noble, 1999)

Dawson, Richard, *Red Terror and Green: The Sinn Fein–Bolshevist Movement* (New York, E. P. Dutton & Company, 1920)

Devoy, John, *Recollections of an Irish Rebel* (Houston, Chas P. Young Co., 1929)

Doherty, Gabriel and Keogh, Dermot, *1916: The Long Revolution* (Cork, Mercier Press, 2007)

Dwyer, T. Ryle, *De Valera: The Man and the Myth* (Dublin, Poolbeg Press, 1992)

— *Éamon De Valera* (Dublin, Gill & Macmillan, 1998)

— *The Squad and the Intelligence Operations of Michael Collins* (Cork, Mercier Press, 2005)

Ebenezer, Lyn, *Fron-Goch Camp 1916 and the Birth of the IRA* (Llanrwst, Gwasg Carreg Gwalch, 2012)

Edmunds, G. J., *The Irish Rebellion: The 2/6th Sherwood Foresters' part in the defeat of the rebels in 1916; Their Early Training* (Chesterfield, Wilfred Edmunds, 1961)

Enright, Seán, *Easter Rising 1916: The Trials* (Kildare, Merrion, 2014)

Esher, Reginald Viscount, *The Tragedy of Lord Kitchener* (New York, E. P. Dutton and Company, 1921)

Fallon, Donal, *John MacBride* (*16 Lives* series) (Dublin, O'Brien Press, 2015)

Fanning, Ronan, *Fatal Path: British Government and the Irish Revolution 1910–1922* (London, Faber & Faber, 2013)

Feeney, Brian, *Seán MacDiarmada* (*16 Lives* series) (Dublin, O'Brien Press, 2014)

Figgis, Darrell, *A Chronicle of Jails* (Dublin, Talbot Press, 1918)

— *The Historic Case for Irish Independence* (Dublin, Maunsel & Co., 1918)

— *Recollections of the Irish War* (New York, Doubleday, Doran & Co., 1928)

Finlay, Ken, *Dublin Day by Day: 366 Days of Dublin History* (Dublin, Nonsuch Publishing, 2005)

Finlay, Ken and Roche, Tom, *Dublin 4, Sandymount – Donnybrook – Ballsbridge – Ringsend* (Donaghadee, Cottage Publications, 2006)

FitzGerald, Desmond, *Desmond's Rising – Memoirs 1913 to Easter 1916* (Dublin, Liberties Press, 2006)

Fitzpatrick, David, *Harry Boland's Irish Revolution* (Cork, Cork University Press, 2003)

Foster, R. F., *Vivid Faces: The Revolutionary Generation in Ireland 1890–1923* (London, Penguin Books, 2015)

Foy, Michael and Barton, Brian, *The Easter Rising* (Gloucestershire, Sutton Publishing, 2004)

Gallagher, Mary, *Éamonn Ceannt* (*16 Lives* series) (Dublin, O'Brien Press, 2014)

Galligan, Kevin, *Peter Paul Galligan: 'One of the Most Dangerous Men in the Rebel Movement'* (Dublin, Liffey Press, 2012)

Gibney, John, *Seán Heuston* (*16 Lives* series) (Dublin, O'Brien Press, 2013)

Gillis, Liz, *Women of the Revolution* (Cork, Mercier Press, 2014)

Greaves, C. Desmond, *1916 as History: The Myth of the Blood Sacrifice* (Dublin, Fulcrum Press, 1991)

Gwynn, Stephen, *John Redmond's Last Years* (London, Edward Arnold, 1919)

Hall, W. G., *The Green Triangle: Being the History of the 2/5th Battalion, The Sherwood Foresters (Notts and Derby Regiment) in the Great European War 1914–1918* (Letchworth, Garden City, 1920)

Hamilton-Norway, Mrs, *The Sinn Féin Rebellion As I Saw It* (London, Smith, Elder & Co., 1916)

Heartfield, James and Rooney, Kevin, *Who's Afraid of the Easter Rising? 1916–2016* (Alresford, Zero Books, 2015)

Henry, William, *Pathway to Rebellion: Galway 1916* (Cork, Mercier Press, 2016)

Herlihy, Jim, *The Dublin Metropolitan Police: A Short History and Genealogical Guide* (Dublin, Four Courts Press, 2001)

Hills, Captain J. D., *Fifth Leicestershire: A Record of the 1/5th Battalion the Leicestershire Regiment, T.F., During the War, 1914–1919* (Loughborough, Echo Press, 1919)

Hinkson, Pamela, *Seventy Years Young: Memories of Elizabeth, Countess of Fingall* (Dublin, Lilliput Press, 1991)

Hobson, Bulmer, *A Short History of the Irish Volunteers*, Vol. 1 (Dublin, Candle Press, 1918)

Hopkinson, Michael, *Irish Narratives: Frank Henderson's Easter Rising, Recollections of a Dublin Volunteer* (Cork, Cork University Press, 1998)

Housley, Cliff, *The Sherwood Foresters in the Easter Rising: Dublin 1916* (Nottingham, Miliquest Publications, 2015)

Hughes, Brian, *Michael Mallin* (*16 Lives* series) (Dublin, O'Brien Press, 2012)

Irish Times, Weekly, Sinn Féin Rebellion Handbook Easter 1916 (Dublin, *Weekly Irish Times*, 1917)

Jamie, Lt- Colonel V. P. W., *The 177th Brigade 1914–1918* (Leicester, W. Thornley and Son, 1931)

Johnson, David, *Executed at Dawn: British Firing Squads on the Western Front 1914–1918* (Gloucestershire, History Press, 2015)

Joly, J., *Reminiscences & Anticipations* (London, T. Fisher Unwin Ltd., 1920)

Jones, Francis P., *History of the Sinn Fein Movement and the Irish Rebellion of 1916* (New York, P. J. Kenedy & Sons, 1920)

Joy, Maurice, *The Irish Rebellion of 1916 and its Martyrs: Erin's Tragic Easter* (New York, Devin-Adair Company, 1916)

Keane, Elizabeth, *Seán MacBride: A Life* (Dublin, Gill & Macmillan, 2007)

Kee, Robert, *Green Flag*: Vol. 1, *The Most Distressful Country*; Vol. 2, *The Bold Fenian Men*; Vol. 3, *Ourselves Alone* (London, Penguin Books, 1989)

Kenna, Shane, *Thomas MacDonagh* (*16 Lives* series) (Dublin, O'Brien Press, 2014)

Kettle, T. M., *The Open Secret of Ireland* (London, W. J. Ham-Smith, 1912)

Kostick, Conor, & Collins, Lorcan, *The Easter Rising a guide to Dublin in 1916* (Dublin, O'Brien Press, 2000)

Kostick, Conor, *Michael O'Hanrahan* (*16 Lives* series) (Dublin, O'Brien Press, 2015)

Litton, Helen, *Edward Daly* (*16 Lives* series) (Dublin, O'Brien Press, 2013)

— *Thomas Clarke* (*16 Lives* series) (Dublin, O'Brien Press, 2014)

Longford, The Earl of and O'Neill, Thomas P., *Eamon de Valera* (London, Arrow Books, 1974)

Lucy, J. F., *There's a Devil in the Drum* (Uckfield, Naval & Military Press, 1993)

Mac Lochlainn, Piaras F., *Last Words: Letters and Statements of the Leaders Executed after the Rising at Easter 1916* (Dublin, Stationery Office, 1990)

Mackenzie, Donald A., *Lord Kitchener: His Life and Work* (London, Blackie and Son, 1916)

MacNamara, Brinsley, *The Clanking of Chains* (New York, Brentano's Publishers, 1919)

Mainwaring, Major A. E., *Crown and Company: The Records of the Second Battalion Royal Dublin Fusiliers* (London, Arthur L. Humphreys, 1911)

Marreco, Anne, *The Rebel Countess: The Life and Times of Constance Markievicz* (London, Phoenix Press, 2000)

McAuliffe, Mary and Gillis, Liz, *Richmond Barracks 1916, We Were There: 77 Women of the Easter Rising* (Dublin, Dublin City Council, 2016)

McCann, John, *War by the Irish* (Tralee, The Kerryman, 1946)

McGarry, Fearghal, *Rebel Voices from the Easter Rising* (London, Penguin Books, 2012)

McGough, Eileen, *Diarmuid Lynch: A Forgotten Irish Patriot* (Cork, Mercier Press, 2013)

McGuire, Charlie, *Seán McLoughlin, Ireland's Forgotten Revolutionary* (Pontypool, Merlin Press, 2011)

McMahon, Seán, *Rebel Ireland: From Easter Rising to Civil War* (Cork, Mercier Press, 2001)

— *Great Irish Heroes* (Cork, Mercier Press, 2008)

McNally, Michael, *Easter Rising 1916: Birth of the Irish Republic* (Oxford, Osprey Publishing, 2009)

Mitchell, Angus, *Roger Casement* (*16 Lives* series) (Dublin, O'Brien Press, 2013)

Mitchell, Seán, *A Rebel's Guide to James Connolly* (London, Bookmarks Publications, 2016)

Moore, William, *The Thin Yellow Line* (Hertfordshire, Wordsworth Editions, 1999)

Mulcahy, Risteárd, *Richard Mulcahy (1886–1971): A Family Memoir* (Dublin, Aurelian Press, 1999)

— *My Father the General: Richard Mulcahy and the Military History of the Revolution* (Dublin, Liberties Press, 2009)

Naughton, Lindie, *Markievicz: A Most Outrageous Rebel* (Kildare, Irish Academic Press, 2016)

Nevin, Donal, *James Connolly: 'A Full Life'* (Dublin, Gill & Macmillan, 2005)

Ní Ghairbhí, Róisín, *Willie Pearse* (*16 Lives* series) (Dublin, O'Brien Press, 2015)

Norman, Diana, *Terrible Beauty: A Life of Constance Markievicz* (Dublin, Poolbeg Press, 1988)

Ó Brolcháin, Honor *Joseph Plunkett* (*16 Lives* series) (Dublin, O'Brien Press, 2012)

O'Brien, Paul, *Blood on the Streets: 1916 & The Battle for Mount Street Bridge* (Cork, Mercier Press, 2008)

— *Uncommon Valour: 1916 & The Battle for the South Dublin Union* (Cork, Mercier Press, 2010)

— *Crossfire: The Battle of the Four Courts, 1916* (Dublin, New Island, 2012)

— *Shootout: The Battle for St Stephens's Green, 1916* (Dublin, New Island, 2013)

O'Callaghan, John, *Con Colbert* (*16 Lives* series) (Dublin, O'Brien Press, 2015)

O'Connor, Frank, *The Big Fellow* (Dublin, Poolbeg Press, 1991)

O'Donnell, Ruán, *Patrick Pearse* (*16 Lives* series) (Dublin, O'Brien Press, 2016)

O'Farrell, Mick, *50 Things You Didn't Know About 1916* (Cork, Mercier Press, 2009)

— *1916: What the People Saw* (Cork, Mercier Press, 2013)

— *The 1916 Diaries of an Irish Rebel and a British Soldier* (Cork, Mercier Press, 2014)

O'Farrell, William, *An Appreciation of Padraic H. Pearse* (New York, Chas. F. Connelly, 1920)

O'Hegarty, P. S., *Sinn Fein: An Illumination* (Dublin, Maunsel & Co., 1919)

— *A Short Memoir of Terence MacSwiney* (New York, P. J. Kenedy & Sons, 1922)

O'Malley, Ernie, *On Another Man's Wound* (Cork, Mercier Press, 2013)

— *The Men will Talk to Me – Galway Interviews* (Cork, Mercier Press, 2013)

Oates, W. C., *The Sherwood Foresters in the Great War 1914–1918. The 2/8th Battalion* (Nottingham, J. & H. Bell, 1920)

Pearse, Patrick, *The Coming Revolution: The Political Writings and Speeches of Patrick Pearse* (Cork, Mercier Press, 2012)

Phillips, W. Alison, *The Revolution in Ireland 1906–1923* (London, Longmans, Green & Co., 1926)

Putkowski, Julian and Sykes, Julian, *Shot at Dawn: Executions in World War One by Authority of the British Army Act* (London, Leo Cooper, 1993)

Redmond-Howard, L. G., *Six Days of the Irish Republic* (London, Maunsel & Co., 1916)

Regan, John X., *What made Ireland Sinn Fein* (Boston, Washington Press, 1921)

Richardson, Neil, *According to Their Lights: Stories of Irishmen in the British Army, Easter 1916* (Cork, Collins Press, 2015)

Ryan, Anne-Marie, *16 Dead Men: The Easter Rising Executions* (Cork, Mercier Press, 2014)

Ryan, Desmond, *The Man Called Pearse* (Dublin, Maunsel & Co., 1919)

Ryan, Meda, *Thomas Kent (16 Lives* series) (Dublin, O'Brien Press, 2016)

Ryan, Meda, *Irish Revolutionaries – Liam Lynch: The Real Chief* (Cork, Mercier Press, 2012)

Sandall, Colonel T., *A History of the 5th Batt. The Lincolnshire Regiment* (Oxford, Basil Blackwell, 1923)

Sheehan, Captain D. D., *Ireland since Parnell* (London, Daniel O'Connor, 1921)

Sheehy Skeffington, Francis, *A Forgotten Small Nationality: Ireland and the Great War* (New York, Donnelly Press, n.d.)

Sheehy Skeffington, Hanna, *British Militarism as I Know It* (New York, Donnelly Press, n.d.)

Simpson, Major-General C. R., *The History of the Lincolnshire Regiment 1914–1918* (London, Medici Society, 1931)

Skinnider, Margaret, *Doing My Bit for Ireland* (New York, Century Co., 1917)

Spindler, Reserve-Lieutenant Karl, *Gun Running for Casement in the Easter Rebellion 1916* (London, W. Collins Sons & Co., 1921)

Stephens, James, *The Insurrection in Dublin* (New York, Macmillan, 1917)

Stiles, Dean, *Portrait of a Rebellion: English Press Reporting of the Easter Rising, Dublin, Ireland in 1916* (self-published, 2012)

Townshend, Charles, *Easter 1916: The Irish Rebellion* (UK, Penguin, 2015)

Tynan, Katharine, *The Years of the Shadow* (London, Constable and Co., 1919)

Valiulis, Maryann Gialanella, *Portrait of a Revolutionary: General Richard Mulcahy and the Founding of the Irish Free State* (Dublin, Irish Academic Press, 1992)

Various, *'The Robin Hoods' 1/7th, 2/7th, & 3/7th Battns Sherwood Foresters 1914–1918* (Nottingham, J. & H. Bell, 1921)

Various, *Dublin's Fighting Story 1916–21* (Cork, Mercier Press, 2009)

Various, *Limerick's Fighting Story 1916–1921, 'Told by the Men Who Made It'* (Cork, Mercier Press, 2009)

Various, *The Capuchin Annual 1966: 1916 Rising Commemoration Pages* (Dublin, South Dublin Libraries, 2016)

Various, *True World War I Stories: Gripping Eyewitness Accounts from the Days of Conflict and Pain* (London, Constable & Robinson, 1999)

Von Clausewitz, Carl, *On War* (Hertfordshire, Wordsworth Editions, 1997)

Ward, Margaret, *In Their Own Voice: Women and Irish Nationalism* (Dublin, Attic Press, 1995)

Wells, Warre B. and Marlowe, N., *A History of the Irish Rebellion of 1916* (London, Maunsel & Co., 1916)

Wheeler, Charles Newton, *The Irish Republic: An Analytical History of Ireland, 1914–1918* (Chicago, Cahill-Igoe Company, 1919)
White, G. and O'Shea, B., *Irish Volunteer Soldier 1913–23* (Oxford, Osprey Publishing, 2003)

E-books

Dorney, John, *The Story of the Easter Rising*, 1916 (2014)
Eddleston, John, *British Executions*. Vol. 4, *1916 to 1920* (2012)
Holbrooke, Philip, *Easter Rising 1916: The Facts* (n.d.)
New Statesman, *Easter 1916: Selected Archive Pieces from New Statesman* (n.d.)
O'Sullivan, Brighid, *Petticoat Rebels of 1916: Extraordinary Women in Ireland's Struggle for Freedom* (2016)
Sinclair, Mark, *United in Arms Divided in Dreams: James Connolly, Patrick Pearse and Easter 1916* (2013)
Woodley, David, *Knutsford Prison: The Inside Story* (2015)

Booklets

Cumann na mBan, *The Fianna Heroes of 1916* (Dublin, Cumann na mBan, 1931)
Reynolds, John J., *A Fragment of 1916 History* (Dublin, Sinn Féin, 1919)
Schuller, G., *'Jim' Connolly: Irish Rising of 1916* (Chicago, Daily Worker Publishing Company, n. d.)
Thurtle, Ernest, *Shootings at Dawn, The Army Death Penalty at Work* (London, Victoria House Printing Co., n. d.)

Journals

Newell, Úna, 'The Rising of the Moon: Galway 1916', *Journal of the Galway Archaeological and Historical Society*, Vol. 58 (2006)
O'Daly, Nora, 'The Women of Easter Week,' *an t-Óglác*, IV, 12 (3 April 1926)

WEBSITES

http://1914-1918.invisionzone.com
http://annual.capuchinfranciscans.ie
http://www.aoh.com
http://www.awm.gov.au
http://www.blackcountry-territorials.org
http://www.bureauofmilitaryhistory.ie
http://www.caucus99percent.com
http://www.communistpartyofireland.ie
http://www.dublin-fusiliers.com
http://www.easter1916.ie
http://www.findlaters.com
http://www.gaelicweb.com
http://gmic.co.uk

http://www.grantonline.com
http://www.heritageireland.ie
http://www.historyireland.com
http://www.inniskillingsmuseum.com
http://www.irishmedals.org
http://irishvolunteers.org
https://issuu.com
http://kilmainhamgaolmuseum.ie
http://kilmainhamtales.ie
http://www.militaryarchive.co.uk
http://www.militaryarchives.ie
http://hansard.millbanksystems.com
http://mountstreet1916.ie
http://www.nam.ac.uk/online-collection
http://www.nli.ie
https://www.paperspast.natlib.govt.nz
https://www.rcpi.ie
http://www.rhk.ie
http://www.richmondbarracks.ie
https://www.royal-irish.com
http://www.royalleicestershireregiment.org.uk
https://www.thegazette.co.uk
http://www.westernfrontassociation.com

BLOGS

http://atlantach.wordpress.com
http://heatseekers.blogspot.co.uk
http://irelandinthecenturies.blogspot.co.uk
http://irishhistory.blogspot.co.uk
http://johnny-doyle.blogspot.co.uk
https://jpkenna.wordpress.com
http://liamlangley.blogspot.co.uk
http://thelondondead.blogspot.co.uk

SPOKEN WORD

RTÉ, *The Story of Easter Week 1916*, RTÉ 273 CD (RTÉ, 2006)

Acknowledgements

DARREN: To my gorgeous wife, Joanne, who in the last year, although not alone, as you knew we were with you each step of the way, has shown me how strong and what a courageous woman you are in dealing with what you had to face. I have nothing but love and admiration for you. Also to my children, Aaron, Liam and Adele, you make me proud to be your father and yet again you made me laugh when I needed it most. I can only say I love you all to bits.

DEREK: Once again the biggest thanks must go to my beautiful and endlessly patient wife, Lisa, and my two gorgeous girls, Shannon and Catriona. You inspire me and make every day a new adventure. Writing about such troubling times makes me aware of what I'm so lucky to have – the three of you – everything else is just window dressing.

Thanks again to both our parents and families for their inexhaustible support.

The authors would like to express tremendous gratitude to Pat Rooney, who once again was so helpful with his unflinching but incisive critique. Time and time again, his input helped to keep us on track – precisely when we needed it to. Thanks also to Mick O'Brien of Senshido Ireland/ Self Protection Ireland for again providing expert military advice and analysis; Johnny Doyle, whose knowledge of Ireland's revolutionary period and British military history is unsurpassed; Marcus Howard for his endless help and boundless enthusiasm; Jean O'Donnell, for putting up with Marcus as well as the pair of us; Brian Kirby MA PhD, Provincial Archivist, Capuchin Friary Dublin; Aoife Torpey, Archivist at Kilmainham Gaol, who went way above and beyond the call of duty to assist us; Berni Metcalfe, National Library of Ireland; Noelle Grothier, Archivist at the Bureau of Military History, Cathal Brugha Barracks; Síle at South Dublin Libraries; Jack Loader of Léonie Press; Norman Lee at the London and North Western Railway Society; Audrey Young and Knutsford Historical Society; Power Drama School; Lusk Heritage Group; Maynooth University; Jenny and all the staff at the Department of Foreign Affairs Registry and Library; Sally Webb and all the staff of the Imperial War Museum; Harriet Wheelock of the Royal College of Physicians in Ireland; Ronan McGreevy and Irene Stevenson of the *Irish Times*; Seán Moncrieff of Newstalk FM; Hugh Linehan of Today FM; Peter and Anne Hearsey.

Thanks to all the following for their help and support: Lorcan Collins, Éamon Ó Cuiv, Conor Dodd, Colin O'Reilly, Maurice & Alison Moran, Paul & Justine Rumens, Las Fallon, Jimmy Sheridan, Muriel McAuley, Donnacha DeLong, Donnchadh Mac Gabhann, Micheal O Doibhilin, Kieran & Christina McMullen, Don Doyle, Niamh McDonald, James Connolly-Heron, Proinsias O Rathaille, Maeve O'Leary, Garbhan De Paor, Petesy Burns, Stevie McLoughlin, Liam Beattie, Sinclair Dowey, Anne Campbell, Cathy O'Sullivan, and all the old Belfast crew who provided such heartfelt encouragement, Dave, Niamh and Nev from Claidheamh Soluis, Tanith Conway, Con and Niamh O'Connor and everyone from the Castlerea Clan, T. J. & Geraldine Moran, Dan and everyone from JLD Self Defence, Stef Thompson from Raw Combat International Essex, Robert Dooley, Jim Barrett, Jane O'Keeffe, Joe Mooney, Liam Ó Briain, Wayne Jenkins, Aidan Gorman, Anthony O'Reardon, Conor Forde, Darren Mulcahy, Derek Jones, Steve & Mia Doyle, Eamon Murphy, Niall Oman, Barry Lyons, Terry Crosbie, Teresa Culleton, Conor Dervan, Cecilia Hartsell, Darragh O'Neill, Paul O'Brien, Liz Gillis, Maria Poole, Terry Cronin, Kevin Brennan, Bróna Uí Loing, Mel MacGiobúin, Diarmuid Breatnach, Cillian Holly, Emily Anne Lucitt and all the Moore Street crew, Marc Daly, Breda Grannell, Therese Cater and everyone from Thomas McCurtain's GAA Club East London & Essex; all at The Collins Press.

Thanks again to all the followers of the Facebook page 'Dublin 1916–1923 Then and Now'. We hope to count on your continuing feedback and support. It is an inspiration to us. The same goes for everyone who helped and encouraged us with our previous book, *When the Clock Struck in 1916*, and to everyone who gave it such a positive response.

Index

NOTE: Illustrations are indicated by page numbers in **bold**.